WHEELS FOR A NATION

WHEELS FOR A NATION
By Frank Donovan

THOMAS Y. CROWELL COMPANY
Established 1834

Designed by Nancy H. Dale

Manufactured in the United States of America

Library of Congress Catalog Card No. 65-23776

1 2 3 4 5 6 7 8 9 10

Acknowledgment is made for permission to quote from the following sources:
(Page numbers are those in this volume.)
Sloan, Alfred P., Jr., in collaboration with Boyden Sparks. *Adventures of a
White Collar Man,* copyright 1940, 1941 by Alfred P. Sloan, Jr., and Boy-
den Sparks, reprinted by permission of Doubleday & Company, Inc. (pages
96 and 121).
Sloan, Alfred P., Jr. *My Years with General Motors,* copyright © by Alfred
P. Sloan, Jr., published by Doubleday & Company, Inc. (pages 85, 86, 225,
and 227).
Sorenson, Charles E. *My Forty Years with Ford,* copyright 1956 by Charles
Sorenson, published by W. W. Norton and Company, Inc. (page 228).

White, E. B. The quotations from "Farewell to Model T" come from an essay, "Farewell, My Lovely!," that first appeared in *The New Yorker* over the pseudonym Lee Strout White. It was suggested by a manuscript submitted to the magazine by Richard Lee Strout, and was written by E. B. White. Quoted by permission. Copyright © 1936, 1964 by The New Yorker Magazine, Inc.; published in book form by G. P. Putnam under the title *Farewell to Model T*, 1936. Reprinted under its original title in *The Second Tree from the Corner* by E. B. White, Harper & Brothers, 1954 (pages 105 and 106).

Sources of other excerpts are as follows:

Boyd, T. A. *Professional Amateur*, published by E. P. Dutton and Company, Inc. (pages 140 and 146).

Chrysler, Walter P., in collaboration with Boyden Sparks. *Life of an American Workman*, published by Dodd, Mead and Company (pages 84, 142, 175, and 176).

Ford, Henry, in collaboration with Samuel Crowther. *My Life and Work*, published by Doubleday & Company, Inc. (pages 55, 117, 120, and 129).

MacManus, Theodore. *Men, Money and Motors*, published by Harper & Row, Inc. (page 85).

Maxim, Hiram Percy. *Horseless Carriage Days*, published by Harper & Row, Inc. (page 36).

Nevins, Allan. *Ford: The Times, the Man, the Company*, published by Charles Scribner's Sons (pages 55, 56, 57, 105, 140, 159, 179).

Stolberg, Benjamin. *The Story of the C.I.O.*, published by the Viking Press, Inc. (page 228).

Sullivan, Mark. *Our Times*, published by Charles Scribner's Sons (pages 110 and 158).

Ways, Max. "The Era of Radical Change," *Fortune*, May 1964 (page 226).

CONTENTS

ILLUSTRATIONS

WHEELS FOR A NATION

Artist's conception of the 1911 automobile show in Madison Square Garden. In lower left corner is the distinctive radiator of a Packard "30." Above this, the five cars facing toward the right are, in order from the bottom, a Thomas Town Car, a Mercer Raceabout, an American Roadster, a giant Simplex, and a Winton Six. Facing toward the front is an elegant Franklin Limousine. The top car facing left is a Flandrau. Below it is a Maxwell Roadster in front of a Baker Electric. The two cars at bottom right are, top, a Case four-door Touring Car, and in lower right, a seven-passenger Chadwick. Painting by Peter Helck.

ONE: MRS. ASTOR'S PET HORSELESS

The evening of November 3, 1900, was a gala night at Madison Square Garden. This was not the ultramodern Garden now abuilding atop Pennsylvania Station. Nor was it the previous, rather tawdry arena on Eighth Avenue, where Mike Jacobs "shoulda stood in bed." This was the authentic, the original Madison Square Garden, so named, quite logically, because it was located on New York's Madison Square. This was the Garden with the tall tower topped by Diana the Huntress—nude but for her bow until the outcry of a few outraged puritans caused a bronze figure-eight drapery to be added, which completely covered her left armpit and nothing else, an addition that endeared her to New Yorkers as "Diana with the Pretzel."

This was the Madison Square Garden in which a premiere was held on that evening late in the last year of the old century—an exhibition that was dubbed by some facetious onlookers "the horseless Horse Show." *The New York Times* reported: "The crowd was one of particular brilliance and animation. The handsome gowns of the women and the multitude of snowy masculine shirt fronts reminded one of the Horse Show at its best." Mr. and Mrs. William K. Vanderbilt were there, as were Mrs. John Jacob Astor, William Rockefeller, Killian Van Rensselaer, D. Ogden Mills, Mrs. Whitelaw Reid, and the Count de Vilaine, to mention but a few of the names that Ward McAlister immortalized as "the Four Hundred." Colonel John Jacob Astor made a dramatic entrance to join his wife after "a rattling fast journey from Staatsburg-on-the-Hudson, a distance of about ninety miles, made in five hours in D. W. Bishop's French racer; a gasoline

Automobile Manufacturers Association

The first automobile show in New York's Madison Square Garden, November 3, 1900. Of the forty brands exhibited, only the Rambler is still in existence.

carriage of twelve horse-power which is only excelled by Albert C. Bostwick's machine."

Society had come to the Garden to admire and play with their new toys at New York's first automobile show. They discussed the respective merits of steam, gasoline, and electric propulsion and the proper uses for *broughams, victorias, surreys, phaetons, cabriolets, traps, carts, brakes,* and *spiders*—model designations that were as meaningful then as today's *convertibles, hardtops,* and *station wagons.* They particularly admired a "handsome victoria with the chauffeur and groom attired in a pearl-colored livery which exactly matched the lining and cushions of the carriage."

Forty makers of self-propelled vehicles exhibited some three hundred cars in this first show. Only one make is still in existence—the Rambler, which went through several name changes between its introduction in 1900 and its rebirth in 1958. Among the others then on view that made early automobile history were the Duryea, the Winton, the Haynes-Apperson, the Pope-Hartford, the Pope-Toledo, the Pope-Robinson, the Autocar, the Packard, the Knox, the Meteor, and the Gasomobile.

Demonstrations of driving skill were a feature of the show. Al Bostwick amused the crowd when he knocked over a straw-filled pedestrian while trying to steer his way between barrels at ten miles an hour. This was not an easy feat; there was a knack to steering even a straight course with a tiller-guided mechanism. Mrs. John Wessley Allison and Mrs. Edward Curtis, Jr., drew polite applause when they raced their electrics around the eighth-mile oval track that encircled the exhibit area. But the hit of the show was the hill-climbing exhibition on the roof of the Garden. A two-hundred-foot wooden ramp stretched partway up the tower toward Diana, and here a Mobile steamer proved twenty times a day that a horseless carriage could master a grade that would faze most horses.

The first New York show was sponsored by the Automobile Club of America, organized in the fashionable Waldorf-Astoria Hotel the

The first auto show featured such demonstrations of maneuverability as the obstacle course. Drivers had to be skillful to steer their tiller-guided cars around the track.

Automobile Manufacturers Association

year before. When the newly formed club later moved to 58th Street and Fifth Avenue one reason seriously advanced by the press was that the new location was more convenient to the Racquet Club, New York Yacht Club, Union Club, Metropolitan Club, and other haunts of its haughty members. Along with worthwhile resolutions for better roads, the early Automobile Club considered establishing elaborate service stations for members only, like small inland yacht clubs. One member of the club, Britton, displayed his high regard for his membership by having "the lamps on his Panhard gold plated, and on each of them the club emblem emblazoned. The emblems were solid gold, set with rubies."

Self-propelled vehicles were not exactly new at the turn of the century. The first electric car had made its appearance in Chicago in 1892 and created such a stir that the press reported: "In a number of instances so great has been the curiosity of those on the streets that the owner, when passing through the business section of the city, has had to appeal to the police to aid him in clearing a way for his carriage." By 1900 a few large cities had electric cabs, and there were reputedly between two and three thousand cars of all kinds in the country, perhaps half of them in and around New York. They ranged from expensive, imported Benzes, Panhards, and Peugeots to makeshift "blacksmith's cars" built during long nights of trial and error in the backs of dingy shops and stables.

It is safe to say that most Americans had seen an automobile by the year 1900, although few had ridden in one. Barnum and Bailey traveled a Duryea with the circus as early as 1896, displaying it with the other freaks and oddities. Montgomery Ward sent a car around the country in a special railroad coach that same year as an advertising stunt, and most state fairs in the last years of the old century displayed at least one of the horseless carriages that almost everyone agreed would never replace the horse.

Although self-propelled vehicles were not new in 1900, "automobiles" were. In 1895 a Chicago newspaper had offered a $500 prize for the best name for the then novel "horseless carriage"—this name was obviously unsuitable because it described what the vehicle was not rather than what it was. Hundreds of literate Midwesterners sent in names ranging from *autowain* to *petrocar*. The prize went to *motocycle*. The French term *automobile* was not suggested, but dur-

Climbing a 200-foot ramp on top of Madison Square Garden—the most popular event at the show. In the sight of passers-by on the street below, the Mobile steamer demonstrated one of its advantages over the horse. Without showing signs of fatigue, it could steam up the incline many times a day.

Fifth Avenue, New York City, at the turn of the century. By 1900 most Americans had seen an automobile, although few had ridden in one.

Automobile Manufacturers Association

Automobile Manufacturers Association

ing the next four years it started to gain some vogue. This enraged etymologists, and a small but bitter controversy developed. The word *automobile* was first used in *The New York Times* in an editorial on January 3, 1899, which condemned not only the name but the subject. Said the erudite *Times:*

"There is something uncanny about these newfangled vehicles. They are all unutterably ugly and never a one of them has been provided with a good or even an endurable name. The French, who are usually orthodox in their etymology if in nothing else, have evolved 'automobile,' which being half Greek and half Latin is so near to indecent that we print it with hesitation; while speakers of English have been fatally attracted by the irrelevant word 'horseless.' Other nations have been equally unfortunate and it really looks as if the dispossessed or to be dispossessed animals are to get revenge on an ungrateful humanity by stumping us to find a respectable name for our noisy and odorous machine."

As the old century ended, the intellectuals admitted defeat. People seemed to like the bastard word *automobile,* derived from the Greek *autos,* meaning "self," and the Latin *mobilis,* meaning "moving." In 1900 the *Times* changed its index to classify these things as automobiles instead of horseless vehicles. It is rather amusing that while this controversy was raging in America, at least one French manufacturer was advertising, in France, a *voiture sans cheval*—a horseless carriage.

By any name these new contraptions did not smell sweet, literally or figuratively, to the vast majority of the American people—which seems strange, because Americans are supposed to be a progressive, forward-looking folk, receptive to new ideas. But it must be remembered that Robert Fulton had trouble getting passengers to ride on his *Clermont* almost a hundred years before, and the Wright Brothers waited five years to get a customer for an airplane a few years later. The initial public apathy toward all three innovations in transportation can probably be traced to the so-called Puritan tradition. They were all "agin' nature."

And there were more specific reasons for the early dislike of the common herd for the automobile. There was the traditional resentment of the "have-nots" toward the "haves" who owned cars. The clanking machines were becoming a disruptive influence that frightened man's second-best friend, the horse. They were (and are) smelly and noisy. An early editorial, speaking of the relation of the man in the street to the automobile, said, "It is his part to inhale the fumes which poison the atmosphere of our best avenues and to be either driven from his home by the noise of the autos or choked by the dust which they raise."

The clergy was against automobiles. Many a sermon was preached on the iniquity of the "devil wagons" by preachers who were forgetful of the Old Testament prophecy of Nahum that "the chariots shall rage in the streets, they shall jostle one against another in the broad ways; they shall seem like torches, they shall run like the lightnings." *The Churchman,* after reminding its devout readers that the coaches of

Farmers, then more than half of the nation's work force, had a special hatred for the automobile. Not only did they associate it with "city slickers," but they also resented the fact that it consumed neither oats nor hay.

Auto Fun, Thomas Y. Crowell

ONE WOMAN WHO DID NOT JUMP

The Farmer: You may remember that you frightened my team last week, and smashed me up, and so I thought I'd rig a little surprise fer ye.

Cartoon satirizing the reckless drivers on Fifth Avenue. Dangers to pedestrians and cyclists caused public resentment toward the idle rich and their high-powered playthings.

the aristocracy had been overturned in the streets of Paris in 1789, proclaimed that the wealthy of America should not be allowed "to buy with money immunity to offend the social conscience and endanger the public safety." Many intellectuals of that day did not support innovations. From his ivory tower at Princeton, Professor Woodrow Wilson declaimed: "Nothing has spread socialistic feeling in this country more than the automobile. To the countryman they are a picture of the arrogance of wealth, with all its independence and carelessness."

The medical profession was, from the beginning, divided in its opinion. There was a school of medical thought that held that the mind might not be able to sustain its equilibrium under the speeds of which some cars were capable. And certainly they were not good for women. Wrote one physician, little dreaming that he was describing the "back-seat driver" of later years: "A speed of fifteen or

Half a block, half a block,
Half a block onward,
All in their 'motobiles
Rode the Four Hundred.
"Forward!" the owners shout,
"Racing car!" "Runabout!"
Into Fifth Avenue
Rode the Four Hundred.

"Forward!" the owners said.
Was there a man dismay'd?
Not though the chauffeurs knew
Some one had blundered.
Theirs not to make reply,
Theirs not to reason why,
Theirs but to kill or die.
Into Fifth Avenue
Rode the Four Hundred.

Tunnels to right of them,
Tunnels to left of them,
Subways beneath them
Volley'd and thunder'd;
Stormed at with shout and yell,

Boldly they rode and well.
Into Fifth Avenue,
While rang the chauffeur's bell,
Rode the Four Hundred.

Flashed all their goggles bare,
Flashed as they cleft the air,
Smashing the people there,
Charging the people, while
All the town wondered.
Plunged in the gasoline smoke,
Right down the street they broke;
Copper and Pedestrian
Reeled from their lightning-stroke
Shattered and sunder'd.
Then they rode back again,
Rode the Four Hundred.

When can their glory fade?
O the wild charge they made!
All the town wondered.
Proud of the charge they made,
Proud of themselves, they said,
Were the Four Hundred.

twenty miles an hour in a motor car causes them acute mental suffering, nervous excitement, and circulatory disturbances . . . extending far into the night and causing insomnia . . . . They are constantly on the lookout for trouble. Each approaching car, each curve in the road hides a disaster beyond; a grade crossing is nothing short of mental agony."

At least one economist theorized that the increased use of leather and rubber in automobiles would raise the price of boots and shoes. "The more people ride," he wrote, "the more the man who walks pays for going afoot. The automobile has developed into an expensive luxury for the man who does not use it."

The American farmers, who then comprised more than half the population and owned 18 million horses and mules, had a special hatred for the chicken-killing, horse-frightening, cattle-disturbing, woman-scaring juggernauts that made occasional appearances on country roads. There was traditional enmity between farm and town, and almost all the early automobiles were owned by "city slickers." Also, automobiles were neither hay feeders nor oat burners; when a car replaced a horse, the farmer lost a consumer for two of his cash crops. Farmers' Anti-Automobile Leagues were formed to combat the evil machine.

Added to all these causes for public resentment against the new plaything of the idle rich was the danger to pedestrians and cyclists, who believed that they had inalienable rights on the public highways. This belief was not shared by the lunatic fringe of the elite, who drove or permitted their chauffeurs to drive through city streets with the reckless abandon of the *grand seigneur* of older days, who tossed a purse of silver from the window of his coach when it ran down one of the peasant's children.

At the Automobile Club organization meeting in the Waldorf, Whitney Lyon, who had called the gathering, had all of this in mind when he told the other poor little rich boys why a club was needed. "We need to organize," he said. "We feel that as a class we are downtrodden and need protection badly. We need protection from the Park Department. We also need protection from that being known as the 'bike cop' who tries to stop our automobiles and tell us to travel so many miles an hour. And, gentlemen, we need a stable or station for our machines. I have been to many stables in New York to find shelter for my machine but the keepers would not take it in at any price. They consider it an enemy of the horse." The reference to the Park Department stemmed from a recent order closing Central Park to automobiles. Chicago had a similar prohibition. San Francisco was somewhat more liberal and permitted electrics only to use certain roads in Golden Gate Park.

A final reason for the distrust of the American public for the automobile was that gasoline-powered cars, the worst offenders in terms of smoke, smell, and noise, were of French origin, and anything French was considered somewhat immoral by most Americans. But not by some Americans. To "society," real or aspirant, what was French was right; and if the automobile was the rage of Paris at the turn of the century, those who set the social pace in the New World could no longer be faithful to the horse. What favored child of Mammon could resist the allure of the prestige of the auto after reading this *Vogue* report from Paris at the close of the spring season?

"You may be sure that today there is a packing of trunks and the automobile stands ready to transport the *mondaine* and her family far from Paris . . . . What a revolution the automobile is causing! The railway carriage is being ignored in certain circles of France, the members of which, when they leave town for some *château* or watering place, make the trip in their own motor cars . . . . The King of the Belgians, who comes up to Paris on the slightest pretext, makes the trip from Brussels to the French capital in his automobile . . . thus avoiding all the crowds at railroad stations and dependency upon time-tables. Is it not truly a royal way of getting about?"

What royalty and nobility could do in Europe, the scions of railroad fortunes, banking fortunes, fur fortunes, real-estate fortunes, and pork-packing fortunes could do in America. Oliver Hazard Perry Belmont imported the first French machine to Newport in 1897. Two years later there were enough of them in the summer society capital to close the season with a motorized lawn fete at Belcourt, the Belmont estate. Footmen and white-aproned maids were distracted from their normal indoor work to assist gardeners in converting the rather ugly vehicles of their masters into flower-bedecked chariots to bear the cream of Newport society.

As the host, Mr. Belmont drove the leading car along a winding path staked out by golf flags through an obstacle course of wooden horses and dummy figures of policemen and nursemaids. Mrs. Stuyvesant Fish rode with him in a car covered with yellow field flowers "surmounted by an arbor of cat-o'-nine tails bearing a stuffed eagle from whose beak ran blue and yellow streamers festooned to a floral pole, upon which were numerous sea gulls." Mrs. Belmont followed in a golf rig set off with blue hydrangeas and piloted by Mr. J. W. Gerard. The hostess gaily urged her mechanical steed on with a whip of hydrangeas and daisies. Mrs. Astor, driven by contemporary playboy Harry Lehr, was more sedate in her smelly hydrangea bower, sporting only a matching floral collar for her lap dog. Her husband, the Colonel, piloted Mrs. Ladenburg in a Stanhope decorated with green and white clematis. According to one reporter the Colonel steered with "the same cool-headed dash that distinguished him while serving under fire at Santiago."

Mrs. Belmont's little circus continued until twelve vehicles had completed the course. Then, followed at a discreet distance by a truckload of mechanics, the gay party drove to the Belmont country place for dinner and dancing, and completed the novel event with a midnight parade in which "every vehicle was brilliantly illuminated with countless little glow-lights interspersed among the floral wreaths, and each in turn let the rays of its headlights play on the many-colored decorations of its forerunner." *The Automobile Magazine* ended its reverent report on these shenanigans with a eulogy: "Thus the procession of scintillating vehicles sped swiftly over the dark country roads, and glided into the sleeping old town of Newport, like a veritable pageant of fairy chariots. A belated stage driver, pulling up his horses on the Post Road, rubbed his eyes in wonder. To him and to his snorting steeds it was like a whiff of the century to come."

Those who were not sufficiently affluent to have a lawn at Newport had to devise less costly ways to use their motorized toys. The society columnist of *Automobile Topics,* writing under the delightful pen name of *La Chauffeuse,* told, in January 1901, of the spectacular exploit of Mrs. "Jack" Gardner of Boston. Apparently Mrs. Gardner was not of the upper echelon of the elite, for *La Chauffeuse* felt it necessary to identify her as "the Mrs. Stuyvesant Fish of the Hub. She is always doing something to startle society, like trotting about the peaceful streets of Boston with a tame lion." Mrs. Gardner deserves better than this of history, for she seems to have devised the first drive-in restaurants.

To top her performance with the lion she got four autos and held the first automobile dinner party. She led her small cortege to the Hotel Touraine. "Here oysters were served, the astonished waiters being compelled to run out with their trays to the autos." The cars next whirled the diners to the Adams House, where they had soup in the street; and so on through ten courses. For a reason not explained by *La Chauffeuse* the tour ended at a Chinese restaurant, where the party had chop suey for dessert.

Automobile gymkhanas became the newest sport in Newport and on Long Island, as they were in Paris. The sponsors of these competitions vied with each other to devise novel events in which blue bloods, male and female, could prove their prowess at driving a car while spearing hoops in the air, knocking over tenpins, picking up parasols

Mrs. Alice Ramsey and party—the first women to cross the continent by themselves in an automobile. They left New York on June 9, 1909, and arrived in San Francisco in August.

on the run, and spearing dummy pigs. The society press took these things seriously; as witness this description of the finale of a pig-sticking contest: "It seems as though all were going to fail when the exquisitely golden haired Comtesse de Beauregard dashed up. The Comtesse in a tense moment poised her big spear carefully, leaned far out of the automobile and sank it deftly, properly, victoriously."

It is to be noted in all this the prominent role played by women. Of course, high society is largely a feminine affair, but even apart from that cars seem to have had from the earliest days an affinity for women—a kind of two-cylinder sex appeal that, in the eight-cylinder days to come, would have the country's most powerful industry turning handsprings to please the little woman. Oldsmobile first used a woman's magazine, *The Ladies' Home Journal,* for automobile advertising in 1903.

In addition to its inherent value as an attention getter, the early auto appealed to a woman as an excuse for a new dress. A motoring costume was a necessity. "The automobile gown has come into existence in Newport," cried a fashion editor, who went on to explain that it had a skirt somewhat longer than that of a golf costume but two or three inches shorter than the ordinary walking skirt and a very tight waist, without any trimming or frills "to prevent the rapid action of the arms and hands on the lever and steering tiller." This was, essentially, the basic costume of the famed Gibson Girl.

In 1899 Paris decreed that *the* color for fall was Automobile Red —the bright, impressive red that French manufacturers were using on car bodies. For milady who really sought a feeling of well-dressed security behind the tiller, New York furrier Revillon Frères offered full-length, sable-lined motor coats.

And to the new woman of the new century the automobile offered opportunity for more freedom with men. A certain romantic reaction was inherent in the shared daring of motoring; but an unanticipated relationship of sex and cars arose during the first decade of the twentieth century. Sensation-seeking newspapers kept standing in type the headline "Beautiful Heiress Runs Away with Humble Chauffeur." They had frequent use for it. When the Y.M.C.A. offered its first course in "chauffeuring" in 1901, it did not realize that this work would offer so many opportunities for interesting and lucrative moonlighting. Not all of these young men were single, and the yellow press reveled in alienation of affection suits brought by less glamorous wives and annulments sought by rich fathers who disdained a chauffeur for a son-in-law. With typical Hearst omniscience the New York *American* attributed the allure of the chauffeur to "the hypnotism of speed, which levels all ranks in the feminine mind and stirs up primitive emotions."

Song writers quickly sensed the possibilities of linking sex with cars. The first ditty to make the connection was published in 1899 under the title "Love in an Automobile." * During the next two years there were scores more; "Let's Have a Motor Car Marriage," "In Our Little Love Mobile," "The Automobile Honeymoon," and "The

---

* Yes, "The Girl in the Low Back Car" long antedated this, but the "Sweet Peggy" whom Victor Herbert's grandfather first saw "upon a summer's day" was riding in a low-backed Irish jaunting car—pulled by a horse.

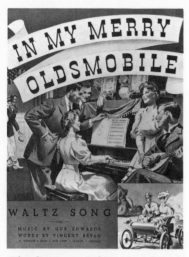
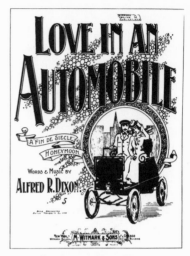

The first song linking the pleasures of cars and romance was "Love in an Automobile," published in 1899. During the next decade, more than two hundred songs appeared on the same subject. The Oldsmobile Company had nothing to do with their best advertisement of all time—"In My Merry Oldsmobile." But they did award the writers a car.

Automobile Kiss" are but a few of the long-forgotten love songs that extolled the pleasures of motorized romance. Most of the almost two hundred automobile songs that appeared during the first decade of the century were on this theme. The greatest, written in 1905 and which may still be heard, implored the singer's Lucille to come away with him in "My Merry Oldsmobile." The Oldsmobile Company had nothing to do with the writing of this, their best advertisement; but after it quickly zoomed to great popularity they felt that the least they could do was to give its writers, Gus Edwards and Vincent Bryan, a car. One Oldsmobile and two writers did not work out very well. The boys sold the car and split the cash.

Theatrical folk were but a short step behind society in patronizing this newsworthy form of transportation. In 1900 it was reported that Lily Langtry—the gorgeous "Jersey Lily"—was tooling around Hyde Park "in a motor carriage which she guides with much skill. She is particularly happy in her choice of costumes and never looks better than when in the garb of a *chauffeuse.*" At the same time

Maude Adams, at the tiller of her new Locomobile, was turning heads in Washington, where she was playing in *L'Aiglon*. And Anna Held, after piloting her Panhard in the *Concourse des Artistes* in the Bois de Boulogne, brought it to America in 1900 and challenged any local woman to a race from New York to Philadelphia. When there was no response to this gambit for attention she made new headlines by taking a much-publicized milk bath. A rather unusual, non-theatrical celebrity to make the news with an automobile was Carrie Nation, who, between saloon smashings, drove a car in Boston's first automobile show.

The automobile quickly became a favorite stage prop. As early as 1897 De Wolfe Hopper played in an opera satire, *Very Little Faust and Much Marguerite,* in which Faust tried to carry off his innocent victim in one of New York's new electric cabs. George Bernard Shaw's *Man and Superman,* in which an automobile figures as a prop, was first produced in London in 1901 and New York in 1905. In that year automobiles graced Broadway stages in eleven plays, including another by Shaw, *John Bull's Other Island,* and two for which Victor Herbert wrote automobile songs.

Annette Kellerman made headlines when she dove in the pool at New York's Hippodrome wearing a skin-tight bathing suit. Here she is more sedately garbed at the wheel of a 1908 Buick in Central Park.

Automobile Manufacturers Association

Advertisements for two stage shows. The automobile quickly became a favorite stage prop as producers saw the public interest it aroused. In 1905 cars appeared on Broadway in eleven plays.

A producer of melodrama named Theodore Kremer took shrewd advantage of the public attitude toward the loathsome new vehicles by casting an automobile as a villain in *The Great Automobile Mystery.* One review of this opus reported that "to see how the audience arise in their seats and all their wrath and call this villain cursed is one of the spectacles which is worth going nearly all the way to Harlem to see. To be sure there are other criminals in the play, but seriously it was an exceedingly clever idea to put an automobile in such a position that as many people as wanted to could curse it as long as they liked for a small price of admission. . . . Think of being able to rid one's chest of all grudges against automobiles for one little dollar. And up in the gallery you can curse the machine even harder for twenty-five cents." Because virtue must always triumph, the car blew itself up in the last act.

The automobile was not always the villain. In the dear, dead days of the theater when production costs did not limit most plays to one set the automobile on a stage treadmill, with a moving diorama behind it, quickly replaced the onstage horse race, chariot race, or galloping fire engine as the thrilling spectacle. In *The Vanderbilt Cup* Barney Oldfield raced his thundering, flame-spitting Green Dragon across the stage while the play's star, Elsie Janis—World War I's one-woman U.S.O.—chewed her nails with anxiety on the side lines.

The race in *Bedford's Hope* was even more thrilling. Ned Bedford gave the villain an order to buy his stock in the Old Pal Mine for a pittance before he learned of the big gold strike. The villain had left in a locomotive. The telegraph line was down, the telephone cable cut. What could Bedford do? With a "honk, honk" from its bulb horn, Bedford's hope came onstage. The curtains closed. When they reopened, the smoke-belching locomotive was center stage, careening along at a mile a minute—or so the moving scenery in the background seemed to indicate. The car crept on from stage left. For a while they raced neck and neck, the car bouncing over bumps on its treadmill while the villain hissed from the locomotive cab and the heroine wrung her hands in the seat beside Bedford. Then the automobile treadmill was slowed down, and the car forged ahead to the thunder of cheers from the audience.

Corny? Perhaps. But *Bedford's Hope* had the S.R.O. sign up, whereas down the block or around the corner one could buy seats to see Ethel Barrymore in J. M. Barrie's *Alice Sit by the Fire,* with brothers John and Lionel in a curtain raiser, Fritzi Scheff as *Mlle Modiste,* or Maude Adams as *Peter Pan.*

Not all of the early blue-blooded automobilists were dilettantes who confined their motoring to city streets or publicity-provoking stunts. In 1900 it was widely reported in the New York society columns that William K. Vanderbilt, Jr., "presented a novel appearance when he arrived in this city at eleven o'clock at night after his ride from Newport in his Daimler gasoline machine. He was attired in leather jacket, large goggles over his eyes and a patent leather cap. Accompanying him were his French chauffeur and a footman. Mrs. W. K., Jr., was waiting at the Waldorf-Astoria for him."

This feat attracted attention because the driver's name was Vanderbilt. A year earlier, when Alexander Winton had made the first recorded cross-country run from Cleveland to New York, nobody paid much attention to him. He covered the 800 miles in ten days, hoping to get some publicity for the cars he was trying to build. When New York ignored him he put his little machine on a freight car and went home, having proved that cross-country touring was possible, though not practicable. In 1901 Roy Chapin—who later

*Early autos were not dependably rugged, but it was the roads rather than
the cars that discouraged many drivers from venturing beyond city limits.
Above, a typical rural road in the early part of this century.*

became Herbert Hoover's Secretary of Commerce—fared no better
when he drove an Oldsmobile from Detroit to New York in seven and
a half days—about five miles per hour, including time out for repairs.
The mud-spattered pioneer was not permitted to use the front door
of the Waldorf. He had to slink in through the tradesman's entrance
to get upstairs, where his boss, Ransom E. Olds, was waiting.

Rugged dependability was not a quality of early cars and tires,
but it was the roads rather than the cars that made it a hazardous
adventure to take one's vehicle beyond the city limits. Roy Chapin
left the road entirely for much of his trip from Detroit and
crossed New York State on the towpath of the Erie Canal. This
exposed him to some very salty language from the drivers of the
mules that towed the canal barges. When they did give him right
of way they moved their animals to the landward side of the path,
so that if the beasts panicked they would not go into the water.

Chapin's trip was interrupted frequently by problems of getting over or under towropes.

Roads were a reason for the French leadership in automobiles. Napoleon had left a legacy of good, paved interurban highways that had been maintained by the government and that cars could use as well as troops. In 1895 some forty self-propelled vehicles had raced from Paris to Bordeaux, a distance of eight hundred miles, at a top speed of fifteen miles an hour. In the United States, paving was limited almost exclusively to the streets of the principal cities—in some cases asphalt, more often Belgian blocks, which are commonly miscalled cobblestones. Of the 2 million miles of country roads only 150,000 were called improved. This meant graveled, after a fashion. Outside the cities there were only 160 miles of hard-surfaced road in the United States at the beginning of the century.

If anything, American roads had retrogressed during the nineteenth century. Railroads and canals had put some early improved toll roads out of business. Most places in the United States were connected by wagon-wide dirt paths, deep in dust in dry weather and deeper in mud in wet. Mud did not bother a horse much, and he could pick his way around chuck holes. He could also plod with ease through two feet of water, so only the deeper streams were bridged. On a day's outing in the country the motorist had to face the possibility of getting stuck in a pothole, bogged down axle-deep in mud, or stranded in a stream. When this happened he hired a farmer to haul him out with a team, while derisive boys screamed delightedly, "Get a horse, get a horse, get a horse."

Still there were daring adventurers who would brave these conditions and go touring to get away from the city congestion and the restrictive regulations that controlled their automobiles. New York City's first speed law was rather liberal: eight miles an hour. In many places it was four or five, and the city of Mitchell, South Dakota, met the menace of the motorcar in a most effective manner by passing an ordinance forbidding automobiles within the city limits.

There were restrictions in the country, too. New York State's first motor vehicle legislation, passed in 1901, required the operator of an automobile to pull to the side of the road and stop on signal from the driver of a horse-drawn vehicle until the latter had passed. If the horse was restive, its driver had the right to require the motorist to shut off his engine. After the horse had passed, the motorist had to get down and start to crank. One ingenious inventor in Battle Creek, Michigan, Uriah Smith, proposed to solve the problem of frightened horses by designing a car on the front of which was mounted a life-sized horse's head. "This expedient," he claimed, "by having the appearance of a horse, would raise no fears in any skittish animal; for the live horse would be thinking of another horse approaching and, before he could discover his error and see that he was fooled, the strange carriage would have passed." Smith proposed to make his design doubly practical by using the horse's head as a reserve gas tank. A piece of Federal legislation that was annoying to tourists prohibited carrying gasoline on ferryboats except in special containers. Where this was enforced motorists were required to drain their tanks and push their cars on and off the ferry.

Together with restrictive legislation came registration. New York State required the 954 automobile owners who registered their cars in 1901 to pay $1 and adorn their vehicles with the "separate initials of the owner's name placed on the back thereof in a conspicuous place. The letters of such initials shall be at least three inches in height." Most states required out-of-state motorists to register locally. In some places this developed into a racket to bilk tourists. Missouri, for a while, required a $2 registration for each county and $10 for St. Louis. It cost about $30 in registration fees to cross the state.

More than anything else, the tourist of the early years of the century needed faith. But even the most optimistic tourist would be foolhardy to take his car far beyond the city limits without making extensive preparations. He carried extra gasoline, because fuel was not readily available, and most country stores that carried it charged exorbitant prices. He also carried a chamois and a pocket hydrometer. If he was forced to buy gas, he first tested it with a hydrometer and then strained it into the tank through the chamois. Car manufacturers supplied a kit of tools with the car to make repairs, but these were not adequate for all probable contingencies. It was well to carry, in addition, a towrope, a block and tackle, a lantern, a pail, a waterproof cover for protection while making repairs in the rain, and possibly a sledge and pry bar. Farsighted tourists also carried spare parts, particularly a fully charged battery.

And even the casual tourist carried at least two spare tires and tubes. On any trip of a hundred miles he felt lucky if two sufficed. Three or four flat tires were nearer the average and eight or ten not unheard of. While he had spares, all he had to do to change a tire was get out a jack, wrench, pry bar, hammer, and pump and force the tire off the wheel, force a new tire back on, then strain at the pump to blow the tire up to about seventy pounds pressure.

After the spares were used up it was a little harder. The tourist then brought out his tube-repair kit. This included patching material, adhesive, a file, sandpaper, small scissors, a little vise, and a tin of canned heat. After removing the deflated tire the motorist reinflated the tube, spit on his finger, and ran it over the tube until a bubble disclosed the leak. He filed around the leak to roughen the rubber, cut a patch, and glued it to the tube. This was put in the vise, and

A frequent scene in the early years. Most motorists carried a full supply of spare equipment, including tires, tubes, tools, and gasoline.

Automobile Manufacturers Association

the canned heat was lighted and the patch vulcanized to the tube. Then the edges of the patch were neatly beveled with the scissors, the area sanded smooth, the tube put back in the tire, the tire on the wheel, and the pumping started. A good man could repair a tube and remount the tire in less than an hour, by daylight. By lantern light it took a little longer.

Perhaps because misery loves company, and to present a united front to unfriendly farmers, much touring was done in groups. By 1901 there were thirty-six automobile clubs in the country. These clubs organized increasingly longer journeys. The New York club first ran to Bridgeport, then to Philadelphia, and finally announced a grand "1,000-mile" trip to the Pan-American Exposition in Buffalo —although it was then, as now, only about 800 miles to Buffalo and back.

Eighty cars started on this epic journey, which was to take seven days. The trip was jinxed from the start when John Jacob Astor ran into a bicyclist. Rain fell hard, and continued to fall hard, day after day. There were no closed cars, and many were without tops. The sodden tourists slithered and wallowed through the mud, grinding along in low gear. Fifty-one of them finally reached Rochester, where, upon learning that President McKinley had been shot at the Fair, they gave up.

In 1904 a more successful run was made to the St. Louis Fair— about 1,250 miles—by seventy-nine cars from several automobile clubs. Some started from New York, and the rest converged along the route. There was a wide variety of makes and sizes of cars available by this time. Among the big machines that lined up for the start were several White Steamers, a Pope-Hartford, a Pope-Toledo, a six-passenger Peerless, an air-cooled chain-drive Franklin, and a big Darracq. The little fellows included a two-passenger Haynes-Apperson, a two-cycle Elmore, an Oldsmobile, a Buckmobile, and a solid-tired Yale. About an hour after the take-off a single-cylinder Cadillac chugged up to the starting point. After asking, in effect, "Which way did they go?" the driver of the little car took off after the pack, which he caught at Poughkeepsie and stayed with all the way to St. Louis.

Colonel Augustus Pope, a "Blizzard Man of '88," an erstwhile actor, opera singer, pioneer balloonist, and an automobile promoter, made the St. Louis tour in a White Steamer and kept a diary. The first casualty was in Yonkers, where a Mr. LaRoche "knocked the fender off a trolley car." Before Poughkeepsie the Buckmobile had to replace its chain and the Pope-Toledo its fan. They all kept going except the Yale, which was disabled when a mechanic left a wrench in the gear box. At Albany the caravan was joined by a contingent from Boston, led by C. J. Glidden in a big green Napier. He had already hit a horse.

West of Albany the roads were so bad that the tourists paused in Utica to write a round robin letter to New York's governor, saying, "It is undoubtedly true that throughout the civilized world there do not exist roads in such wretched condition." The troupe was cheered somewhat by a dinner in a Syracuse hotel at which was served "air-cooled green turtle soup, double-cylinder clams, jump-spark sauterne and gasoline cocktail." At Buffalo there was a mass meeting to protest the action of the Pope-Toledo, which always started out early so as to get to the next stop first and hog the headlines. The tour was not supposed to be a race, but scorchers, trying to burn up the road, continued to give so much trouble that the operation was almost abandoned outside Chicago.

Near Eire, Ohio, Mr. Glidden was faced by a farmer standing in the road over a dead chicken, killed by a previous car. The rustic held a shotgun at his head until Glidden passed over a dollar. At Perrysville, Ohio, the Mercedes driven by H. W. Whipple, president of the A.A.A., was demolished by a freight train—Whipple, unhurt, continued as a passenger in another car. At Pontiac, Illinois, a mechanic set fire to F. A. Benson's Olds, and the gas tank blew up. Between South Bend and Chicago three cars overturned in ditches and there were two runaway-horse incidents.

A great difficulty was finding the route on roads unmarked by signs. The A.A.A. Blue Book was not much help with directions like: "Upgrade over several bad rocks, caution for many bad water bars during next four miles, curve left and immediately right after cheese factory; *do not take this road.*" The tourists were led by pilot cars from each city, from which local litterbugs marked crossroads with strewn confetti. This worked except when the wind blew away the paper. At South Bend an ingenious pathfinder sought to avoid this by using white beans instead of paper. The lead cars found the

Contestants in front of Mt. Washington Hotel, turning point of the first Glidden Tour, 1905. Starting from the Plaza Hotel in New York, the tour ran 870 miles to Bretton Woods, New Hampshire, and back. Entrants included Percy Pierce, R. E. Olds, and other auto makers who sought publicity for their products.

road well marked by chickens eating the beans. Later cars followed the feathers from the chickens that the earlier cars had killed. One driver toward the rear of the cortege commented that all such marking was unnecessary for him; he followed the route of broken spring leaves.

On the rainy morning of August 10, 1904, sixteen days out of New York, sixty-seven cars lined up four abreast to parade through St. Louis. The iniquitous Pope-Toledo was sent to the back of the line for jumping the gun, as was a Mercedes. Five cars came in later; seven did not finish. Next day they were escorted by two hundred local cars to the fairgrounds, where the mayor of St. Louis proclaimed the day Automobile Day, and everybody rode on the giant Ferris wheel.

The success of the St. Louis tour led retired millionaire C. J.

Glidden to donate an elaborate silver trophy for a series of annual reliability tours that started in 1905 with an 870-mile run from New York to Bretton Woods, New Hampshire, and return. Mr. Glidden had assumed that this would be something of a social event, and every morning two baggage trucks left well before the tourists so that their evening clothes would be at the next stop in time to dress for dinner. He was rather disturbed that the automobile manufacturers saw in his tours a great opportunity for publicity. When the entrants for the first tour lined up in front of the Plaza Hotel, Percy Pierce was driving a Pierce-Arrow, Walter White was piloting a White Steamer, R. E. Olds was at the wheel of a Reo, J. D. Maxwell was handling Jack Benny's favorite car, and three members of

Whether this Glidden Tour Pathfinder ever got back on the path is not on record. It is on record that it sat stuck in mud up to the hub caps, one of many victims of the primitive American roads.

American Automobile Association

the Pope family had entered various species of the hyphenated Pope cars.

The Glidden tourists battled their way to Bretton Woods despite the opposition of New England farmers and constabulary. Rural automobile haters had learned that the weak point of the car was its pneumatic tire and that the pernicious vehicles could be reduced to impotence by glass or barbed wire placed in their paths. One fiendish farmer buried a crosscut saw blade in the road that was not discovered until four cars had impaled all their tires on its teeth. Then there were the farm boys who were not dissuaded by their parents from stretching a wire across the road at the height of the motorists' necks, at dusk, to see whether they could decapitate some of the invaders from the city.

Several New England towns sought to fill their coffers with fines by laying traps for visitors who exceeded the eight-mile speed limit in their outskirts. In one case constables dressed as workmen took positions on a measured quarter mile of fairly good road with a rope that could be swung across the highway to stop unwary speedsters. The radar of today's state police is not a new technique. The police chief of Leicester, Massachusetts, more knowledgeable than most about motors, merely posted himself at the foot of a hill and collected $15 fines from all who briefly accelerated to make the grade.

The general attitude of New England toward these self-propelled visitors from the metropolis was expressed by the Manchester, New Hampshire, *Union,* which editorialized that they were an "unmitigated nuisance" and an "outrage which ought to be stopped once and for all . . . . If these people think of coming here another year we hope the law against speeding and scorching will be promptly and vigorously enforced. Let a few of them stay in jail two or three days and all the rest of us will be better for it."

The Glidden Tours were the forerunners of today's sports car rallies. They were not races. In the point system that determined the winner, penalties were imposed for exceeding the speed limit or arriving at a control point too early. To achieve a perfect score a tourist had to check in at each control point on time and without mechanical trouble. When the tourists returned to New York from the first Glidden Tour seven had perfect scores, and the trophy

Automobile Manufacturers Association

Another Glidden Tour Pathfinder bites the dust—or, in this case, the water.

was awarded by having each contestant cast two votes for the winner. After first voting for themselves, seventeen contestants voted for Percy Pierce, and the trophy went to Buffalo to rest in the Pierce-Arrow plant. The Glidden Tours, which continued annually until 1913, did much to convince America that the automobile was a dependable means of transportation.

Another early endorsement for the practicality of the new vehicles came, surprisingly, from doctors—usually a conservative lot. But local transportation was an important element in the doctor's life. Speed, dependability, and cost were all factors; as was convenience—none but physicians had much occasion to hitch up a horse at 2 A.M. In 1906 the *Journal of the American Medical Association* published a special section, "Automobiles for Physicians," in which doctors related their experiences and expressed their opinions.

Fifty-nine physicians endorsed the new method of transportation, five opposed it, four were on the fence, and one rugged medic averred that the only way for a doctor to get around in the twentieth century was on a motorcycle. Most doctors who endorsed the

Doctors, usually a conservative group, were among the first to endorse the automobile. In 1906, Maxwell offered a "doctor's model," based on specifications requested by physicians making house calls. Price, without top, $1,300.

automobile added that a really practical car for physicians had not yet been built, and they proceeded to describe such a car. Because many physicians are individuals with strong opinions, there was little agreement as to specifications. Some insisted that only a heavy, multicylinder car would serve a physician, others that the single- or dual-cylinder runabout was ideal. Some claimed that pneumatic tires were works of the devil, others that solid tires would not do. More favored an air-cooled over a water-cooled engine. One doctor proposed that the profession get together on specifications and offer an order for a thousand or more vehicles to the manufacturer who would make a "doctor's car." By 1907 Maxwell was offering a "doctor's" model. The *Journal of the American Medical Association* was rather noncommittal in its editorial endorsement of the automobile but came out strongly with one recommendation—all drivers should be required to take a medical examination. This would be very good business for doctors.

As the first ten years of the new century passed, the attitude toward the automobile changed. It was not yet by any means a way of life for every man, but, except in some die-hard areas, distrust, derision, and detestation slowly changed to desire in the breasts of many Americans. In fact, despite all the evidence of early opposition, there had probably always been an underlying urge to accept this new thing—if it was for real, and attainable.

With the dawn of the twentieth century America was spiritually ready for the automobile but did not know it. Bicycles had paved the way. The cycle craze of the nineties had given 10 million Americans a taste of personal transportation that would take them at least a little way toward the horizon. And cyclists had done some spade work for the automobile in another direction. They, too, needed better roads, and 10 million votes carry a lot of weight in a democracy. At the turn of the century seven states had organized road departments. Although they had as yet done little to pull America out of the mud, the groundwork was laid to meet the increasingly vehement demands of the motorists.

By 1910 the automobile was no longer an exclusive, or nearly exclusive, plaything of the rich. Its exploits were published as news, not in the society columns. True, more were still driven by socialites

Baseball's "most valuable player" award began as an effort to publicize the Chalmers car. Hugh Chalmers announced in 1910 that he would give a car to the champion batters of each league. He was delighted when Ty Cobb, a Detroiter, won the American League championship. But his elation turned to fury when Cobb promptly sold his prize.

and sports than by small-town bankers; but in most sizable communities some of the professional men and merchants argued the respective merits of their Buicks, Oldsmobiles, Cadillacs, Ramblers, or Fords—the only cars of that era which are still in existence. As early as 1901 there was some evidence of this trend away from the domination of the new vehicles by the elite in New York. In that year the Automobile Club of America proposed an alliance with thirty other clubs—with A.C.A. dominating the amalgamation. This proposal from New York received a cold reception in the hinterlands, but a counterproposal from another club, that a meeting be held in Chicago, was warmly received. So the American Automobile Association was formed on March 4, 1902—not in the lush New York Club, but at a meeting in the plebian Coliseum in Chicago. And the American Automobile Club changed its name to the Automobile Club of New York.

During the first ten years of the century the American automobile grew from a toddler to a teen-ager. It was not yet a fully responsible member of society, but it was beginning to look like an adult. The two-seated, tiller-steered, bicycle-wheeled buggies of 1900, with their one- or two-cylinder engines of six or eight horsepower, had advanced to five-passenger, four-cylinder cars of forty or more horsepower. The tonneau, or after-body, had made the transition from a pair of jump seats reached through a rear door to an honest back seat with side doors. For a while, doors on the side were considered a foreign affectation, principally because few American cars had a long enough wheelbase to accommodate them. Dim kerosene headlights had been replaced by bright beams of gas. The steering wheel had replaced the tiller, and fenders, running boards, tops, and windshields were standard equipment in the higher-priced cars. The 1910 Overland was the first car in the $1,000 class to carry a top, windshield, and headlights as standard equipment.

By 1910 domestic production had increased from 4,192 in 1900 to 187,000, and there were a total of 469,000 cars and trucks on what could not yet be called highways. Prices had not materially changed. In 1901, when foreign cars and some American makes were selling at $4,000 or up, the little curved-dashboard Oldsmobile was priced at $650, and this was still about the range in 1910, although several foreign and a few American makers offered models priced over $7,000. But the buyer got a lot more for his money. The few producers of dependable low-priced automobiles could not make enough cars to supply the demand.

Although it cannot be said that America was on the move at the end of the first decade, it was certainly on the way. And, drooling in the wings, so to speak, stood every small boy in America, dreaming that someday he might sit behind a steering wheel. No one would have then believed that practically every boy who dreamed that dream in 1910 would fulfill it within the next two decades.

Henry and Clara Ford in the shed where he built his first car. Painting by Norman Rockwell.

TWO: RULE OF THUMB

Faithful as the swallows of Capistrano were the bobolinks of Dearborn, Michigan, which always returned on April 2—or so said Henry Ford in his autobiography. That is how he could be so sure of when he first operated his gasoline buggy. He wrote that it "first ran successfully in the spring of 1893. I was running it when the bobolinks came to Dearborn."

The Automobile Manufacturers Association does not quarrel with Mr. Ford's knowledge of ornithology, but it does challenge the accuracy of his memory. "Henry Ford," says the Chronicle of the Association, "successfully operated his first motor vehicle in Detroit on June 4, 1896."

Charles Duryea said that he first drove on April 19, 1892 the automobile he designed. His brother Frank, who built the car, claimed that he, not Charles, first drove it on September 20, 1893. Most authorities endorse this latter date as that on which the first American-made gasoline-powered automobile was publicly demonstrated. But people in Allentown and Bethlehem, Pennsylvania, insisted that a gasoline-powered vehicle built by Henry Nadig was running on the streets of these communities in 1891.

This conflicting and confusing testimony as to precedence is important only to the hairsplitting historian. It is cited to point up the strange fact that we seem to know more specifically what Caesar did with Cleopatra in Egypt two thousand years ago than we do about the development of the automobile in America seventy-five years ago. It is certain that during the early 1890s many mechanics and tinkerers, craftsmen and crackpots, were laboring in lofts, shops, barns, and kitchens to create what would later be called automobiles. In its first issue in 1895, *Horseless Age* estimated that there were then three hundred self-propelled vehicles planned, built, or abuilding.

All of the pioneer automobile builders were unknowns. With few exceptions they had no formal training in any kind of engineering. Automotive engineers, of course, did not yet exist. The best of the early entrepreneurs were self-taught, like Henry Ford, and seemed to have an almost instinctive ability to handle tools and devise machinery. Hiram Percy Maxim, who later gained fame as the inventor of the silencer for a gun, offered one explanation of why so many started experimenting almost simultaneously:

> As I look back I am amazed that so many of us began work so nearly at the same time, and without the slightest notion that others were working on the problem. In 1892, when I began my work on a mechanical road vehicle, I suppose there were fifty persons in the United States working on the same idea.
>
> Why did so many different and widely separated persons have the same thoughts at the same time? In my case the idea came from looking down and contemplating my legs and the bicycle cranks while riding along a lonely road in the middle of the night. I suppose not another of us pioneers had its original inspiration come to him as mine came to me.
>
> It has always been my belief that we all began work on a gasoline engine propelled road vehicle at about the same time because it had became apparent that civilization was ready for the mechanical vehicle . . . . It has been the habit to give the gasoline engine all the credit for bringing the automobile . . . . In my opinion this is the wrong explanation. We have had the steam engine for over a century. We could have built steam vehicles in 1880, or indeed in 1870. But we did not. We waited until 1895.
>
> The reason why we did not build mechanical road vehicles before this, in my opinion, was because the bicycle had not yet come in numbers and had not directed men's minds to the possibilities of independent, long distance travel over the ordinary highway. We thought the railroad was good enough. The bicycle created a new demand which it was beyond the ability of the railroads to supply. Then it came about that the bicycle could not satisfy the demand which it had created. A mechanically propelled vehicle was wanted instead of a foot propelled one, and we know now that the automobile was the answer.

Maxim ignored the few self-propelled vehicles that had long been

Many conflicting claims have been made as to who built the first American car and when he demonstrated it. One such claim is that Henry Nadig drove his gasoline-powered auto on the streets of Allentown and Bethlehem, Pennsylvania, in 1891.

in use. Indeed, because he was no farm boy, he may not have known about them. Henry Ford did. He traced his first interest in automobiles to the year 1875, when he saw a steam engine used for powering sawmills and threshing machines on which a chain had been run from the engine to the rear wheels so that it could propel itself from job to job. At the age of sixty Ford wrote, "From the time I saw that road engine as a boy of twelve right forward to today, my great interest has been in making machines that would travel the roads."

Most of the successful pioneers were country-reared and of about the same age—in their early or middle thirties. Elwood Haynes was born in 1857, Ransom Olds in 1864. The birth dates of Henry Ford, Charles Duryea, and Alexander Winton fell between these years. In the strictest sense, none of these creators of the first cars was an inventor, except of his own vehicle. All of the main components of the automobile existed, and all of the principles involved were in use at the time they started to work.

A French artillery officer named Nicholas Joseph Cugnot is often called the father of the automobile because in 1770 he built the first known self-propelled road vehicle. This was a steam-powered tractor with which Cugnot hoped to haul guns. It made one successful run of three miles and then, on a second attempt, ran into a wall and upset in the world's first automobile accident. There were other experimental steam vehicles during the late eighteenth cen-

The first self-propelled road vehicle was built by Nicholas Cugnot in 1770. A French artillery officer, he designed a steam-powered tractor to haul guns. After a successful three-mile run, his tractor crashed into a wall and again made history in the world's first automobile accident.

America's first self-propelled vehicle—an amphibian that ran on either water or land—was built by Oliver Evans in 1805. It ran on steam power to its launching in Philadelphia, sailed on the river, then returned to land, where its owner drove it around Independence Square.

General Motors Corporation

For a short time in the early nineteenth century, steam coaches were making regular hauls on roads going to and from London. But the "Red Flag Act," sponsored by stagecoach interests, forced them out of business. This law required a man carrying a flag to walk ahead of each bus using a public road.

tury. The first in America was built in 1804 by Oliver Evans. The City of Philadelphia contracted with Evans to build a steam-powered floating dredge to clear garbage away from the docks. Like Robinson Crusoe, Evans built his boat back from the water. To launch it he put axles and wheels under it, ran a belt from the engine, and took it to the river under its own power. He then sailed it to Philadelphia and ran it up the bank and around Independence Square. He advertised this exploit in a Philadelphia newspaper, asking people who came to see it to pay twenty-five cents. So America's first automobile was the subject of the first automobile show. It was also the first amphibian.

Before the middle of the nineteenth-century steam-propelled coaches were running on regular schedules on lines radiating out of London. One such line carried 12,761 passengers a distance of 4,200 miles in one three-month period. Well-entrenched stagecoach interests first caused road tolls for buses to be raised to an exorbitant figure and then caused the passage of the "Red Flag Act," which required a man with a flag to walk in front of a self-propelled vehicle using a public road. This put the buses out of business and set automobiles back a half century. There was a similar law in the

United States, but it was applied principally to railroad trains within city limits. Until a very few years ago "Paul Revere" was a familiar figure in New York City. This was the rider who listlessly waved a red flag as he plodded down Tenth Avenue on a sorry nag, ahead of New York Central freight trains.

The contribution of the early steam engines and vehicles to the development of the automobile was twofold. Improvements in metallurgy, tools, and standards of workmanship brought about by the steam engine were available for the pioneering of the gas engine. And problems of transmission of power to wheels, and changing of speed and steering that had been worked out for steam-powered vehicles, could be applied to gas-powered vehicles.

Use of the internal combustion engine may be traced back to the end of the seventeenth century, when some unsuccessful experiments were made to operate a machine by a series of explosions, using gunpowder as the fuel. This did not work, and a better starting point for the gas engine is probably the experimental work with the properties of gases inspired by Joseph Priestley in the late eighteenth century. A John Barber secured a patent in England in 1791 on a means of procuring motion by exploding "inflammable air," and Robert Street secured an English patent in 1794 on the principle of the internal combustion engine, operating on gas from burning tar or turpentine.

When illuminating gas from coal was developed, several engines were built in Europe using this for fuel. The first commercially successful internal combustion engine was built by Jean Etienne Lenoir in Paris in 1860—a two-cycle engine fueled by liquid hydrocarbons that did not compress the gases within the cylinder. Nicholas August Otto heard of the Lenoir engine and, in Germany, developed a somewhat similar one operating on illuminating gas under compression. Next in point of time came French engineer Alphonse Beau de Rochas, who, in 1862, wrote a detailed treatise describing a four-cycle internal combustion engine. He did nothing about building one. In 1877 Nicholas Otto did, and built the first commercial four-cycle engine.

Lenoir put one of his engines in a carriage in about 1864 and made a journey of twenty-four kilometers from his factory to Paris and back. Perhaps because the engine was too heavy, he did nothing more about developing the automobile. In Vienna, Siegfried Marcus, impressed by de Rochas' treatise, built a four-cycle engine and mounted it in a car that became a familiar sight on the streets of Austria's capital. Seeing no commercial possibilities for the vehicle, Marcus turned to other things.

The vehicles generally considered the prototypes of the modern automobile were constructed by Gottlieb Daimler and Karl Benz. Daimler, an associate of Nicholas Otto's, had a disagreement with the latter, built a much lighter, higher-speed four-cycle engine and proclaimed, "I have created the basis for an entirely new industry," an understatement that was then brushed off as an egotistical boast. Working independently, but doubtless using his knowledge of the Otto engine, Karl Benz, also a German, developed a very similar power plant. Some years later *Automobile Topics* described the Daimler engine, which was then on the market in America:

"The Daimler motor uses for its fuel a light hydro-carbon, usually called gasoline. The engine is a vertical one, double cylinder, and works on the well known 'Otto' cycle, e.g., the downward stroke of the piston sucks in an explosive charge, which at the upstroke is compressed and 'fired' by a platinum tube heated to a bright red heat by a burner from the outside, or the charge is fired by an electric spark. The sudden pressure caused by the firing of the charge forces the piston downward at the next stroke, i.e., the working stroke. At the second upward stroke the exhaust valve is opened by a tappet or cam, and the products of combustion pass out of the cylinder through the exhaust valve. This cycle of operations, known as the 'Otto' cycle, is then repeated in the same order."

And it is still being repeated in powering almost every passenger car in the world today. The differences between the modern internal combustion engine and those built by Marcus, Otto, Daimler, and Benz are developments and refinements; the principle of operation is exactly the same. Of course, without the refinements, the automobile would not be practical. For instance, this is how the Daimler engine was started. "The starting of the motor is performed as follows. The burners have a small cup at the bottom. This cup is filled with gasoline, which is then lighted. When the flame is about to go out the gasoline supply to the burners is turned on, when a blue flame is seen at the mouth of the burner. This flame heats the ignition tubes to a red heat, the gasoline supply to the carburetor is turned on and, if the air is properly adjusted, a few turns of the starting handle are sufficient to start the motor, which should then run until the gasoline supply becomes exhausted."

Daimler mounted one of his engines in a motorcycle in 1885 and in a four-wheeled vehicle late in 1886. Benz mounted one of his engines in a tricycle early in 1886. This led to a long wrangle as to who was the first. Benz advocates pointed out that a motorcycle was not an automobile. Daimler supporters claimed that neither was a tricycle. All ignored Siegfried Marcus, who was running a four-wheeled vehicle powered by a four-cycle engine, which still sits in the Vienna Museum, twenty years before either of them.

But, unlike Marcus, Benz and Daimler did something about their creations. Daimler gave the French rights to his products to the carriage-building firm of Panhard and Levassor, which started turning out horseless carriages in 1889. Benz teamed up with another Frenchman, named Emil Roger, who started making the Roger-Benz the same year. Both cars were exhibited in the Paris Exposition that year, together with a streetcar powered by a Daimler engine. The public did not seem much interested, except in the streetcar, which provided a comfortable place to eat lunch. Panhard and Levassor made a deal with the Peugeot firm to produce another Daimler-powered car. In the early 1890s these were the Big Three of the automotive industry: Panhard & Levassor, Roger-Benz, and Peugeot.

The American automotive pioneers undoubtedly knew what was happening in Europe, which was reported regularly, though rather sketchily, in *Scientific American*. There is no evidence that they were much influenced by the car builders, but they did borrow freely from the European engines, which were widely used in America as stationary power plants long before the automobile experimental work started. There were also some American engines. Twenty-one-year-old Ransom Olds helped his father design one in 1885, which they manufactured in Lansing, Michigan. One that was exhibited by H. K. Shanks at the Ohio State Fair in 1886 inspired Charles Duryea to design his car.

The best-known American engine, which *Scientific American* considered superior to the two-cycle Otto, was built by George B.

Brayton in 1873, used to power a streetcar in Providence in 1876, and advertised for sale by the Pennsylvania Ready Motor Company that same year. Brayton used a wick type of vaporization, in which a felt was saturated with gasoline vaporized by a jet of compressed air. Ignition was by an open flame burning continuously within the cylinder.

By the time Americans started to create automobiles the four-cycle engine had made Brayton's obsolete; but not before it indirectly became the source of much trouble and more publicity for Henry Ford. In 1876 George B. Selden, a patent attorney with engineering training, built an engine on the Brayton principle and designed, on paper, a road vehicle in which to mount it. He applied for a patent in 1879 and kept the application alive by repeated amendments until 1895. This would later lead to the most famous patent suit in American history. Selden built no car until many years later, and then only to prove a point in the patent suit.

But other Americans were building cars in the early 1890s. First in point of time were the Duryea brothers, Charles and Frank. In

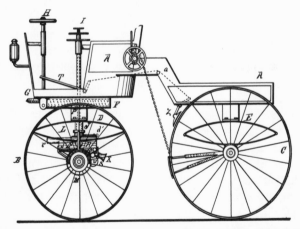

Automobile Manufacturers Association

Sketch for a "master patent." In 1895, George B. Selden, who had never built a car, obtained a patent for a gasoline automobile. Most manufacturers paid royalties to Selden until the U.S. Court of Appeals ruled against him in 1911.

1891 they were in Chicopee Falls, Massachusetts, where Frank worked as a toolmaker for a bicycle manufacturer. Charles, the bookish brother, had designed bicycles. Now he designed an engine of the two-cycle Otto type. He promoted $1,000 from Springfield businessman Erwin P. Markham, bought an old phaeton horse carriage, and hired brother Frank to build the engine and convert the phaeton to self-propulsion.

Frank built the engine to Charles' specifications, although these did not include an ignition system, an exhaust pipe, or a means of starting. The brothers tried to test it by inserting a crude ignition tube heated by an alcohol lamp and spraying gasoline into the cylinder with a perfume atomizer. When it did not work, Charles left for Peoria, Illinois, to go into the bicycle business. Frank had more faith. Although interrupted by a bout with typhoid, he continued to tinker with the engine. He devised a carburetor and a flame ignition system, and by early 1893 he had it operating on a test bench. He then mounted it in the phaeton and, with a belt transmission, drove the vehicle around the loft where he had built it.

Frank was still not satisfied. He wheedled more money out of Markham and continued tinkering to install electric ignition and an improved piston and flywheel. He then took his crude prototype downstairs, dragged it to the edge of town behind a horse, and on the night of September 20, 1893, spun the flywheel. For several spins nothing happened. Then the engine caught. Frank jumped into the seat, grasped the tiller, took up the slack on the transmission belt, and started on what is generally credited as the first trip in an American-made gasoline-powered automobile. The car went twenty-five feet and stalled. Started again, it covered 200 feet, to complete that night's motoring.

Frank Duryea should be accorded the distinction of being the automobile industry's first perfectionist. He was still not satisfied with the car. After promoting more money from Markham to install a gear and clutch transmission he retired the first vehicle—now in the Smithsonian—designed an entirely new machine and secured a new backer, H. W. Clapp, to finance its building. This was a much more advanced vehicle, with a four-cycle engine. It was a trim-looking buggy with wooden wheels, solid rubber tires, and all of its machinery neatly boxed out of sight. Its water-cooled engine

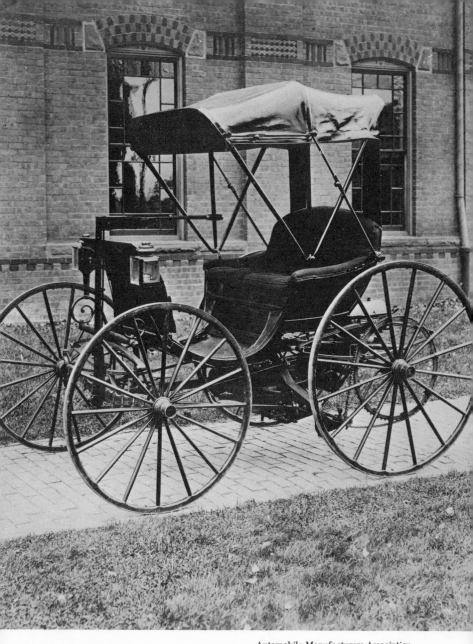

The car that the Smithsonian Institution recognizes as first workable American-built gasoline-engine vehicle. Designed by Charles E. Duryea, it was built and driven, in 1893, by his brother Frank.

Automobile Manufacturers Association

Frank Duryea behind the tiller of his second car at the start of America's first automobile race, from Chicago to Evanston and return, in 1895. In spite of two breakdowns, he outpaced the other five entries for an average speed of 6.66 miles an hour.

was in the rear, and its clutch and gear transmission provided three forward speeds and a reverse. It had a top speed of about eighteen miles an hour.

Shortly after this car was built, fifteen cars completed an eighty-seven-mile road race from Paris to Rouen under the sponsorship of a Paris newspaper. This inspired the publisher of the Chicago *Times-Herald* to offer $5,000 in prizes for an American road race from Chicago to Evanston and return, to be run on Thanksgiving Day, 1895. Applications for entry blanks to compete for this fat purse poured in. Eighty-nine engine builders, carriage builders, makers of bicycles, wheelchairs, and baby carriages—and just plain people —entered cars they hoped to build in time for the race. But when

Thanksgiving Day dawned there were but six cars at the starting line; three Benzes, two electrics, and the Duryea. There was also, in Chicago, eight inches of unexpected snow.

The race was a dramatic event—if anything in such slow motion could be so described—although only three cars really competed. Both electrics had battery trouble, and one Benz was defeated by the snow. The Duryea, first away at the start, kept a commanding lead, with brother Frank at the tiller and brother Charles following in a sleigh, until a part of the steering apparatus broke. Both brothers took to the sleigh and coursed the holiday streets seeking a machine shop where the owner lived in. By the time they found one and repaired the part the Benz entered by New York department store owner R. H. Macy was in the lead, and the other Benz, entered by Oscar Mueller, was coming up behind.

While Frank doggedly drove on to make up lost time, Charles stopped to eat and rest the horses. After lunch he could not find Frank and ranged the streets until he located him, off the course,

Elwood Haynes in the car he first demonstrated on July 4, 1894.

Automobile Manufacturers Association

crouched over a charcoal fire repairing a part of the electrical system. At the halfway point the Macy car was still in the lead, but shortly after the turn the Duryea caught up and passed it. Then the Macy car dropped out of the race. From that point on the Duryea breezed home. In the afternoon the sun came out and Chicagoans took to the streets to enjoy the season's first sleighing, creating an attractive Currier and Ives scene as they followed the chugging little car. Frank crossed the finish line in the dark, at 7:18 P.M., completing the fifty-four-mile run at an average speed of 6.66 miles per hour. The remaining Benz came in an hour and a half later, with the umpire driving, and Mueller collapsed beside him from the strain of the long, cold drive.

There would have been two American-made cars in the Chicago race if Elwood Haynes in his recently built vehicle had not tangled with a trolley car en route to the starting line. Haynes, who had studied at Worcester Polytech and Johns Hopkins, had some formal engineering training and had perfected a steel-producing process before he became interested in automobiles. His interest in a horseless vehicle probably stemmed from the endless hours he spent creeping around in a horse and buggy as a field superintendent for a natural gas company in Kokomo, Indiana. Early in 1893 he designed a car and took his plans to Elmer and Edgar Apperson, capable rule-of-thumb mechanics who ran a machine shop in Kokomo. Using an adaptation of a stationary gas engine made by Claude Stintz they hammered out the rest of the car as though the assignment was an ordinary machine shop order. Like the first Duryea it was crude in appearance, with large bicycle type wheels, a chain drive, and a conventional buggy seat and steering tiller perched atop the works. Unlike Frank Duryea and, later, Henry Ford, both of whom sneaked out at night for their first tests, Haynes and the Appersons were so confident of the success of their vehicle that they boldly announced that they would demonstrate it publicly on July 4, 1894. And they did. The skeptical holiday crowd formed an awed lane to watch the unbelievable horseless carriage chug along at six miles an hour.

Haynes—with the Appersons—and the Duryea brothers formed companies to make automobiles and started the industry on the competitive road of claims of precedence and superiority that still marks the business. Charles and Frank organized the Duryea Motor

Wagon Company and made thirteen cars in 1896—the first time that more than one car was made from a single design in the United States. Although there is some conflicting opinion, the first commercial sale of an American-built gasoline-propelled car seems to have been made by the Duryeas in February 1896 to George H. Morrill, Jr., of Norwood, Massachusetts.

The Haynes-Apperson Company was organized in 1895 and was also producing in 1896. From the early automobile factories it would be impossible to envision the later industry. In 1899 Haynes queried the Hyatt Roller Bearing Company in Newark about their product. The Hyatt sales manager visited Kokomo and returned to tell his partner that the cars "were made in a dirty little factory about as primitive as our own place. Most of the work is being done on a dirt floor." The partner to whom he imparted this information was young Alfred Pritchard Sloan, Jr., who, as President and Chairman of the Board of General Motors, would later contribute more to automotive development than any of the pioneers except Henry Ford.

In 1896 the Duryeas advertised in *Horseless Age* that their new models were "the finest specimens of carriage makers art ever produced for motor vehicles, embodying the handsome lines of a high grade carriage, yet having a 'complete' appearance—not 'a carriage-without-a-horse look'—and yet not a machine in appearance." Some-

American Manufacturers Association

Charles Brady King grasping the tiller of the first automobile to run on the streets of Detroit, in March 1896.

what later Haynes advertised with the slogan "Haynes—America's First Car," and the initial vehicle that the Appersons built was so labeled in the Smithsonian Institution until 1912, when Charles Duryea convinced the National Museum that his car deserved this honor.

Meanwhile, up in Detroit, Charles B. King was building a car. King was an engineer rather than a mechanic, and his contribution to the development of the automobile is of interest for only two minor reasons. He was the first man to build and drive an automobile in the city of Detroit, and he gave much advice, encouragement, and assistance to Henry Ford. King saw a Stintz two-cycle engine at the Columbian Exposition in Chicago in 1893 and bought one with the idea of using it in a road carriage. He soon discarded it and designed a four-cycle engine of his own. He entered in the Chicago race the car he planned to build but withdrew it when he realized that it could not be finished in time. Instead he rode in the race as Mueller's umpire and brought the Benz across the finish line after its owner collapsed.

King's work lagged through shortage of funds and the press of other duties in connection with the production of a pneumatic hammer that he had developed, until, early in 1896, a carriage works gave him an experimental iron-tired wagon to convert into a self-propelled vehicle. King mounted his engine in it, thus making it the crudest of all the early automobiles. He later said that it was not a car, merely a testing wagon. Before he obtained the wagon he had been working on a well-engineered chassis. This he later sold to a man named Carter, who was superintendent of the machine shop at the state prison. Carter procured a design for an engine and had it made by prison labor, and from this developed the Cartercar, a make later absorbed by General Motors.

King made some secret tests starting on March 1, 1896, and on March 6 announced a public demonstration. On March 7 the Detroit *Free Press* reported, "The first horseless carriage seen in this city was out on the streets last night." Generally, the press of the future Motor Capital expressed little interest in automotive transportation. The longest account of King's feat was a quarter column on an inside page of the *Journal*. The *Tribune* gave it only three lines.

But one who was vitally interested was the bicyclist who, with

Automobile Manufacturers Association

Alexander Winton at the tiller of a "dos-à-dos," which he demonstrated in 1899.

derby perched squarely atop his head, pedaled after King's crude wagon. This was Henry Ford, whose first vehicle was nearing completion.

There is a prevalent impression that Henry Ford's life was a typical Horatio Alger story, from rags to riches. The riches part is true enough—Ford was, at one time, the richest man in the Western world. But the rags part is purely legendary. His father was a fairly prosperous farmer who was never parsimonious with his son. There is also the belief that, in the Alger tradition, Henry achieved his first success by incessant, solitary labor. This is true to the extent that Ford never loafed. But neither was he a drudge. In his autobiography he explained his aversion to farming by writing, "My earliest recollection is that, considering the results, there was too much work on the place." In building his first car much of the actual work was done by several helpers, while Ford designed and directed.

Young Ford left the farm and Dearborn's one-room school at the age of seventeen to work in a Detroit machine shop. Long before this he had evidenced a skill with tools and machinery amounting to genius. In his early teens he had become a self-taught expert watch repairman, using tools he made himself. At this time he had little interest in the gasoline engines that were coming into use. He later reported that he "followed its progress, but only from curiosity." He worked at various jobs, all involving machinery, until 1888, when he married a young lady named Clara Bryant—a noteworthy event in the development of the automobile, because Clara's faith had much to do with Henry's success. His father gave him forty acres of timber land on condition that he would give up machinery for farming. Henry provisionally agreed to the extent of cutting and sawing the timber and building a house. He also built a shop in which he experimented with steam engines and devised a steam tractor that ran about forty feet.

In 1891 Ford was asked to repair a four-cycle stationary Otto engine in a bottling plant. He came home and told Clara that this engine could be adapted to propel a vehicle and that he wanted to do it. First, however, he needed to know more about electricity. He proposed that they move to Detroit, where he "might" get a job with the Edison Illuminating Company. Clara was aghast. They had a new home and a pleasant life among old friends. Yet she made no protest. She was sure that Henry could do what he set out to do, and if this required giving up the security of the farm and moving to a strange city, so be it. Actually there is evidence that Henry took the job as night engineer with the Edison Company before he told Clara, but that is beside the point.

The Fords finally settled in a two-family house on Bagley Avenue, with a brick woodshed in back. Henry set up a shop in his half of the shed and started to build an automobile. There is conflicting testimony about the date for this. All of the pioneers were vague or forgetful as to when they succeeded, and all put the dates earlier than more reliable evidence indicates. King once said that he had his car on the road in 1894. When asked why, then, he did not compete in the 1895 race in Chicago, he pondered for a while and then said, "That's a thought, isn't it?" But Clara Ford had no such urge to prevaricate. Her testimony dates one aspect of her husband's developmental work.

It was Christmas Eve, 1893, in the kitchen of the house on Bagley Avenue. After putting her seven-weeks-old son Edsel to bed, Clara was busy with the preliminaries of Christmas dinner, to which her folks were coming. Henry came in with a board to which he had fashioned a cylinder reamed out of a piece of one-inch gas pipe in which was fitted a home-made piston. This was connected to a crankshaft that led to a flywheel taken from an old lathe. A gear operated a cam that opened intake and exhaust valves. The ignition system was a piece of bare wire mounted atop the piston and another that projected through a piece of fiber into the top of the cylinder. This latter piece was connected to the house current. When the piston came up and the two pieces of wire approached each other a spark jumped the gap—an application of the "theory of points" that Benjamin Franklin had developed 150 years before and a forerunner of the spark plug.

Henry did not have enough hands to make his gadget work, so Clara had to drop dinner preparations to drip gasoline into a cup mounted on the cylinder and feed the fuel into the intake valve by twisting a screw at her husband's direction. Henry spun the flywheel, and the engine coughed into action. Clara, a true believer in her husband's destiny, made no objection to this interruption of Christmas dinner preparations or to the flame, smoke, and stench that filled her kitchen and the noise that must have awakened the baby. Henry took his toy back to the shed. "I did not stop to play with it," he said later. "I wanted to build a two-cylinder engine which could be used to propel a bicycle."

Ford built this engine but never mounted it in a bicycle. Instead he started developing a four-cycle engine from drawings he found in the *American Machinist* and with the help of two fellow employees at Edison—Jim Bishop and George Cato. The latter, an expert electrician, devised the "make-and-break" ignition system used in the engine. By this time Ford had met King and frequently sought advice and borrowed parts and tools from the trained engineer. An employee of King's, Oliver Barthel, took a night course at the Y.M.C.A. on machine shop practice, of which Ford was the instructor, and worked with Ford to build the car, as did another friend, Edward Huff. Ford the genius had at least these five helpers and associates in his pioneering efforts, all of whom made some contributions to his first car.

Ford called this vehicle a quadricycle, and in appearance it resembled two bicycles side by side, with a buckboard body between and the engine mounted ahead of the rear axle. A chain transmission, con-

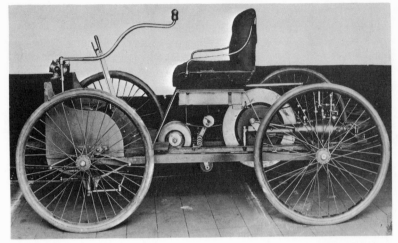

Ford Motor Company

The first car built by Henry Ford after he replaced a bicycle seat with a buggy seat and made other minor changes. No picture exists of the car as he first drove it on June 4, 1896.

trolled by a clutch, provided two speeds, ten and twenty miles an hour. There was no reverse, and the seat was a bicycle saddle. Ford's car, before remodeling, looked less like an adaptation of a horse-drawn vehicle than any of the others. Later he substituted a double seat for the bicycle saddle, added a dashboard and boxed the machinery, giving the car more of a buggy appearance. His car, which weighed 500 pounds, was lighter than any of the others. Duryea's weighed 700 pounds, Haynes's about 820, and King's over 1,300.

Work on the car was completed about 2 A.M. on the rainy morning of June 4, 1896. Ford was ready for a trial run—but he discovered that genius had overlooked one little detail. The car was wider than the shed door. This was quickly solved by knocking out the brickwork of the door frame with the back of an ax.

With Jim Bishop helping him and Clara holding an umbrella Ford pushed his car through the damaged door onto the wet cobblestones of the lane. He spun the flywheel, mounted the bicycle saddle, and grasped the tiller to steer the little quadricycle into the street. Bishop pedaled ahead of him down Grand River Avenue until the car suddenly stopped. Investigation disclosed that a spring in the ignition system had failed. Bishop cycled to the Edison plant for a new one, and the test continued to Washington Boulevard, which was wide enough to let the car turn around and come home. Sometime after 4 A.M. a happy Henry and a contented Clara went to bed for the few brief hours until Henry had to go to work.

If Ford expected any recognition for his feat he was disappointed. There was never a word in any Detroit paper about Henry's first car. The car as it is now displayed in Greenfield Village bears little resemblance to the vehicle he drove in that predawn trial. A few weeks later a man named David Bell applied for work at the Edison Company, saying that he had been a carriage blacksmith. Ford promptly hired him and set him to work, evenings and weekends, fashioning metal elements to replace the wooden chassis and making a new steering mechanism. Ford, with help from Bishop and Huff, rebuilt the car with these parts and added the buggy seat and dashboard. Bell later said, "I never saw Mr. Ford make anything. He was always doing the directing."

Now that the quadricycle could carry a passenger, Ford rode his friends around town. Detroit's mayor was an old family friend and Henry later said, "I had to get a special permit from the mayor and thus for a time enjoyed the distinction of being the only licensed chauffeur in America." It was probably a verbal permit, but Ford was proud of it. He delighted in parking the car and hiding behind bushes to hear the comments of the crowd it attracted. He recalled: "If I stopped my machine anywhere a crowd was soon around it before I could start up again. If I left it alone for even a minute some inquisitive person always tried to run it. Finally, I had to carry a chain and chain it to a lamp-post whenever I left it anywhere."

His first long trip in the rebuilt vehicle was out to Dearborn to see his father. His sister Margaret described the occasion:

"My first sight of the little car was as it came along what is now Ford Road. The wheels on one side were high in the center of the road. Henry had built the car in such a way that the distance between the wheels was less than that of wagons and carriages so [they] drove in this way on a road which had a rut. Clara and Edsel were in the front seat with him and all of them were sitting on the slanted seat. I remember Edsel was a very small boy in dresses at this time and he was held tightly by his mother on her lap . . . . I well remember the peculiar sensation of what seemed to be a great speed and the sense of bewilderment I felt when I first rode in this carriage which moved without a horse . . . . After I had ridden in the car I wondered more than ever at the cool confidence and nerve which Clara displayed in trusting herself and Edsel to Henry's little car for the first time in the country."

William Ford, Henry's father, lacked the confidence of his daughter and daughter-in-law. Margaret wrote: "He examined the car, listened to Henry's explanations, but he wouldn't get into the car. Father was a conservative farmer . . . . He saw no reason why he should risk his life at that time for a brief thrill from being propelled over the road in a carriage without horses."

Ford claimed that he ran the little quadricycle about one thousand miles before he sold it to a Detroiter named Charles Ainsley for $200 to finance a second car. He wrote: "It was not my idea to make cars in any such petty fashion. I was looking ahead to production, but before that could come I had to have something to produce." It took more than three years to find a group of speculatively inclined Detroiters, who put up $15,000 to organize the Detroit Automobile Company. Ford quit his job as chief engineer of the Edison Company to become production superintendent of the new company, with a minor stock interest and little authority.

The Detroit Automobile Company was dissolved after little more than a year, during which Ford produced about twenty cars. The reason for the failure of the company is not clear. Ford was certainly having production difficulties that he did not anticipate, but he claimed that the lack of success was the interest of his associates in making quick money. "I could get no support at all," he wrote, "toward making better cars to be sold to the public at large."

After the failure of his first business venture Ford decided to build a racer, although he later wrote, "I never thought anything of racing, but the public refused to consider the automobile in any light other than as a fast toy." A successful racing car would get him publicity and help him to build a reputation on which he might capitalize commercially. And there was prize money to be made at the track— some meets offered $10,000 in purses.

Ford's first race car was a skeleton chassis with a two-cylinder engine that developed twenty-six horsepower. This was not as powerful as others already in existence. Alexander Winton had a seventy-horse-power car in which he had set an American record of a mile in 1 minute, 14½ seconds—an average of better than 48 miles per hour. But Ford's car was much lighter. It made its first appearance in what turned out to be—after other contestants withdrew—a ten-mile match race with Winton at the Grosse Pointe horse track in October 1901.

Winton already had a considerable reputation as a race driver, but Henry was a home-town boy, and the announcement that "the Detroit chauffeur, Henry Ford" had entered the competition brought the crowd out. Winton, the experienced driver with the bigger, more powerful car, pulled ahead and hugged the rail as he slid around the turns. The novice Ford had to decelerate and swing wide. He fell steadily behind until Winton's car started to pour a cloud of smoke from a hot box and slowed down. Ford passed him to win with an average time of 1 minute, 20⅘ seconds per mile—not too bad for his first race. Henry acknowledged his lack of skill as a race driver and announced that he would never race again. "Put Winton in my car," he said, "and it will beat anything in the country."

The race had the desired effect. Some of the backers of the defunct Detroit Automobile Company financed a new venture—The Henry Ford Company, in which Henry was to have a one-sixth interest and again be in charge of production. A letter of Clara's at the time indicated an attitude of her husband's that would later develop into an obsession—his antipathy toward and distrust of financiers and bankers. "The race has advertised him far and wide," she wrote, "and the next thing will be to make some money out of it. I am afraid it will be a hard struggle. You know rich men want it all."

Henry made no money from this venture. Although he had said that "I never thought anything of racing," he was now bitten badly by the racing bug, because he believed that here lay fame and big money. He wrote his brother-in-law, "My company will kick about me following racing but they will get the advertising and I expect to make $s where I can't make ¢s at manufacturing."

His associates did "kick" at Henry devoting so much attention to developing a new race car that he had only spare time for work on a commercial car. When Ford accomplished little toward producing a car that they could sell, they called in Henry M. Leland as an adviser. Ford blamed his associates for the failure of the enterprise, saying

Ford Motor Company   General Motors Corporation

The conflict between these two automobile pioneers resulted in great cars at opposite ends of the scale. Left: Henry Ford in 1901. Right: Henry Leland, Ford's replacement in the company that was reorganized as the Cadillac Automobile Company.

that "the whole thought was to make to order and get the largest possible price for each car. The main idea seemed to be to get the money. And being without authority other than my engineering position gave me, I found that the new company was not a vehicle for realizing my ideas but merely a money making concern that did not make much money." He never explained the inconsistency between this statement and his avowed interest in making quick "$s" from racing.

It is probable that his principal cause of dissatisfaction was Henry Leland, who was the guiding genius of Faulconer and Leland, undoubtedly the best machine shop in the country. Leland, the precisionist, had little faith in Henry's tinkering and cut-and-try methods. Ford, the rule-of-thumb mechanic, had little patience with Leland's insistence on conforming to blueprints. By March 1902 Ford was out, and later, Leland was in. A condition of Ford's leaving was that the company would not continue to use his name. It was reorganized as the Cadillac Automobile Company.

Many years later Leland resigned as president of Cadillac to organize the Lincoln Motor Car Company. When Lincoln was in trouble in 1922 Ford bid it in at a receiver's sale for $8,000,000. No one knows why Ford, who was committed to the mass production of cheap cars, suddenly bought a company making one of America's fine, expensive cars. There are cynics who say that his purpose was to "get even" with Leland for what had happened twenty years before—although the Lelands, father and son, stayed with Lincoln for a short time after Ford bought the company.

Ford's third venture in the automobile game was with a bicycle-racer-turned-automobile-driver named Tom Cooper. Ford and Cooper started to build two identical seventy-horsepower race cars, The Arrow and 999. They were the biggest racers in America, with a wheelbase of 9 feet 9 inches and a tread width of 5 feet 5 inches. Each engine had four 7" by 7" cylinders, and the exhaust made so much noise that Ford said "it was enough to half kill a man." The cars consisted of large pneumatic-tired wheels, a steel and oak frame, a finned radiator, the bellowing engine mounted in the front, a drive shaft, and a gear transmission. Steering was controlled by a heavy iron bar. All of the works were exposed, and the driver rode in a constant spray of oil from the drive shaft.

Most of the testing was done by Cooper and Ed Huff, but a week before a race scheduled for Grosse Pointe in October 1902, another young bicycle racer named Barney Oldfield joined the group. Oldfield had never driven a car, but he induced Cooper to let him try 999. To everybody's amazement the daredevil Barney made better time than either Cooper or Huff.

When 999 approached the starting line of the five-mile event at Grosse Pointe, Barney's hamlike hands clutched the ends of the steering bar. With his four exhausts thundering and flaming, the young bicycle racer hugged the rail in a cloud of oil and dust, taking the turns in a series of sliding skids without decreasing power. Alexander Winton in his big Bullet kept on his tail until engine trouble forced him out of the race. Oldfield easily lapped a Geneva Steamer and was about to lap the fourth car in the race, a Winton Pup, when the contest ended.

Although Ford subsequently built more racers, this was the high point in his racing career. He shortly sold 999 to Cooper and parted company with his partner. Clara may have had something to do with this. She wrote her brother about Cooper: "I am glad we are rid of him. I would not like you or Henry to travel with him. He thinks too much of low-down women to suit me."

While the racers were being built, Harold Wills, a new associate of Ford and an expert draftsman, was drawing the plans for a "family horse" with a novel two-cylinder opposed engine that Ford had developed. With these under his arm and the publicity from the race behind him Ford toured Detroit looking for money to build a pilot model. When he secured it in 1903, seven years after he had made his first car, he started his fourth attempt at production. This, The Ford Motor Company, was successful.

By the time Ford finally got underway he was a long way behind the parade of motor car producers. Leading it was Ransom Eli Olds, who by this time was making the most popular car in America. Olds was a mechanic who had grown up in his father's machine shop, which, by 1892, he had taken over and was manufacturing stationary and marine gasoline engines. On the side he was developing a self-propelled tricycle. Surprisingly, in view of his main business, it was steam-powered. He drove this on the streets of Lansing in 1887 and by 1893 had built a very dependable four-wheeled vehicle. This was so favorably described in *Scientific American* that he received an order for it from India. Although most accounts say that he sold it to an Indian maharaja, the actual buyer was a patent medicine company in Bombay.

Olds built his first gasoline car in 1896, a two-seat, four-passenger vehicle. Like all the rest, he later said that he sold one in 1895, but there is no record of any Oldsmobile prior to the one now in the Smithsonian, which was built the following year. Feeling that Lansing did not have sufficient labor and facilities for automobile production, Olds went East to seek a factory site in Newark. When the Eastern

Ford Motor Company

Just one week after the first time he had driven a car, Barney Oldfield drove Ford's famous 999 to a victory in a race at Grosse Point, Michigan. The biggest racer in America, the car had a 9'9" wheelbase, a steel and oak frame, and a heavy iron tiller.

money men whom he approached showed no interest in his venture he returned to Detroit and propositioned copper millionaire S. L. Smith. In addition to millions, Smith had two unemployed sons. In return for jobs for his sons, Smith put up most of the $200,000 needed to finance the Olds Motor Works.

Olds started to produce in 1899. He later wrote:

It was our plan at that time to put out a model that would sell for $1,250. I had fitted it up with some very up-to-the-minute improvements —pneumatic clutch, cushion tires and electric push button starter. We thought we had quite a car, but we soon found that it was too complicated for the public. The first year we ran behind $80,000.

The prospects of the industry were not very bright. Winton was making some cars down in Cleveland, Ohio, and Duryea, Haynes and Apperson were all in the market. But the public persisted in the idea that it was not a practical proposition and would be a thing of the past within a year or two. Finally, after a long sleepless night, I discarded all my former plans and built a little one-cylinder runabout, for I was convinced that if success came it would be through a more simple machine.

This was the famous "curved dash" Oldsmobile—the first car produced in volume in America. But it is possible that the concentration of Olds on this model came about by accident rather than Ransom's prophetic vision. In March 1901 the Olds plant burned to the ground. The only thing saved was the prototype runabout, which an alert timekeeper pushed from the burning building. When the plant was rebuilt this was the only thing he had to make, and when Roy Chapin drove one from Detroit to exhibit in the second New York show it

Of the many pioneer American cars, only five have survived since the turn of the century. Below, the original models for four. The fifth is Henry Ford's first car, shown on page 54. Left to right: the prototype

was an immediate success. In 1901 Olds produced 425 of them; by 1905 production was 6,500.

Olds was certainly right about one thing. When he started to build cars at the turn of the century there was no assurance that automobiles were here to stay; or if they were, that they would be gasoline-powered. Contemporary opinion rather favored electric or steam power. There are no statistics of guaranteed accuracy for the period, but one respectable set claims a production of 4,192 cars in 1900— 1,691 steam-powered vehicles, 1,585 electrics, and only 936 gasoline cars. Of eleven cars advertised in *Auto Topics* early in 1901, four were electrics, three were steam, and four were gas.

Theoretically, the electric motor was vastly superior to any heat engine as a power unit, but in a self-propelled vehicle it had to carry its own source of energy. This meant heavy, heavy batteries that had to be recharged about every twenty-five miles. In the city, where charging stations could be established at intervals, the electrics were popular as cabs, light delivery trucks, and private cars. At an early automobile show one inventor exhibited a coin-operated charger for use in the country. The driver of an electric could park beside it, hook in, deposit a quarter, and wait for his batteries to charge. This never came into general use.

The steam engine had several advantages over the gasoline engine. It was simpler and more reliable. It was quieter and emitted no objectionable smoke or odor. Steam cars accelerated more smoothly. But they had the same drawbacks as electrics—excessive weight and limited range of operation. The steam engine itself could be made

Cadillac, built in 1900; the first Oldsmobile, built by Ransom Eli Olds in 1896; David Dunbar Buick's first car, built in 1903; Thomas Jeffrey and the Rambler which he built in 1900.

General Motors Corporation

American Motors Corporation

General Motors Corporation

The "curved dash" Oldsmobile runabout, the first car produced in quantity—built from 1900 through 1904.

light in weight, but it needed both water and fuel—usually kerosene or gasoline—to make steam. If the tanks for these were made large enough to give the car a respectable range, the weight far exceeded that of a gasoline-powered car of equal range. Most of the early steamers had to replenish their water supply about every thirty miles, and if the water was not chemically pure the boiler pipes soon became encrusted or corroded. And—a most important drawback—it took from a quarter to a half hour to build up pressure in the early steamers.

Then there was a certain nervous tension in sitting atop a high-pressure steam boiler, or even in the soft hiss of steam when the car was parked with the pilot light burning. The danger of explosion was more imagined than real, but after a few pressure gauges blew up, some manufacturers took them off the dashboard and put them on the side of the car facing outward, so that when they exploded, passersby, rather than the driver, would be showered with broken glass and scalding water.

Electrics did not last long beyond the first few years of the century except for a few that were bought by little old ladies. Steamers continued to compete with gasoline cars for several years. The most famous was made by F. O. and F. E. Stanley, of Newton, Massachusetts. The sight of a crude steamer at a county fair convinced the twin brothers that they could build a better one. They bought an engine, a boiler, and a buggy body and built a bicycle-wheeled frame that was far too light for their 750-pound power plant. But they put it all together and fired it up, and sometime in September 1897 they were ready for their first ride. Neither had ever driven a steam vehicle, but F. E. seemed to be a little bolder than F. O. and so took the tiller. With identical beards and identical derbies perched on identical heads, they drove through Newton, the car making a sound like a peanut stand and becoming more shrill as the speed increased.

They next developed a new power plant that weighed only 125 pounds and entered the car in a race in Cambridge, which they won easily. When they started to receive letters from people who wanted to buy a car, they bought an abandoned bicycle factory and started to make automobiles. There is a legend that the first bodies they ordered from a carriage maker were delivered with whip sockets, but this same story is told about every car that had its bodies made by a carriage factory. Whether there ever was an automobile with a whip socket is questionable.

The Stanley Steamer was a dependable, smooth-running automobile and, after they licked the problem of the peanut whistle, a remarkably quiet one. And it was fast—it was said in those days that nobody had ever driven one as fast as it would go. For publicity purposes the

Automobile Manufacturers Association

Identical twins F. O. and F. E. Stanley built the first dependable, fast, smooth-running steam car. It was rumored that none of their cars had ever been driven as fast as it would go. For many years, the Stanley Steamer competed with gasoline engines.

twins made a few racers called Wogglebugs, which did well on the track and dominated hill-climbing competitions. In 1906 one of them made a mile in 28.2 seconds at Daytona Beach—a record that stood for four years, until Barney Oldfield shaved it by only 0.87 of a second in a Benz. Until well into the second decade of the century there was a small group of faithful addicts who would own nothing but a steamer, but after those first few years steamers never seriously challenged the gasoline car.

Most of the pioneers of the rule-of-thumb era never reached production, but early in the twentieth century new automobile companies were coming into existence so rapidly that it was almost impossible to keep track of them. One reliable source cites seventy-two automobile companies in 1900, thirty-eight more in 1901, another forty-seven in 1902, and fifty-seven more in 1903. But soon more were going out of business than were coming in. *Motor* made an exhaustive study of the business from 1900 to 1908 and reported that 502 companies had been started to make automobiles of which 302 had failed.

The statistics for this early era can be misleading. Lists have been published containing the names of over 3,000 cars and trucks that were supposedly made in America. There were never anything like this number of automobile manufacturers in America by any reasonable definition of the word *manufacturer*. Many of them were entrepreneurs who made a pilot model, named it, and incorporated with a large capitalization and a few hundred dollars paid in. This is as far as many of the so-called manufacturers went before they folded.

Also the number of makes of cars was vastly greater than the number of car makers, as is indicated by a thumbnail history of the present American Motors Corporation. Thomas B. Jeffery started to produce Ramblers in Kenosha, Wisconsin, in 1902—the second early "mass-produced" car. After the founder died the name of the car was changed to the Jeffery. Charles W. Nash, who had come up through Buick, left General Motors, bought the Jeffery Company, and started to produce the Nash. Meanwhile, Roy Chapin had left Olds and organized the Hudson Motor Car Company. In 1954 Nash and Hudson were combined to form American Motors. In all of this there were two original automobile manufacturers involved—the Jeffery Company and Hudson. But, at one time or another, they produced nine different cars: Rambler, Jeffery, Hudson, Nash, Essex,

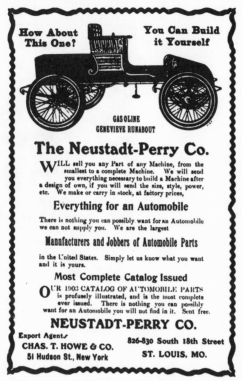

The early cars were not difficult to put together. One company in St. Louis advertised a complete line of parts and even entire engines and cars to "build in your own home." All the builder had to do was specify the size, style, and power he wanted.

Terraplane, LaFayette, Ajax, and Dover—and now, Rambler again.

In the early days it was not difficult to produce a single car by rule-of-thumb methods. If the prospective builder was not a really ingenious mechanic, he could order the parts by mail from the Neustadt-Parry Company in St. Louis, which advertised: "You Can Build It Yourself—we will send you everything necessary to build a machine if you will send the size, style, power, etc." After the first car was built in a barn its owner could use it to amaze and impress his fellow townsmen; or he could seek financial backing to build more cars—to go into the fascinating new "automobile game."

The National Automobile Race.

THREE: THE AUTOMOBILE GAME

They used to start drinking early at the bar of the Pontchartrain Hotel in Detroit. By the time the ornately carved, marble-framed clock behind the bar said 11:30, the mosaic floor of the barroom was crowded with contestants eager to play the automobile game. The patrons of the Pontchartrain were not drunkards. They thronged to the bar early because nobody wanted to miss any of the gossip; and this was the gossip center of the game.

Among those who bellied to the bar were parts manufacturers and salesmen, prospective dealers, agents, brokers, and others who were seeking an entree to some aspect of this chancy business. At the tables along the other side of the room, hopeful creative geniuses explained the merits of their brain children to dubious prospective financiers. Proprietors of machine shops huddled with designers of cars sketching details of crankshafts, motors, transmissions, and chassis on tablecloths. It is alleged that some Pontchartrain waiters retired rich from selling this linen instead of sending it to the laundry; the doodles that decorated it might contain valuable new ideas.

This was Detroit early in the first decade of the century. It had not yet become the Motor Capital, but unpretentious buildings with high-sounding names were beginning to rise around town and in nearby South Michigan. The name Ford was there, and Olds, and Cadillac. The name Dodge was on a substantial machine shop owned by brothers Horace F. and John E. From Warren, Ohio, had come Packard, and David Buick was building cars in nearby Flint.

Still, nobody could have foretold that Detroit was on its way to-

1901

BUY A SKENE,

A successful steam automobile built by reliable makers, and enjoy the fascination of a horseless carriage. We will be pleased to demonstrate the many points of superiority which our machine possesses to any one who is interested. There is a small amount of **TREASURY STOCK** in this Company still unsubscribed. Those who are looking for a "good thing" will do well to correspond with me immediately.

ARTHUR C. EDDY, Treasurer

Skene American Automobile Company

Carr Bldg., Harrison Ave., Springfield, Mass.

Denied access to Wall Street money, some early car companies tried to sell stock, as well as cars, to the public.

ward housing the nation's leading industry. New England, the center of much of the nation's metalworking, seemed far more logical. Machine shops, arms plants with a superior knowledge of metallurgy, and the largest bicycle factories were all there, as was the labor skilled in these trades. And Boston and New York had the wealth to finance new ventures.

But this wealth was not available to the automotive pioneers. Eastern money was old money that had become conservative. Its possessors wanted no part of this speculative game nor its fly-by-night crackpots who seriously claimed that their machines would replace the horse. The newly rich Midwesterners had not yet learned the basic Boston axiom: "Never touch your capital." Many of them had made their money in their own lifetimes and still had the pioneering, gambling spirit that had brought their first millions. And it was surely coincidental that men like Olds, Buick, and Ford happened to be in the same place as men like Smith, Durant, and Malcomson.

The relationship of Ransom Olds and S. L. Smith is indicative of what happened to many of the rule-of-thumb creators when they tried to play the automobile game. The name of the company was the Olds Motor Works, and the car was called Oldsmobile—but Smith held 19,961 shares of the original 20,000 issued. To Smith's sons, whose employment had been a condition of the financing, the little curved-dash runabout, the largest-selling car in America, looked puny beside the lush foreign models at the automobile shows. They sought the prestige of making larger, more expensive vehicles—the type of cars their rich friends would buy. The elder Smith could not conceive of a true mass market for the little car and decided that the company should build bigger ones.

Olds protested vehemently, to no avail. When he threatened to resign he was taken at his word and by 1903 was out of the company. Unlike Ford he did not retain the right to use his own name; so the Olds Motor Works went on without Olds to build four- and six-cylinder cars. By 1908 they were making only one thousand units a year. Friends of Olds in Lansing set him up in a new company, using his initials to name its product, the Reo, a car of which Mr. Olds said, immodestly: "The car I now bring out is regarded by me as close to finality. I do not believe that a car materially better will ever be built."

One pioneer who never even got to play the game for high stakes was James Ward Packard. In 1899 Packard bought a car from Alexander Winton. After driving it a while he wrote the maker: "I got one of your damn cars. It's no good. I could make a better one myself." Packard, a graduate mechanical engineer and owner of a successful electric cable business, had been toying with designs for a car since the early 1890s. Now he hired two of Winton's best technicians, built a one-cylinder runabout, and formed the Ohio Automobile Company, to build a few cars in Warren.

Rich Detroiter Henry Joy went to the New York automobile show in 1901 to buy a steam car. When a gauge blew up and showered him with hot water he lost interest in steam. Next day he was inspecting a Packard parked at the curb when a fire engine went past. The Packard driver spun his crank once and took off after the engine. When he came back Joy bought the car, which he liked so well that he drove to Warren to see the maker. Packard told him that he could sell two hundred cars a year if he had the money to make them but that his bankers said he was crazy. Joy and some associates bought the Ohio Company and moved it to Detroit as the Packard Motor Car Company. Although Packard was titular president, he stayed with his electric cable business in Warren.

From this point Packard's experience paralleled that of Olds. Joy imported a French engineer and made a fine, big, four-cylinder car— so fine that it sold for $7,500, and Joy lost $200,000, until changes brought the price down under $5,000. Opposed to deserting the little car, Packard resigned from the automobile company, which continued to make cars bearing his name.

In justice to the Smiths and Joys it must be said that the one- or two-cylinder cars could not have lasted in their original form despite their initial success. They were neither rich man's toys nor utilitarian vehicles. They were literally horseless buggies, with all of the limitations of the buggy. Evolution was inevitable. But few, other than Packard and Cadillac, made the transition to big cars successfully. Only Ford made the change from the buggy to a practical small vehicle. Henry later said that he was extremely lucky in his competitors, because after making a success with small cars they all went into big cars, leaving him practically alone in the field under $1,000.

Olds made his million before he left Oldsmobile. Packard, too, became a millionaire when he sold his cable company, Packard Electric, to General Motors. But one man whose name still graces a modern car was frozen out of the automobile game without winning a hand and died penniless. In 1900 David Dunbar Buick was a partner in a successful plumbing supply business in Detroit. He had perfected a method of affixing porcelain to metal that gave birth to the modern bathroom. But bathtubs are dull things. Buick found internal combustion engines much more fascinating and used up the resources of his plumbing supply business to develop and manufacture a stationary and marine valve-in-head engine.

This operation was fairly successful, but Buick poured all the profits into designing a two-cylinder car. By 1903 he was $3,500 in debt to the Briscoe brothers, Frank and Benjamin. They reorganized the operation and promptly sold the Buick Motor Company to the Flint Wagon Works for the amount of their loan plus interest. Ben Briscoe would later say, ruefully, that "Buick made over a hundred millionaires." The new company was capitalized for $75,000, and a little factory was built, but it soon became evident that although David Buick could make *an* automobile, he could not manufacture automobiles. Production in 1903 was sixteen cars, in 1904, thirty-seven. Flint Wagon could no longer support the company. They sought another buyer and found him in the incredible William Crapo Durant.

Billy Durant had started in his grandfather's lumber business as a boy, but before he was twenty-one he had his own insurance agency. This was a business he liked, because it was something he could sell, and William Crapo Durant was one of the world's great salesmen. While hustling through the Michigan hinterlands he saw a road cart that impressed him. He bought the patent rights for $50, went into partnership with Dallas Dort, a young hardware clerk, and ordered 10,000 carts from a Flint wagonmaker at $8.50 a piece. This was an unheard of quantity, but Durant quickly sold them at $12.50 a piece. By 1904 the Durant-Dort Carriage Company was one of Flint's leading industries, and Billy Durant was a millionaire.

Durant had no technical knowledge or mechanical skill. When he was approached to take over Buick he took a car and drove it around Michigan on the worst roads he could find for two months. He experienced all of the motoring mishaps that were to be expected in those days, but he came to the conclusion that it was a good car. Had it not been he probably would have made some other deal to acquire an automobile property, because Billy Durant and the automobile game were made for each other.

The manner in which he assumed control of Buick in November 1904 presaged the role he would later play. Capitalization was immediately increased fourfold to $300,000, with old stockholders getting preferred stock plus a 25-percent bonus of common for their holdings —no cash. Almost before the deal was concluded, capitalization was upped to $500,000, and before a year was out, to $1,500,000. The lawyer who drew up the corporate papers later explained that, no matter how much he padded assets, he was still $60,000 short of the amount required for this capitalization until he included "Ownership of invention of combustion engine construction not patented for business reasons—$60,000." He added, "The fact that I was very well acquainted in Lansing, the state Capital, may have been beneficial in getting such a hazy item passed."

But hazy or not, Durant now had something to sell. It is said that he sold $500,000 worth of stock to his Flint neighbors in a single day. By 1905 Buick Motor Company was off and running, but by 1906 David Dunbar Buick was out. He was one of the many rule-of-thumb pioneers who did not play the automobile game well. It is ironic that in his recent best-selling book, *My Years with General Motors,* Alfred P. Sloan, Jr., does not mention the names of David Dunbar Buick or Ransom Olds. Buick was the backlog of General Motors and Oldsmobile its next acquisition.

An exception among the pioneers was one who did play the automobile game very well indeed—Henry Ford. The "angel" who, in 1902, backed Ford in his fifth production venture was a Detroit coal dealer named Alexander T. Malcomson. Ten years before he had started by buying a small coalyard on credit and delivering with a single horse and wagon. Now he served most of Detroit with wagons bearing the legend HOTTER THAN SUNSHINE. He owned yards throughout the city and thousands of acres of coal land. Malcomson was a plunger and an enthusiast. Ford had met him when he was buying coal for Edison Illuminating.

Malcomson liked Ford's plans for the two-cylinder opposed engine well enough to promise to finance its development. It had to be a promise—despite his extensive holdings he had little cash and was never out of debt. He and Henry formed the partnership of Ford and Malcomson, with the latter putting up $500 cash and promising more when he got it. Ford agreed not to tell Malcomson's uncle, bank president John S. Gray, about the deal, because Malcomson owed so much money to the bank. Malcomson also contributed one of his employees, James Couzens, to manage the business end of the enterprise. Ford drew no salary, but there is a belief that Ford's associate, Harold Wills, split with his boss the salary of $125 a month, which he received from Malcomson.

Wills and Ford set up a shop to build the first commercial Ford. With two lathes, two drill presses, a planer, a saw, a grinding wheel, and a forge, this first Ford factory was rudimentary indeed, but a step above the brick woodshed on Bagley Avenue. While they were building the first car, Malcomson, with great faith and enthusiasm, induced a carpentry contractor named Albert Strelow to remodel a wagon shop on one of his coal lots to assemble cars in quantity. Strelow financed the remodeling under an agreement that Ford and Malcomson would pay him $75 a month rent on a three-year lease.

Ford finished the first car in December 1902. It had a wheelbase of six feet and could be either a roadster or a touring car, depending on whether one bought the separate tonneau that slipped on the back. There was no top, no windshield, no running board, no doors. The steering wheel was on the right, with two levers for throttle and ignition adjustment underneath. Power for the spark was from two sets of six dry cell batteries. It had two speeds forward and a reverse through a planetary-type transmission that Ford would cling to stubbornly through the years. It had a bicycle chain drive. Its greatest claim to fame was its engine, an advanced design for the time. The car was to sell for $750 without the tonneau, which cost $100 extra.

The partners had a car, but no money to make more. This did not faze Malcomson. He made a contract with the Dodge brothers to produce 650 complete chassis, including engines, transmissions, frames, and axles. The brothers were to receive $250 a chassis in the form of progress payments as they tooled up for the job and made deliveries.

The Dodge boys were unusual associates for Henry Ford, although the alliance continued for twelve years until the brothers started to produce a car of their own. Straight-laced would be a fitting description of Henry. The Dodge brothers were in the way of being hellions. Starting as uneducated factory hands, always working together, they had worked their way up to having a machine shop that was second, perhaps, only to Leland and Faulconer. They were both quick-tempered, argumentative, and always ready to fight—with each other, if necessary. John was the more aggressive of the two and on Saturday nights went looking for trouble in the saloons of Detroit's less desirable neighborhoods. He usually found it, and his almost equally pugnacious brother was always there to back him up.

Malcomson made other contracts. The C. R. Wilson Carriage Company would supply wooden bodies for $52 and cushions for $16. The Hartford Rubber Company would supply tires at $40 a set and the Prudden Company wheels at $26 a set. The Ford operation, after designing the car, would be entirely one of assembling—all parts of the car were made by somebody else. This was not unusual at the time. Originally most of the early automobile companies were largely assemblers rather than manufacturers.

When the time came, Malcomson could not make payments to the Dodge brothers—he had run more heavily into debt extending his coal business. The Dodge boys threatened to pull out unless they got their money. With much hesitation, Malcomson went to his banker-uncle Gray, who, to protect the money the bank had already loaned his nephew, agreed to guarantee the Dodge payments up to $10,500 on condition that a company was formed of which he would be president and in which he would hold 10.5 percent of the stock.

Meanwhile, Couzens and Malcomson were beating the bushes for

The first production model Ford, 1903. The car was designed and assembled by Ford, but built entirely by other companies. The Dodge brothers made the chassis; a carriage company, the body; and a rubber company, the tires.

Ford Motor Company

other investors. They thought they had the financial problems of the infant venture solved when Charles H. Bennett, a principal of the Daisy Air Rifle Company, came to Detroit to buy a car and visited Malcomson. A phone call brought Ford with the pilot car, and the coal dealer so enthused Bennett that the latter agreed that the air rifle company would put up half the capital to form the Ford Motor Company. Daisy's lawyers quickly squelched this by pointing out that the company's corporate charter did not permit it. Bennett personally invested $5,000.

The Ford Motor Company was finally incorporated on June 16, 1903. One thousand shares of stock were issued, with a nominal value of $100 per share. Ford and Malcomson each received 255 shares, a total of 51 percent, for work done, patents, and so on. Gray was made president and received the promised 105 shares. Bennett gave his note for fifty shares. Two of Malcomson's lawyers, Horace H. Rackham and John W. Anderson, each took fifty shares, paying part cash and part with a note. The Dodge brothers each received fifty shares, for which they contributed $7,000 in materials and a note for $3,000. A cousin of Malcomson's, Vernon C. Fry, put up $3,000 and gave a note for $2,000 for fifty shares. Albert Strelow, the carpenter who had built the assembly plant, paid cash for fifty shares. A friend of Malcomson, Charles J. Woodall, gave a note for ten shares.

James Couzens had been very cool toward the Ford enterprise when Malcomson assigned him to it, but he had now warmed up to the point that he put in $1,000 and gave a $1,500 note to secure twenty-five shares of stock. Couzens did not have all of the $1,000. His sister, a schoolteacher, had $200 in a savings bank. After much soul searching, she decided to risk half of her savings and buy one share. She ultimately received $355,000 for her $100 investment.

The company started with $28,000 in cash. While driving away from the organization meeting in the pilot car, Ford is supposed to have turned to Couzens and said, "Jim, what do you think we ought to ask those fellows in the way of salary?" Such a remark would be typical of Ford's attitude toward his backers. He and Couzens were insiders, concerned with building and selling cars. The rest of the stockholders were "those fellows"—outsiders who were merely money men. At the first directors meeting Ford was voted a salary of $3,600 a year; Couzens got $2,500.

The earliest photo of Ford manufacturing, 1906. The forty workers turned out fifteen cars a day.

Early in July 1903 the Dodge brothers started to deliver chassis on horse-drawn hay ricks to the converted wagon shop. Dumped on the floor, they were handled in groups of four by three workmen to a car. After inspecting, running up, and adjusting the engine, two men picked up the body and bolted it on while the third attached the fenders—which, one worker said, "were so light you could wear them for ear rings." Then the car was painted. Another worker later recalled, "We worked our hearts out to get fifteen cars a day."

For the first weeks the new company ran nip and tuck with bankruptcy. On July 11 the bank balance was $223.65, and not a car had been sold. Then, on July 15, a check came in from a Dr. E. Pfennig, the buyer of the first commercially produced Ford. Other checks followed in a steady stream. During its first year the company billed about $1 million and was never thereafter in financial difficulties except, briefly, in the postwar depression of 1920.

At this time the total work force was about forty, working a nine- or ten-hour day for a base rate of $1.50—a day, not an hour. Behind a partition at one end of the ground floor Ford and Wills labored longer hours, six days a week, in the company's "development department." Ford was frequently on the factory floor, and both bosses helped deliver the finished machines to the railroad and pack them in freight cars. Couzens had an office partitioned off with raw lumber on the second floor.

The Ford Motor Company might not have survived its infancy without James Couzens. He managed, with an iron hand, every aspect of the business except design and production. He was sales manager, advertising manager, office manager, and purchasing agent and performed the actual duties of secretary and treasurer. He signed up dealers and made closely bargained contracts with suppliers. Although he was Ford's close associate for thirteen years, it is safe to say that the two men never really liked each other.

Ford, at forty, was described by one worker as "an agile, friendly man; a man that nobody need be afraid to approach at all." He was a backslapper who got results by encouraging his men and working with them. He was fond of playing practical jokes, like electrifying door knobs. Harold Wills told a story of the time when he was drafting the plans for the "family horse" and Ford was building 999. They worked nights in a shop that had no heat. When they got too cold to hold a pencil or a tool they put on boxing gloves and flailed at each other until they were warm. There was none of this humanness or playfulness in tough, irascible, hot-tempered Couzens. He was a humorless, merciless slave driver. One employee commented, "I called Couzens 'Sunny Jim' because he was so God damn mean!" It was said that when he smiled his annual smile the ice broke up in the Great Lakes. But, through the years, Couzens was the only man who sometimes made Henry Ford back down.

Henry was helping to load the day's production on freight cars on July 26, 1903 when somebody showed him an advertisement in the Detroit *News* signed by the Association of Licensed Automobile Manufacturers. After characterizing the twenty-six member firms of the association as "the pioneers of the industry" the advertisement stated: "No other manufacturers or importers are authorized to make or sell gasoline automobiles, and any person making, selling or using such machines made or sold by any unlicensed manufacturers or importers will be liable to prosecution for infringement." George Baldwin Selden had struck—or rather, the New York financiers who now controlled Selden's patent had struck.

Selden is usually regarded as a wily legal eagle who contributed nothing to the development of the automobile and who, after sixteen years of stalling, through inconsequential amendments that kept his application alive, had accepted the patent in 1895 solely to impose a legal but unfair tax on those who had done the actual work. Although this was the effect of what he did, it may be unduly harsh to say that it was his purpose. He *did* build an engine, and he made several unsuccessful attempts to secure financing to build an automobile.

In the same year that Selden took out his patent the country's largest bicycle maker, the Pope Manufacturing Company of Hartford, had started experimental work on electric and gasoline cars. By 1899 they were making both types. In New York, financiers William C. Whitney and Thomas Fortune Ryan had organized the Electric Vehicle Company to operate electric taxicabs. Pope was the only operation that seemed substantial enough to build the 1,600 cabs that they wanted, and the New Yorkers acquired the automobile interests of Pope. One of Pope's lawyers had been saying for four years that their gasoline cars infringed Selden's patent. No one paid any attention to him until Whitney came into the picture. With the typical New York money man's attitude toward eliminating any possibility of legal difficulties, Whitney went to Rochester and acquired Selden's patent for $10,000 plus a very small percentage of any royalties collected.

The Electric Vehicle Company, now an $18,000,000 corporation, filed suits against five automobile, engine, and importing companies, including Winton, who started to fight back until the others gave in, and seven companies who had not been sued applied for licenses. Winton then compromised before the case came to trial. Meanwhile ten other companies, principally in Detroit, had come together under the leadership of F. L. Smith of Olds to seek an agreement with Electric Vehicle. In Whitney's Fifth Avenue mansion they made a deal to pay 1.25 percent royalty on every car manufactured, 40 percent of which was to be retained by their own organization, the Association of Licensed Automobile Manufacturers. One clause in the agreement took the matter far beyond the mere payment of royalties. It provided that the Association "shall say who shall be licensed and who shall not be licensed under the agreement." If this held up, member companies could monopolize the automobile business.

By 1903 the A.L.A.M. was almost justified in its claim that its members were "the pioneers of the industry." The Duryea brothers had split by this time, and the companies with which each was connected were members. Haynes had split with the Appersons, and both were members, as were Olds, Cadillac, Packard, Pierce-Arrow, Winton, Pope, Autocar, Peerless, Franklin, Locomobile, and most others who were in quantity production. The principal holdouts were Thomas Jeffery, who was building Ramblers in Kenosha, and Henry Ford.

Smith later claimed that Ford approached him for a license and that he told Ford, "I did not think an application from the Ford Motor Company would be considered favorably." Ford told a different story. He claimed that at a luncheon meeting with Smith to discuss a license Couzens roared, "Selden can take his patent and go to hell with it," to which Henry added, "Couzens has answered you." In any case, two days after the Association's first warning advertisement appeared in Detroit, Ford indicated his intention to fight by publishing an answering advertisement addressed to "Dealers, Importers, Agents and Users of our Gasoline Automobiles" that promised: "We will protect you against any prosecution for alleged infringement of patents." Further, Couzens published an open letter containing a devastating attack on the Association that virtually taunted them to take action. On October 22, 1903 the Electric Motor Vehicle Company and George B. Selden filed suit against the Ford Motor Company and its New York dealer. Before the suit got well underway both the Pope Manufacturing Company and the Electric Vehicle Company went bankrupt. The actual fight was between Ford and the Association.

The suit dragged through the courts for eight years. As a law case it was extremely dull. Through the early years it was a series of hearings before examiners rather than a trial. All of the industry pioneers gave evidence at these hearings, which ultimately filled thirty-eight very thick volumes. It was here that most of them made their sworn, but inaccurate, statements as to when they had first successfully operated their automobiles.

But in the newspapers the case was by no means dull. Here it was not necessary to stick to evidence, and both sides made wild claims and counterclaims. Ford advertisements screamed: "We will protect you against the 'Trust,' " and flag-waving news releases proclaimed: "We possess just enough of the instinct of American freedom to cause us to rebel against oppression." Selden was castigated as being "willing to prostitute his profession and avail himself of the blind alleys of the law to gain an end." When the case started, Henry Ford was known, if at all, as the builder of the race car that Barney Oldfield drove so well. Before it was very far advanced, Henry was widely esteemed as the valiant little David who was fighting the fearsome Goliath of "the interests."

The case came at just the right time, for Ford. Teddy Roosevelt had started his trust busting. The public was convinced by things like Ida Tarbell's exposé of the Standard Oil monopoly, which John D. Rockefeller had created, and was beginning to believe that the private enterprise system was at the mercy of cartels, trusts, and "the interests" in Wall Street. Henry Ford, with his new company, which had only $28,000, was a perfect example of the enterprising little man whom these iniquitous and unscrupulous interests were seeking to crush for their own further enrichment. True, by the time the case was decided Henry was several times a millionaire, but that did not affect his public image in the early years. And the publicity sold cars. For every chickenhearted individual who bought a licensed car to avoid possible trouble, there were several who deliberately bought a Ford to express their sympathy for the underdog.

An interesting aspect of the case that was not dull were the cars built by both sides to prove certain points. The complainants constructed two cars that they said were built to the specifications of the Selden patent. The defendants said that they were not—that they incorporated more recent devices. It did not matter; the cars ran only haltingly for a few feet at a time. Not so with the vehicle Ford constructed to prove that a car could have been built with things that were in existence prior to Selden's original application in 1879. An expert for the complainants had testified that the Lenoir engine could not have powered a car in the 1860s. The car that Ford built had a Lenoir engine and a carburetor patented in 1875. It ran happily up Fifth Avenue, through Central Park, around Columbus Circle, and down Broadway. In fact, it worked better than some of what were then considered modern cars.

It would be impossible to summarize, in a few paragraphs, the legal aspects of the Selden patent case—and presumptuous to comment on it, for legal experts still argue its merits. In 1909 a Circuit Court judge handed down a decision against Ford. In 1911 the Appellate Court partially reversed the decision, ruling that the Selden patent was valid but that Ford did not infringe it: a clear-cut victory for Ford. Which court was right depends on "which paper you read," but it may be significant that F. L. Smith, who headed the Association prosecuting the case, later said, "By what miracle that flimsy patent was ever sustained in the lower court I know not."

The difference between the two verdicts was based on varied interpretations of what the patent covered. Selden's claim, which was allowed by the Patent Office, covered "any vehicle propelled by a hydrocarbon engine with disconnecting device between the driving engine and the vehicle and having a receptacle for fuel." The lower court accepted this broad interpretation, which obviously covered every gasoline-fueled automobile with a clutch and tank.

The upper court ruled that the patent covered only cars powered by the type of engine that Selden described in his specifications—a two-cycle, external-compression engine with a flame ignition, of the Brayton type. Ford was using a four-cycle, internal-compression engine with spark ignition, of the Otto type. Selden's case was not helped by an incautious diary entry he had made before filing for his patent. After examining an Otto four-cycle engine he had written, "That is another of those damned Dutch engines." Regardless of what he later claimed, Selden had obviously drawn a distinction between his engine and the Otto engine and believed that his was superior.

Three things happened in 1908 that foreshadowed the end of the "automobile game" era, although its big inning was yet to be played. First, Walter P. Chrysler bought his first automobile—an act that had no immediate bearing on changing the game to a solid industry but which would culminate in the establishment of the third, in point of age, of the Big Three.

Walter Chrysler, son of a railroad engineer, had started as a sweeper and then an apprentice mechanic in the shops of the Union Pacific Railroad in Kansas. Like Ford, he had an innate love for and understanding of tools and machinery. He made his own tools and built a perfect scale model of his father's locomotive. He progressed steadily from journeyman to roundhouse foreman, to general foreman and, by 1908, Superintendent of Motive Power on a section of the Chicago and Great Western at Oelwein, Ohio. Then he used his railroad pass and went to Chicago to the Automobile Show.

To quote Chrysler: "That is where it happened. I saw this Locomobile touring car; it was painted ivory white and the cushions and trim were red. The top was khaki and supported by wood bows. Straps ran from that top to anchorages on either side of the hood. On the running board was a handsome tool box that my fingers itched to open. Beside it was a tank of gas to feed the front headlamps; just behind the hood on each side of the cowling was an oil lamp, shaped quite like those on horse drawn carriages. I spent four days hanging around the show, held by that automobile as by a siren's song. The price tag meant just what it said, I found out by repeated inquiries: $5,000 cash. I had $700." Chrysler might have added that his salary was $350 a month and that he had a wife and two children.

Chrysler knew the vice-president of a Chicago bank who, somewhat reluctantly, lent him the $4,300. Years later this banker was a member of a syndicate that had $50 million in the Willys-Overland Company, which was headed for the rocks. He hired Chrysler at a fee of $1 million a year for two years to save the company.

Walter put his machine on a freight car for Oelwein—he did not know how to drive. Then he went home and broke the news to his wife. Della Chrysler did not seem to have quite as much faith as Clara Ford. Her husband said that when he told her about the car "she did not scold me, but it did seem to me that when she closed the kitchen door it made a little more noise than usual. Maybe she slammed it."

When the car arrived, Walter hitched a hired team to it and sat behind the wheel as it was hauled to his barn. Then he started to take it apart. Every night and every Saturday and Sunday for three months Chrysler took the car apart and put it back together. It had the best-tuned engine of any Locomobile in America—but it never left the barn. It was Della who finally insisted that if they were going to own a car they should at least ride in it, and Walter took his family for a memorable first ride.

This was the beginning of the end of Chrysler the railroad man.

He went on to become works manager of the American Locomotive Works. But three years after he bought his first car, he was plant superintendent of the Buick Division of General Motors.

That was the second event of 1908—Billy Durant started to put General Motors together.

Perhaps fifty years from now William Crapo Durant can be evaluated objectively and unemotionally. It is yet too soon, for many who knew and worked with him have told conflicting stories of the man. What he did and how he did it are clear; but his motivations, personality, and ethics are variously reported. Theodore MacManus, an advertising man who worked with Durant, wrote this description:

He ruled his little world and all the ants in it. He delighted in obeisance of men. His arrogance was equal to his luck. In later days, when he bestrode the world like a motor car colossus, it was his delight to demonstrate his vigor and vitality by laboring from seven o'clock one morning until one, two, or three the next—and keeping a host of sleepy satellites attendant on his needs. There is—or was—a sense of Gallic vainglory in this man and a sense of the dramatic which did not permit him to do things in the ordinary way.

He traveled with a retinue of retainers and took impish delight in seeing them bewildered while his quick brain steered its way through a maze of conflicting projects and appalling detail. Time and again he would give an audience across his desk to one man while three, four, five or six, each with a separate proposition to present, anxiously awaited their turn in various corners of the same room. He did not keep them waiting in an anteroom but grandiosely herded them together in his office if the whim seized him, knowing perfectly well there was heartburn, anxiety, and even jealousy in each conflicting breast. These were big men, men of consequence, with deals to discuss running into millions and tens of millions, but they all stood about like schoolboys awaiting his beck and nod.

Alfred P. Sloan, Jr., who surely knew Durant better than MacManus, paints a more kindly picture. "Mr. Durant," says Sloan, "was advanced for his time in general methods of production . . . . [He] showed a considerable sophistication in economic matters, very different from the popular image of him as a mere stockmarket plunger . . . . Mr. Durant was a great man with a great weakness—he could create but he could not administer—and he had, first in carriages and then in automobiles, more than a quarter century of the glory of creation before he fell. That he should have conceived a General Motors and then been unable himself in the long run to bring it off or to sustain his personal, once dominating position in it is a tragedy of American industrial history."

In a semiofficial history of General Motors, published in 1934, Arthur Pound wrote this description:

This small spare man seemed to draw upon irresistible sources of energy. He worked more hours than any of his employees, did with little sleep, yet came to his labors fresh and smiling every morning. There was a gaiety and resilience in him which overcame all obstacles. The press began to speak of him as the "Little Giant." His worshipful associates might call him Billy, but among themselves they fell into the habit of calling him "The Man." . . . He was the first among equals rather than the autocrat and no captain has ever been followed by more devoted troops . . . . There are innumerable instances that he cared little for money for its own sake. His tastes were simple and he had no time to spend money; already well off, he had serene confidence that he would always be successful and that nothing could stop him from amassing an immense fortune in the automobile game. I use the word "game" advisedly; if he was not the man who invented that expression to describe the early activities of what has since become a most precise and responsible business, he at least played that great game most completely as an adventure of the human spirit.

Durant has been called a wheeler-dealer, a plunger, a promoter, a stockjobber. He was all this. But he was also the one man with the imagination to envision what the automobile would come to mean to America. No one has ever accused him of dishonesty or of taking unfair advantage, in a deal, for his personal gain. And it is quite possible that, of all the makes of cars in the United States today, only four would now exist were it not for Durant. He started Chevrolet. He put Buick on its feet. Oldsmobile and Pontiac (then Oakland) would almost surely have passed from the scene but for Durant. Cadillac might have gone the way of Packard, Pierce-Arrow, and so many others that were then doing well. Durant brought Charles Nash into the automobile business from Durant-Dort Carriage Company, and Nash went on to create the foundation for American Motors and the rebirth of Rambler. Durant gave Walter Chrysler his opportunity as president of Buick, from whence Chrysler went on to save Willys-Overland, which later brought forth the famous Jeep, and to create

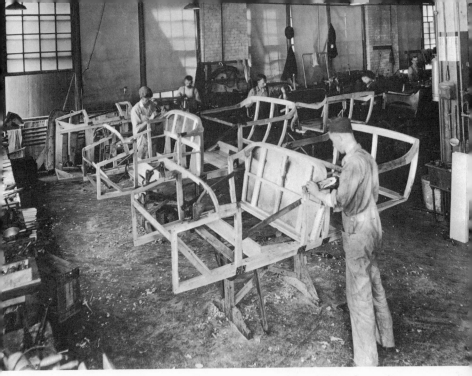

Body manufacturing in the early years was based on carriage-making techniques.

the Chrysler and Plymouth. Only Ford, Lincoln, Mercury, and Dodge were not, in one way or another, affected by William Crapo Durant.

By 1908 Buick was the country's leading producer, with 8,487 cars built that year as compared to 6,181 Fords and 2,380 Cadillacs. Durant was ready for bigger things. So was Ben Briscoe. After getting his feet wet with Buick, Briscoe plunged into the automobile game by financing J. D. Maxwell to make the Briscoe-Maxwell— later simply the Maxwell, which, still later, became the starting point for Chrysler Corporation. Durant and Briscoe devised a deal to merge Maxwell, Buick, Ford, and Reo. At a meeting to discuss this, Henry Ford and Couzens demanded $3 million cash. Not to be outdone, Ransom Olds made a similar demand. Because nothing like this amount of cash was available, the deal fell through.

Briscoe, through his sheet metal business, had some dealings with J. P. Morgan and Company. He and Durant asked Morgan to underwrite $500,000 of $1,500,000 to start what would become General

Motors. The House of Morgan had little regard for Billy Durant. The story goes that Durant had said, in the presence of Morgan partner George Perkins, "The time will come when five hundred thousand automobiles will be manufactured and sold in this country every year." Perkins stamped out of the room, growling, "If he has any sense he'll keep those notions to himself if he ever tries to borrow money." When Morgan turned down the entrepreneurs Briscoe went on alone to put together United States Motors, which had some 130 corporations under its banner when it went bankrupt in 1912.

During the talks with the House of Morgan, Perkins had suggested the name International Motors. When the deal fell through he asked Durant not to use that name, because he had proposed it. In a huff, Durant crossed out *International* and scribbled in *General*. That is how the world's largest corporation got named. Durant incorporated it in New Jersey as the General Motors Company, with an initial capitalization of $2,000, which was soon raised to $12,500,000.

Durant transferred Buick to General Motors by trading $3,750,250 of the new company's stock for the shares of the Buick Motor Company plus $1,500 in cash. A month later Durant traded $3,023,-574 of General Motors stock and $17,279 in cash for the Olds Motor Works. By 1908 Olds had sunk so low that Durant is said to have commented, "That's a hell of a price to pay for a bunch of road signs." Olds was a large user of billboards. Durant did not get

The 1908 models of the General Motors cars that are still in existence. Left, Buick. Right, Cadillac.

General Motors Corporation   General Motors Corporation

Cadillac so easily. He secured a ten-day option to buy the company for $3,500,000, but Wilfred C. Leland, Henry's son, wanted a half million in cash. Durant could not raise the money, and the option lapsed. This was repeated six months later, but this time the price was $4,125,000. Finally, in October 1909, Durant paid $500,000 cash and $5,169,200 in General Motors stock and brought Cadillac into the fold.

Durant made another effort to buy Ford in October 1909. Now Henry wanted $8 million—$2 million in cash and the rest in one and two years. General Motors directors approved the acquisition, but no banker would advance the cash. Although the Ford Motor Company had earned almost $2,700,000 in 1908 on sales of $9 million and expected to do a business of $15 million in 1909, the distrust of the big money men for the automobile game was such that none considered The Ford Motor Company worth $8 million.

Between 1908 and 1910 Durant brought twenty-five companies into General Motors. Many of them were "dogs" that Durant acquired for reasons best known to himself. His theory was that General Motors should cover every base and not be left out in the cold no matter how the industry developed. He bought Cartercar—the automobile that started in a prison—because it had a disk transmission he thought might have a future. He bought Elmore because it had a two-cycle engine that might have promise. No one knows why he bought the Marquette, the Ewing, the Randolph, the Welch,

Left, Oldsmobile. Right, Oakland, which became Pontiac. The first Chevrolet did not appear until 1912.

General Motors Corporation   General Motors Corporation

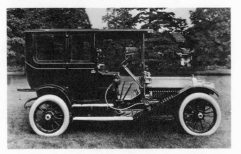 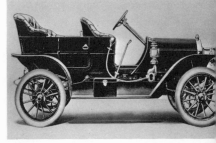

and several others. Two truck companies purchased at this time became, much later, GMC Trucks. He also bought the Oakland Motor Car Company, which later became the Pontiac Division.

Another theory in which Durant pioneered was integration of parts production within the company. He bought motor companies, an axle and wheel company, and other parts suppliers. He personally financed a French race driver named Albert Champion, who had an idea for a ceramic spark plug and later turned over his 75-percent interest in what became the AC Spark Plug Division to General Motors without a personal profit.

Those who would attribute Durant's maneuvers to luck or unguided chance point out that some of his acquisitions were subsequently written off as total losses. Particularly, they point to the Heany Lamp Company, for which Durant traded some $7 million in General Motors stock—more than he had given for Olds and Buick combined. Heany's sole asset was a patent application on a tungsten lamp that was later thrown out by the patent office. Without the patent the company was worthless.

By 1910 General Motors was doing 20 percent of the industry

Billy Durant (far right, wearing derby) with the first production Chevrolet, 1912. Durant had quietly backed Louis Chevrolet (front row center, without hat) in the development of a small car. The car was a success from the start, and helped Durant regain control of General Motors.

General Motors Corporation

business, mostly on Buicks and Cadillacs; the rest of the cars were then of little consequence. But the company was vastly overextended and strapped for cash. The Cadillac payroll was raised on one occasion by an emergency meeting of Detroit bankers to provide a short-term loan. A Buick payroll was met by having the Boston distributor express suitcases full of currency to Flint. Durant sought money from Eastern bankers, but he was still *persona non grata* in New York. He toured the West. Kansas City, Chicago, and St. Louis turned him down. His unfailing, cheerful optimism was evident from a little story told by one of two associates who made the Western swing with him: "The train stopped in Elkhart, Indiana in a pouring rainstorm. Far down the dark and dismal street shone one electric sign, BANK. Durant shook Goss, who was dozing dejectedly in a corner. 'Wake up, Goss,' said the leader. 'There's one bank we missed.' "

Durant again went East and offered to relinquish his control of the management of the company in return for a loan that would save it from receivership. Investment bankers J. & W. Seligman of New York and Lee Higginson of Boston agreed to this proposition, with the further provision that the affairs of the company be administered by a trusteeship dominated by the bankers. They issued $15 million in 6-percent notes, covered by mortgages on all the company's real property, for which they advanced $12,750,000—making the real interest over 7 percent. In addition they received a bonus of $6,169,-200 in General Motors stock. In short, they received over $21 million plus 6 percent interest on $15 million for advancing $12,750,000. And the risk was not great; the real properties, if liquidated, would probably have covered their investment. It was deals of this kind that were behind Henry Ford's distrust of money men.

Under the trusteeship General Motors was soon on more solid ground, largely because management retrenched and waited for the market for cars to catch up to their inventories and ability to produce. General Motors stock was listed on the New York Stock Exchange in 1911—the first automobile stock on the Big Board. By 1915 sales had declined to 10 percent of the total market, but the market had so increased that unit production was up from 40,000 to 100,000. In that year General Motors paid its first cash dividend of $50 per share on the common stock, the largest per-share cash dividend ever declared on a stock listed on the New York Stock Exchange.

By this time the automobile game was over; the industry had become a respectable business—to everybody except William Crapo Durant. He had stayed on as vice-president of General Motors when the bankers took over. But quietly, on the side, he had backed Louis Chevrolet in the development of a small car. The Chevrolet brothers, Louis and Arthur, were race drivers who had come from France to drive for Buick. Durant had them race each other on a dirt track behind a plant. When Louis won, Durant hired Arthur as his personal chauffeur because he had lost by taking no chances. Louis joined the Buick race team and worked on the design for the car that would bear his name. After the car went into production, Louis faded from the picture and turned his attention to building Frontenac race cars.

The Chevrolet was a success from the start, but Durant was more interested in it as a means of regaining control of General Motors than as a separate entity. In this he had, at last, some help from Eastern money—ironically as a result of his great mistake in Heany Electric. One of the original stockholders of Heany had made a fortune from the General Motors stock that Durant had traded for the company. Obviously, he thought very highly of Billy Durant, and he was a power in the Chatham and Phoenix Bank in New York.

Durant offered General Motors stockholders a trade of five shares of Chevrolet for one share of General Motors—a deal that assured an immediate profit. In 1915 the banker's trusteeship expired, and a new Board of Directors was to be elected for General Motors. Durant walked into the meeting and announced that he controlled the company. Today, Chevrolet is one of the most valuable properties owned by General Motors. But in 1915 General Motors did not own Chevrolet—Chevrolet owned General Motors with 450,000 shares of the 825,000 outstanding.

Durant came back as president, and in the words of Alfred P. Sloan, Jr., "the big show was on again." Capitalization was upped from $60 million to $100 million. The name was changed to General Motors Corporation—instead of Company—and the corporation became an operating company, with the manufacturing companies as divisions, rather than merely a holding company. At about this time John J. Raskob, treasurer of the du Pont Company, recommended General Motors as a good investment for his company's war profits, and du Pont ultimately acquired almost 29 percent of General Motors common.

Durant, with Raskob's full support, was quickly up to his old tricks. He bought the Sheridan car, Fisher Body, and a couple of tractor companies and started General Motors Acceptance Company. He made one little investment with his own money. There was a small company in Detroit called Guardian Frigerator Company, which was experimenting with domestic electric refrigeration. Durant bought it for $56,000 and later turned it over to the Corporation for what he had paid for it, and it became the Frigidaire Division. The domestic electric refrigeration industry grew from this transaction. At one time most people called all electric refrigerators Frigidaires, just as they used to call all record players Victrolas.

Perhaps the most important trades that Durant ever made, both for General Motors and the industry, were for two relatively small companies—Dayton Engineering Laboratories and Hyatt Roller Bearing Company. To the great complex of General Motors these were rather insignificant additions; but with Dayton, GM got Charles Franklin Kettering, and with Hyatt, Alfred Pritchard Sloan, Jr.

The Hyatt Company of Newark made an antifriction bearing used, originally, in mine cars, sugar-crushing machinery, printing presses, and similar equipment. John Wesley Hyatt was not active in the company that bore his name. While seeking a substitute for ivory to win a $10,000 prize offered by a billiard ball manufacturer he had invented Celluloid, the egg from which the plastics industry hatched.

With a fresh B.S. degree in electrical engineering from M.I.T., Alfred P. Sloan, Jr., went to work at Hyatt in 1895. One of his early weekly chores was to take the train to Hoboken, the ferry to New York, and wait in the anteroom of the American Sugar Refining Company until Hyatt's backer, John Searles, sent out a check to cover the difference between the bank balance and the Hyatt payroll. Searles finally tired of signing checks, and Sloan's father and some friends put up $5,000 to acquire control of the business and keep it going.

In 1899 a letter came to Newark from Kokomo. Elwood Haynes wanted to know whether Hyatt could make a bearing to be used in an automobile axle. Olds followed, then Cadillac, then Ford. As the early years of the century passed, Hyatt could scarcely expand fast enough to fill its automobile orders.

In 1916 Billy Durant phoned Sloan to ask whether the Hyatt Roller Bearing Company was for sale. Sloan did some quick thinking. About half of Hyatt's sales were to Ford, the bulk of the remainder to General Motors' divisions. Sloan saw the handwriting on the wall for independent parts manufacturers—the automobile companies were integrating parts suppliers. If Hyatt lost either Ford or GM business, it would be in a bad way. He met with Durant and boldly demanded $15,000,000 for the company. Durant smilingly told him he would think about it. The deal was finally concluded for $13,500,000, half in cash and half in the stock of United Motors Corporation, a subsidiary Durant had set up to acquire parts companies. Sloan's father and his friends wanted most of their share in cash, so Alfred, Jr., ended as a major stockholder in, and president of, United Motors. When this was later absorbed by General Motors, he became vice-president and a large stockholder in that company.

Durant continued down the road of expansion, aided and abetted by Raskob at every step. Raskob, who has never been considered a plunger or an "operator," shared Durant's faith in the future of the automobile industry. By 1920 the company was so big that it could no longer be properly managed by Durant's hit-or-miss methods. Sloan prepared and presented to Durant a carefully studied plan for administrative reorganization. Durant brushed it aside; he was not interested in reasoned administration. He continued to make all important decisions, sometimes, it seemed, whimsically. Serious internal weaknesses were developing. Henry Leland quit as head of Cadillac. Walter Chrysler, after stormy disagreements with Durant over the operation of Buick, walked out and slammed the door. Sloan very seriously considered liquidating his interest. To top the internal difficulties the postwar business depression struck, and the stock market broke.

Durant tried desperately to support the market for General Motors stock. He pledged his shares in the company for loans from brokers to buy more stock and to protect the holdings of his friends. As the price continued to tumble there were frantic calls for margin from brokers all over the country. Durant had no more to give. If Durant was wiped out, not only the corporation but several brokers might

After the Model A, Ford gave each new car he designed a successive letter of the alphabet, whether or not it actually went into production. The Model N, being inspected above, was one of the last models before Ford's famous Model T.

collapse. In this crisis the du Ponts stepped in and, through J. P. Morgan, advanced the money to take over Durant's personal obligations.

"In this way," wrote Alfred P. Sloan, Jr., "2,500,000 shares of General Motors stock passed from the ownership of W. C. Durant to the du Ponts. In this episode W. C. Durant, a man of genius, of courage, of vision and great wealth, is seen sacrificing all he had in a fruitless effort to protect, according to his way of thinking, his creation, General Motors—loyal to the very end.

"There was a meeting of the Board. Mr. Durant presided as usual. You knew he was grief-stricken, but no grief showed in his face. He was smiling pleasantly, as if it were a routine matter, when he told us he was resigning as president of General Motors. Our board meeting broke up. Later, as Mr. Durant left, followed by one or two devoted secretaries, there was only sadness and regret. A true friend had departed from among us. An epoch in General Motors history was concluded."

Pierre du Pont became titular president of General Motors, with executive vice-president Alfred P. Sloan, Jr., to install and operate the internal reorganization plan he had previously proposed to Durant to bring order out of chaos. A new epoch in General Motors history was starting.

But Billy Durant was not through playing the automobile game; for him there would be an extra inning. Less than a month after he left the corporation he organized the Durant Motor Company. He built up a new group of automobile and parts companies, and during the 1920s he made the Flint, the Durant, and the Star—the last sold well, briefly, in competition with Ford and Chevy. But they were not very good cars, and Durant was still no administrator. The depression that started in 1929 finally finished him in the automobile game. In 1935, at the age of seventy-five, Durant filed a petition in bankruptcy, listing $250 in assets and $914,000 in liabilities.

That same year a newspaper reporter in Asbury Park, N. J., saw an old man helping to clean up a supermarket on the night before its grand opening. His sob story that the man who had founded General Motors was reduced to sweeping floors for a living brought much business to the market—for which William Crapo Durant was grateful. He owned the supermarket.

The third event of that critical year of 1908 that portended the end of the automobile game was the introduction of a new model by Henry Ford. The first commercial Ford, in 1903, had been labeled Model A. Each new development car, whether or not it went into production, was given a successive letter. By 1907 Ford was producing Models N, R, and S. The new car was labeled Model T— the car that was the great leap forward in changing the entire concept of the automobile and its relation to life in America.

The Lamp, Standard Oil Company (N.J.)

Henry Ford's Model T, the car that put a nation on wheels. This model was so popular that Ford continued it for nineteen years, during which time he sold 15 million cars. He streamlined production and pared the cost from $850, when the car first appeared in 1908, to a low of $295 in 1924. Painting by Leslie Saalburg.

FOUR: THE MECHANICAL COCKROACH

October 1, 1908, was the official birthday of the Model T Ford. On the thirtieth of that same month Mrs. William Waldorf Astor died quietly in her home on Fifth Avenue. There was no connection between these two events, but Mrs. Astor's passing was symbolic of a changing social and economic pattern in American life that created a situation in which the Model T—or something like it—could hardly fail of spectacular success.

With Mrs. Astor passed "society" in the old sense. The affluent aristocracy, luxuriating on hoarded wealth, was starting to decline. A new era had dawned in which the gulf between the idle rich and the common man would cease to yawn so widely. Ultimately the former would virtually disappear, and the latter would take for granted a way of life previously reserved for a privileged class. The Model T played two roles in this changing pattern of life. It provided the common man with his first and biggest symbol of freedom and power. And it accelerated a new development of the industrial system that diffused wealth in a manner that made the new order possible.

The Model T was the first *volkswagen,* but, unlike Hitler's, it was born at a time and in a place where the "volk" were ready for wagons. Had it been created a few years sooner it might have languished until the times caught up. Had its birth been delayed, something else would surely have filled the need. This ungainly vehicle spurred the Industrial Revolution to a gallop and sparked an agrarian reform that would have far-reaching influence on American life.

The Model T came into being when it did because Henry Ford now had undisputed say over the kind of a car the company would make. He had long talked of a "universal car," but Malcomson had insisted that, in addition to small cars, they make the Model K— on which the company lost money at a sale price of $2,800. There were other differences between the coal dealer and the native genius. Although Malcomson was titular treasurer of the Ford Motor Company, he had concentrated on his coal business and left the affairs of the automobile company to Couzens. When he realized that he was running the tail while Couzens was running the dog, he tried to change places. Ford would not agree. Then Henry, Couzens, and the Dodge brothers organized the Ford Manufacturing Company, of which Malcomson had no part, to make engines and parts for the Ford Motor Company. Because, in effect, they were selling to themselves, they could drain the profits of the Motor Company into the Ford Manufacturing Company. In July 1906 Malcomson sold his interest in the automobile company to Ford for $175,000. Woodall, Fry, and Bennett followed him out, and Strelow—the carpenter who had built the first plant—sold his fifty shares to Couzens for $25,000. Ford then had 585 of 1,000 shares, Couzens 110.

As soon as Malcomson was out Ford, assisted by Harold Wills, started to design the "family horse." The car they conceived was probably the homeliest vehicle in America—unless one could see beauty in pure functionalism. Stubby and boxlike, it was far too high for its length by any aesthetic standards. But to Henry Ford, clearance of obstructions on rural roads was far more important than well-balanced proportions. Its creators had no thought in mind other than to create a car to serve a purpose—which the Model T did so well that it lasted for nineteen years, during which over 15 million were made. It still holds the record, by a wide margin, as the world's most widely used single piece of large mechanical equipment.

The Model T weighed 1,200 pounds. Its four-cylinder vertical engine generated twenty horsepower—enough to give it a top speed of about forty miles an hour. Its three-point suspension made it amazingly loose-jointed, another concession to rough roads. Mechanically, it was as simple as simple could be. Fuel feed was by gravity from a tank under the seat. Water circulation was based on the principle that warm water rises and cold water sinks; there

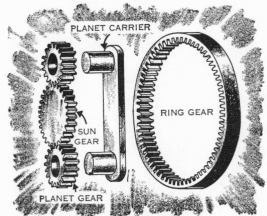

PLANET CARRIER

SUN GEAR

PLANET GEAR

RING GEAR

One mechanical distinction of Ford's Model T was the planetary transmission. Ford clung to this contrary contraption long after other makers switched to more effective types — but the planetary came back to supply the mechanical foundation for modern automatic transmissions. The basic elements in the planetary transmission are a ring gear with internal teeth, a sun gear, two or more planet gears, and a planet carrier. If the sun gear is connected to the crank shaft and the planet carrier is connected to the drive shaft, the drive shaft will turn at a slower rate than the crank shaft. This produces strong power at low speed for starting. If, through clutching, the relation of the planet carrier and sun gear is reversed, the drive shaft will give high speed at lower power.

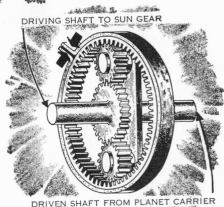

DRIVING SHAFT TO SUN GEAR

DRIVEN SHAFT FROM PLANET CARRIER

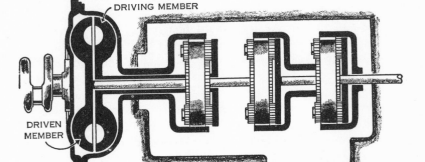

DRIVING MEMBER

DRIVEN MEMBER

Henry Ford Museum

The Model T's three-point suspension system was designed for the rough roads of the day. The car had an eel-like ability for twisting and turning.

was no water pump. Anyone but a mechanical dunce could repair it with a screwdriver, pliers, wrench, and hammer. Vanadium-alloy steel made it strong far beyond its weight.

In addition to its rugged simplicity the Model T had several popular features. It was one of the first vehicles with lefthand drive: Ford realized that it was more important that the driver have a good view of the car coming toward him on his left than of the ditch on his right. It had a double system of braking, hand and foot, and unusually strong transverse springs—another concession to the realities of roads. Two important mechanical advantages were its planetary transmission and its low-tension magneto mounted on the flywheel. At a time when inexperienced drivers had trouble shifting without grinding and stripping gears the simple planetary transmission was received with acclaim. The magneto, revolved by the flywheel, supplied a steady electric current without batteries.

Early Model T advertisements proclaimed that "no car under

$2,000 offers more, and no car over $2,000 offers more except in trimmings." All things considered, this was a justifiable brag.

Initially, the Model T was far from the cheapest car in America. The 1908 touring car sold for $850. This price covered the chassis, body, four wheels, four tires, and three oil lamps. There was no provision for carrying a spare, and the windshield, top, and headlights were extras. At the time, the Hupmobile, similarly stripped down, was selling for $750. The Brush, which was advertised as "Everyman's Car," sold for $485. The Sears-Roebuck catalogue offered a "large, roomy, two passenger, piano-box buggy pattern . . . . Three bow Morocline auto top fitted with complete side curtains and storm front . . . . Any lady or child can start and run a Sears Motor Car. Price $395 to $495." Sears made cars from 1905 to 1910, then gave up and made much more money selling accessories for Model Ts.

The price of the Model T went down through the years as production mounted, and the car, which had seemed to be as basic as possible to begin with, was further stripped of nonessentials. Until 1912 the radiator and lamps were brass, then they changed to black-painted steel. In 1913, when front doors were added to the touring car, only the one on the right worked. The "door" on the left was a dummy embossed in the metal; it did not open. It was 1914 before Henry said, "The customer can have any color he wants as long as it's black." In 1908 buyers could get a red touring car or a gray roadster; later all cars were Brewster Green, with black trimmings and red striping. By 1914, the first year in which over half a million Model Ts were made, the price was down to $490. It reached an all-time low of $290 in 1924.

In 1909, the first full year of the Model T, Ford made 18,664 cars—about 8 percent of the industry production of 123,990. In 1913 a quarter million Model Ts were made, almost 40 percent of the industry total. In 1921 production passed the 1 million mark; in 1923, the 2 million. From the end of World War I until 1925 approximately half the cars made in America were Model T Fords, and because they were so rugged, they represented far more than half the cars on the road.

During much of the reign of the Model T the old saw "It's not the initial cost; it's the upkeep" applied to most other cars. Dealers knew little and cared less about service. Parts, made in small quantities for constantly changed models, were costly if not unattainable. Not so with Ford. Parts made by the million were warehoused in branches throughout the country. A muffler cost $2.00, a front fender $3.00, a front spring $4.00. And if the Model T owner was too lazy or incompetent to make repairs himself, a dealer would do it for little more than pennies. By the early teen years prospective dealers were approaching the Ford Motor Company on their knees to obtain a lucrative Ford franchise, and the company made them toe the mark on service. The charge for replacing a muffler was 60 cents, for installing a fender 75 cents.

Driving a Model T should have been as simple as the car itself,

Ford showroom, Omaha, Nebraska. For the decade after World War I, half of the cars made in America were Model T Fords, and because they were so rugged, they represented far more than half the cars on the road.

Henry Ford Museum

but this was not always so, because each Model T had a personality of its own, and many were highly temperamental. There are those who say that no piece of machinery can have such human characteristics; but those who say this never owned a Model T. Perhaps the feeling that the car had a personality came from the owner rather than the car. Brought up with horses, which do have personalities, many an owner treated his Model T like an animal—petted it, talked to it, and developed a deep affection for it. But there is no doubt that the Model T was temperamental. At times it was docile, obedient, and seemed to return one's affection. At other times, seemingly under the same conditions, it displayed mulelike stubbornness about starting or otherwise doing its owner's bidding.

The horselike quality of the Model T was attributed to its planetary transmission by Lee Strout White in his famous eulogy, "Farewell to Model T." He wrote, "Because of the peculiar nature of this planetary element, there was always, in Model T, a certain dull rapport between engine and wheels, and even when the car was in a state known as neutral it trembled with a deep imperative and tended to inch forward. There was never a moment when the bands were not faintly egging the machine on. In this respect it was like a horse, rolling the bit on its tongue, and country people brought to it the same technique they used with draft animals . . . . Often, if the emergency brake hadn't been pulled all the way back, the car advanced on you the instant the first explosion occurred and you would hold it back by leaning your weight against it. I can still feel my old Ford nuzzling me at the curb, as though looking for an apple in my pocket."

Allan Nevins, in his studious report on Henry Ford and the company, attests to the idiosyncrasies of the individual Model T. "No two cars," he says, "were quite alike. Mastery of any one involved highly personal qualities of courage, skill, intuition, and luck. As of Cleopatra, it could be said that time could not wither nor custom stale the infinite variety of the flivver; with all its superior dependability and simplicity it combined an arch and mercurial eccentricity. It was more like a human being (of feminine gender) than any car ever known to man. To buy one was to embark on a great adventure."

The driving controls of the Model T consisted of a horizontal hand accelerator under the steering wheel, a vertical lever beside the left hand, and three pedals. There is no truth in the legend that three feet were required to manipulate the pedals—nor that the car could go forward and backward at the same time, although it often seemed to, because many drivers used reverse as a brake, sometimes making the car go from a forward to a rearward direction seemingly without a pause. The operation of the controls was explained in the Instruction Book supplied with the 1909 car:

The foot pedal at the right marked "B" operates the brake on the transmission; the foot pedal on the left marked "C" is the control lever acting on the clutch. The pedal in the center operates reverse. The hand lever when thrown forward engages high speed; when pulled back operates the emergency brake. Hand lever is in neutral when almost vertical and clutch is in a released condition. Throwing the control lever forward engages the clutch in high speed; a light pressure on foot pedal "C" throws in neutral; a full pressure on this pedal throws in low; a partial gradual release of the pedal again engages high speed.

This may have been the way that Henry Ford drove the Model T. Most others did not find it that definite. Lee Strout White, writing in *The New Yorker,* gave a much better description. He wrote:

To get under way, you simply hooked the third finger of the right hand around a lever on the steering column, pulled down hard, and shoved your foot forcibly against the low-speed pedal. These were simple, positive motions; the car responded by lunging forward with a roar. After a few seconds of this turmoil, you took your foot off the pedal, eased up a mite on the throttle, and the car, possessed of only two forward speeds, catapulted directly into high with a series of ugly jerks and was off on its glorious errand. The abruptness of this departure was never equalled in other cars of this period . . . .

The driver of the Model T was a man enthroned. The car, with top up, stood seven feet high. The driver sat on top of the gas tank, brooding it with his own body. When he wanted gasoline, he alighted, along with everything else in the front seat; the seat was pulled off, the metal cap unscrewed, and a wooden stick thrust down to sound the liquid in the well. There were always a couple of these sounding sticks kicking around in the ratty sub-cushion regions of a flivver. Refueling was more of a social function then, because the driver had to unbend, whether he wanted to or not. Directly in front of the driver was the windshield— high, uncompromisingly erect. Nobody talked about air resistance, and the four cylinders pushed the car through the atmosphere with a simple disregard of physical law . . . .

In 1909 two Model T's came in first and second among the six cars that completed a transcontinental race. This is one of them, marooned in a stream. The mechanic holding a rifle is looking for a rattlesnake hidden behind the car.

The Fords were obviously conceived in madness: any car that was capable of going from forward into reverse without any perceptible mechanical hiatus was bound to be a mighty challenging thing to the human imagination. Boys used to veer them off the highways into a level pasture and run wild with them, as though they were cutting up with a girl.

First to find the Model T as the beginning of a new way of life were America's farmers. Most did not buy it primarily as a pleasure vehicle—it was a business investment. A man in Maine stated very simply what the Ford meant to the farm. "Before I got my Ford," he said, "it took me a whole day to get my produce into town. Now I load the rear seat with butter, eggs and vegetables, seat myself on a fine soft cushion instead of a hard board covered with horse blankets, and away I go without a jolt hard enough to crack one of my eggs. I can make the trip to town and back by noon, and besides saving half a day's time, I get twenty percent better prices by being to market before the rest."

The Ford was the farmer's friend because it could negotiate any road—or no road. It could churn along through deep mud or sand in low gear, its radiator steaming, for mile after mile, if the driver did not mind keeping his foot constantly on "pedal C." It could claw its way up steep grades, and its high clearance kept the works dry in fording unbridged streams. Under the conditions of its day, it was a better car than any made in this day. No modern car could cope with the situations the Model T took in its stride.

The farmer also used his Model T as a portable power plant. With rear wheels jacked up and a power take-off attached, a Ford could saw wood, pump water, grind feed, make cider, and do countless other farm chores. And when the work was done, the family could go to town to see how people lived far from the farm on that other recent development, the silver screen. Within five years after the Model T was born the density of automobiles in relation to population had shifted from the cities and industrial states to the farming and ranching areas of the plains and the Pacific coast.

Although the Model T wrought its greatest magic in rural America, it was not confined to the farm. It was equally the doctor's car, the sportsman's car, the storekeeper's car, the engineer's car, and the minister's car. As the first really dependable, truly utilitarian low-

Model T's were used in many ways: Right, a snowmobile. Below, a railroad work car; a Model T carrying livestock. Below right, hunters carrying their kill.

Ford Motor Company

Ford Motor Company

Henry Ford Museum

Ford Motor Company

priced vehicle it was the car of the common man everywhere. It changed the automobile from a high-priced luxury or a low-priced gadget to a national necessity, or at least an indispensable convenience. To nothing else can the word *ubiquitous* be so aptly applied as to the Model T in the late teen years and the early 1920s.

Because it represented half the cars in America at the time of the "automobile explosion," the Model T was a leading factor in the social and economic change that was taking place in America. In his exhaustive history of the United States during the early years of the century, Mark Sullivan makes the point that there was a political trend at the time designed to redistribute wealth by edict, "the direction of bringing it about that the man who had two horses should give up one . . . . At that very time, men in another world than politics, men unnoticed by the politicians or the public . . . were conferring upon both the man who previously had no horse and the man who formerly had two, not only the power of one horse but of twenty or a hundred . . . . Had all the proposals of restraint ever devised by Bryan or LaFollette been enacted into law, the sum of their effect . . . would not have procured for the average man even a tiny fraction of the enrichment that Henry Ford conferred upon him."

Few people called the Model T by its proper name. Among non-Ford owners the most common contemptuous appellation was the Mechanical Cockroach. Other terms of opprobrium were the Detroit Disaster, Bouncing Betty, Leaping Lena, the Galloping Snail, and the Spirit of St. Vitus. Many Ford owners expressed their affection for their individual vehicles by giving them names, usually feminine. The most common names were Flivver and Tin Lizzie. Exhaustive research has failed to disclose the origin of the latter. The tin part is obvious—but none knows from whence came *Lizzie*. An improbable explanation is offered for the word *flivver*. There were some who believed that the vibration of riding in a Model T was good "for the liver"—which was abbreviated to *f'liver*, or *flivver*. This seems far-fetched, but there was a limerick that went:

> There was a fat man in Fall River,
> Who said as he drove his Ford "flivver,"
>   "This bouncing and jolting,
>   To me is revolting!
> It's hell, but it's good for the liver."

Although it had many supplementary uses, the Model T was principally what Henry Ford had envisioned as a "family horse"—a car that moved back the horizon for the common man and his kin.

Regardless of its origin, *flivver* became part of the language. In the 1927 supplement to Webster's Dictionary the lexicographers decided that *flivver* meant "a small and inexpensive automobile; hence anything that is small of its kind and cheap or insignificant." Not a very good definition; the Model T had great significance.

More ubiquitous than Fords were Ford jokes; collectively they were a national mania that reached its peak about 1914 and raged unabated until after the war. If one were to pile all the recent elephant jokes on the older moron jokes and place these atop the ancient mother-in-law jokes, "Pat and Mike" jokes, and "two Jews" jokes, the result would not approach the proportions of the Ford jokes. Nowhere was one safe from them. In schools and at sewing bees, from rostrums and at Rotary Clubs, Americans laughed and chuckled at the latest Ford quip—and, next day, there was another latest. A Ford joke was part of a doctor's bedside manner; in countless sermons it proved that clerics were *au courant*. Ford jokes were published in cheap, paperbound books. Nobody knows how many of these were issued or how many millions were sold. There are eight in the Library of Congress, but these represent only the few that were copyrighted.

Most jokes kidded the Ford rather than extolled it, probably because satire is an easy form of humor to contrive. Basically they represented a form of American folk humor; few were vicious, and virtually none was dirty. The most popular aspect of the Model T with humorists was its size.

It was said that Ford was going to paint his cars yellow and sell them in bunches like bananas. It was further said that letter carriers quit their jobs when they heard that Ford was going to sell cars by mail and that garbage men complained that their lives were getting harder—"Dead cats is bad enough and broken bottles is hell, but the worst is sorting out them damn little Fords." Junkmen amended their cry to "Any old rags, old bottles, old Fords today?" There was the joke about the Model T owner who approached a toll gate, got out, put his Ford in his pocket, and walked through for pedestrian toll, and the Cadillac owner who carried a Ford in a tool box for use in an emergency.

One quip alleged that Fords did not need to carry lamps—"they're light enough without them." And there was this fellow who was standing under a tree looking up mournfully into the branches. When asked what the matter was he replied, "I was cranking my Ford and it flew off the handle." There was the story of the clergyman who, annoyed by the buzz of a whispering congregation during the sermon, rebuked it by saying, "I don't mind your bringing your Fords into the pews, but in deference to the Lord and to me I must ask you not to run them during the service." And finally there was the one about the fellow who drove up to a pump and asked for a pint of gas for his Model T. "You sure you don't want more?" asked the attendant. "Uh-hunh," said the Ford owner, "I'm weaning it."

Next to tinyness came tinniness as a basis for Ford jokes. There was a woman who saved tin cans for years and sent them to the Ford Company; they sent her a new car and returned the five cans that were left over. Then there was the farmer who tore the old tin roof off his barn and sent it to Detroit. He received a letter saying, "Your car is the worst wreck we have ever seen; it will take us two weeks to fix it." And many said that Ford was going to make the car without doors and supply a can opener so that the owner could cut them to suit himself.

Then there were the "rattling good car" jokes, like the one claiming that Henry Ford was a great evangelist because his cars had shaken hell out of more people than Billy Sunday ever saw. When the brass radiator was dropped it was said that the new Fords would be quieter than the old, because they had taken the brass band off the front. Because Fords were supposed to shake themselves apart, Henry was going to supply a trained squirrel with each car to retrieve the nuts that fell out on the road. Somewhere there was supposed to be a garage that advertised "Automobiles repaired, Fords mended." And there was a mythical junk dealer who watched a Ford owner tow his inert car to the door and root around in the stock until he found a length of old pipe, part of an old perambulator frame, a piece of hose, a broken bird cage, and some other odds and ends. The car owner paid thirty cents for his treasures, took them out to his car, fiddled around for a while, and then drove off. After a few minutes' thought the junk dealer went to the back of his shop and painted a new sign. He took down the one that said "All Kinds of Junk" and replaced it with "Ford Parts and Accessories."

Irvin S. Cobb told a story about the crazy man who stole a Ford and picked up two Chinese laundrymen to go for a ride. The lunatic could not drive, and the vehicle wove an erratic course down the road until it reached a grade crossing at the same time as a train. When the train crew came back to investigate all they could find was a nut and two washers.

There were jokes based on the Model T's dependability, like the one about the farmer who specified in his will that his car be buried with him "because I've never been in a hole yet that my Ford could not get me out of." And there were jokes about Lizzie's temperament, like the jingle that advised:

> Speak harshly to your little Ford
> And kick it when it freezes;
> It does it only to annoy,
> Because it knows it teases.

Any compendium of Ford jokes always ends with the one about the traveler who said to a stranger on a train, "Have you heard the last Ford joke?" The stranger replied, fervently, "I hope so." Some versions of this have it that the stranger was Henry Ford. But this was not the last Ford joke. When Ford bought Lincoln, long after the Ford joke craze had died down, there was the one about the fellow who said, "I've got a new job in the Ford plant." "What do you do?" he was asked. "Paint whiskers on Fords to make them look like Lincolns."

Companions to the Ford jokes were Ford legends. At various times it was said, and widely believed, that Fords would be sold for $100 on Mr. Ford's birthday, on Edsel's wedding day, on the day that the Province of Ontario went dry, at a certain fixed hour all over the country, and if a million people each sent their name to the Ford Motor Company with $1 enclosed. The most widespread legend had to do with four dimes. It was said that Ford would give a free car to anyone who sent in four dimes on which the mint letters spelled *FORD*. Countless small boys—and innumerable adults—clung to dimes lettered *F, O,* and *D,* waiting for the elusive *R* which never came. *R* was never used as a mint mark. An interesting follow-up on this is the legend during World War II that Ford would give a car to the first one who sent him a 1943 copper penny for his coin collection. The Ford Company was deluged with queries on this—but received no pennies. Due to wartime shortage, no copper pennies were minted in 1943.

Butt of thousands of jokes, hero of dozens of legends, the Model T was the only car ever to be the subject of a symphony. When the ten millionth car was produced composer Frederick Converse wrote a fantasia in honor of the occasion. Its movements included "Dawn in Detroit," "Call to Labor," "The Din of the Builders," "The Birth of the Hero," and others that musically depicted the Hero wandering across the country to become involved in "America's Romance" and "America's Joy-ride." When Sergei Koussevitzky conducted the Boston Symphony in the first rendition of "Flivver Ten Million" he objected strenuously to the inclusion of a Ford horn in the orchestra, but the composer was adamant.

As Model Ts swarmed across America and reached out into the rest of the world, the Ford Motor Company amassed fabulous profits

In its final years the Model T ran into flaming youth as the 1920s started to roar.

—over $25 million in the first four years. Capitalization had been increased to $2 million by issuing additional stock to the remaining stockholders, and the regular dividend policy was 15 percent per quarter. The money poured in so rapidly that Couzens had it spread in fifty banks throughout the country. Special dividends were declared every few months; first 30 percent, then 50 percent, then 100 percent, and finally a whopping 500 percent—$10 million. Henry Ford was well on his way toward colossal wealth from the lion's share of these dividends. Clara Ford told of finding a check for $75,000 that Henry had forgotten in a suit that she was sending to the cleaners. Other stockholders had become millionaires. The car-buying public had benefited from steadily reduced prices; at one point Ford even rebated $50 per car to old buyers when production exceeded estimates. Then he decided that the worker, too, should share in this bonanza. On January 5, 1914, representatives of the Detroit press were called to James Couzens' office to hear an announcement that rocked the business world.

While Ford sat quietly in a corner, Couzens read a prepared statement. "The Ford Motor Company, the greatest and most successful automobile manufacturing company in the world, will, on January 12th, inaugurate the greatest revolution in the matter of rewards for its workers ever known to the industrial world. At one stroke it will reduce the hours of labor from nine to eight, and add to every man's pay a share of the profits of the house. The smallest sum to be received by any one man twenty-two years old and upward will be five dollars a day. The minimum is now two dollars and thirty-four cents per day for nine hours."

There was more to the statement telling how the bonus of $10 million over and above their regular wages would be distributed to the men, but the reporters could scarcely wait to put this sensational news on the wire. In the words of Allan Nevins, Ford's announcement "was like the dazzling burst of a rocket in velvet skies. Headlines blazed throughout the globe." Specifically, the press of New York City devoted fifty-two columns to the so-called Ford Plan during the next seven days.

Generally, the comment was highly laudatory. It was "an epoch in the world's industrial history," said the *Herald;* "a bolt out of the blue sky, flashing its way across the continent and far beyond, something unheard of in the history of business," said the *Sun.* The *Times* caught the popular imagination by noting that "the lowest paid employees, the sweepers, who in New York City may claim from $1.00 to $1.50 a day, are now to receive $5 in Ford's plant."

There was some unfavorable comment. Ford did it only as an advertisement; it was a cunning scheme to take advantage of his competitors; it would rob workers of independence through paternalism; the workers would squander their wealth in riotous living. In one ironic contrast *The Wall Street Journal,* the organ of capital, sneered at Ford's idea as an attempt to "apply Biblical principles where they do not belong," which would "return to plague him and the industry he represents, as well as organized society." At the same time a meeting of Socialists condemned the idea by resolving that "Ford had purchased the brains, life and soul of his men by a raise of a few dollars a week."

To this day there is argument as to why Ford, from the blue, doubled wages. At the time he told reporters it was "a plain act of social justice." Eight years later, in his autobiography, he caused his ghost writer to discourse at length on the theory of wages:

There is now a definite demand that the human side of business be elevated to a position of equal importance with the material side. And that is going to come about. It is just a question whether it is going to be brought about wisely—in a way that will conserve the material side which now sustains us, or unwisely and in such a way as shall take from us all the benefit of work of the past years. Business represents our national livelihood, it reflects our national progress, and gives us our place among other nations. We do not want to jeopardize that. What we want is a better recognition of the human element in business. And surely it can be achieved without dislocation, without loss to anyone, indeed with an increase of benefit to every human being. And the secret of it all is in a recognition of human partnership. Until each man is absolutely sufficient unto himself, needing the services of no other human being in any capacity whatsoever, we shall never get beyond the need of partnership. Such are the fundamental truths of wages. They are partnership distributions.

An interesting aspect of the above, in the light of today's political and economic philosophies, is that the middle of it sounds like Barry Goldwater and the beginning and end like Walter Reuther—opponents whose views would seem to have no common denominator.

There are those who say that Ford's plan was not motivated by social justice, that it was designed to reduce labor turnover, an extreme problem in the automobile industry. But Ford's turnover had been reduced to a negligible figure by enlightened labor practices that were in effect before the $5 a day plan. The Ford plant was a good place to work. Ford had some ideas on labor that were ahead of his time—perhaps ahead of our time. No man was ever refused a job because of a physical handicap; jobs were classified so that there was work for blind men, for deaf men, for legless men—even for armless men. No man was refused work because of "previous condition of servitude." Henry said that a man was "equally acceptable whether he has been in Sing Sing or Harvard." Facts do not bear this out. There were more ex-convicts working for Ford than college graduates; Old Henry did not have much reverence for a college degree. And he had other foibles. He would not employ a married woman whose husband had a job. In Henry's opinion, her place was in the home.

The idea that higher wages would make the worker a potential buyer for the product he produced is often advanced as the basis of the $5 a day wage. In general, Henry Ford believed this at a time when most employers thought it heresy. He wrote: "If we can distribute high wages, then the money is going to be spent and it will serve to make storekeepers and distributors and manufacturers and workers in other lines more prosperous and their prosperity will be reflected in our sales. Country-wide high wages spell country-wide prosperity, provided, however, that the higher wages are paid for higher production."

If Ford hoped that his act would cause others to follow his example, he was disappointed. The only immediate benefit to labor outside the Ford plant was inspirational. The convergence of prospective workers on Detroit to seek jobs at Ford assumed gold rush proportions. The result (in addition to a riot) was to so glut the labor market that other companies could get all the men they needed at whatever they chose to pay. But the public reaction to the wage boost had an effect on Henry Ford that was to have a far-reaching influence on the automobile industry.

Before the wage announcement Henry Ford, the man, was not widely known outside Detroit. His name was a brand on a piece of merchandise, like Singer on a sewing machine or Ingersoll on a watch. Contemporaries Edison, Rockefeller, and Morgan were known, for better or worse, as individuals; Ford was a make of a car. To that time his name had not appeared in *Who's Who*.

With that announcement Henry Ford flared to international prominence. Reporters flocked to Detroit as to Delphi to seek his opinion on every conceivable subject. He was invited to the White House to consult with President Wilson. He was no public speaker and disliked making public appearances, but he courted personal publicity. He freely offered didactic opinions on anything from smoking—he was "agin" it—to the world monetary system—he was "agin" that too; from books, which, he said, "muss up the mind," to world peace. He knew nothing about most of the things on which he pontificated, and he was not disposed to learn. He distrusted and avoided men of erudition, in whose presence he was ill at ease. But his public image of dedication to the people and the worker caused his every utterance to be received with reverence.

This public deference may have had much to do with the change that came over Henry Ford after the age of fifty. During the next ten years the back-slapping, prank-playing Henry of earlier years gave way to a remote and isolated autocrat who would neither accept advice nor brook criticism. This change certainly influenced the departure from his presence of the few men whose cooperation had contributed to the success of earlier years—principally the Dodges, Couzens, and Wills.

The Dodge brothers were the first to go. Their business was at the mercy of Ford, who took their entire production. They cancelled their contract with Ford to make a car of their own. Couzens was next. Canadian-born of English parents, he was wholeheartedly pro-Ally in World War I; Ford was violently pacifistic. There were other differences between the two chief executives of the company, but when Couzens resigned in 1915 as vice-president and treasurer he gave as his reason Ford's views on "peace, the Allies' war loan and national preparedness." He added, "The friendly relations that have existed between us for years have been changed of late, our disagreements becoming more violent." He attested to Ford's new character by adding, "I will be willing to work with Henry Ford, but I refuse to work for him."

Early in 1916 Ford confounded the minority stockholders by announcing that there would be no further special dividends; all profits would be plowed back into the business to finance the vast industrial complex he planned to build on the River Rouge. The Dodge brothers sued and secured a decision compelling Ford to pay $19,000,000 in dividends. Ford then decided that he must own the company outright. His first move was to announce, while visiting in California, that he was leaving the Ford Motor Company to form a new organization to make a better car and sell it at a lower price. The new venture would be entirely owned by the Ford family. When queried about the old company he replied, "I don't know what will become of that; the portion that does not belong to me cannot be sold to me, that I know." Shortly after he made this pronouncement, smooth-talking gentlemen from Boston's Old Colony Trust Company approached the minority stockholders with a view to buying them out.

At first it was thought that Billy Durant was behind this move. The stockholders were jittery, as well they should be. A new Ford company, with the Master at the helm, would surely sound the death knell of the old one. Only Couzens held out long enough to learn that Henry was behind this move and to demand $500 a share more than the $12,500 offered the other stockholders. Couzens received $29,308,857.90, the heirs of banker Gray $26,250,000, the Dodge brothers $25,000,000, and Anderson and Rackham each $12,500,-000—truly a handsome profit on their original investments of $5,000 to $10,500.

Henry Ford was now the complete autocrat, and men who would not tolerate his dominance dropped away or were dismissed. Quiet, studious Harold Wills, who had helped to design the first Model A and the Model T, and who had personally devised the famous *FORD* script trade-mark, left in 1919 to develop a new car, the Wills-Sainte Clair. Among other capable men who would not be yes men was the genial Dane, William S. Knudsen, whose dismissal was ordained by Ford. This was a double blow to the Ford Motor Company. It not only lost the Dane's great ability, but Knudsen was shortly working at General Motors—in charge of Chevrolet.

In 1922 Henry Ford described his theory of how a business should be run. He wrote:

That which one has to fight hardest against in bringing together a large number of people to do work is excess organization and consequent red tape. To my mind there is no bent of mind more dangerous than that which is sometimes described as the "genius for organization." This usually results in the birth of a great big chart showing, after the fashion of a family tree, how authority ramifies. The tree is heavy with nice round berries, each of which bears the name of a man or an office . . . .
Now a business, in my way of thinking, is not a machine. It is a collection of people who are brought together to work and not to write letters to one another . . . . It is not necessary to have meetings to establish good feeling between individuals or departments. It is not necessary for people to love each other in order to work together . . . . And so the Ford factories and enterprises have no organization, no specific duties attached to any position, no line of succession or of authority, very few titles, and no conferences.

That is how business was run in Dearborn. In the soaring new General Motors building in Detroit, Alfred P. Sloan, Jr., had very different ideas. In describing the reorganization of his company in the early 1920s he wrote:

> We realized that in an institution as big as General Motors . . . any plan which involved too great a concentration of problems upon a limited number of executives would . . . mean an autocracy, which is just as dangerous in a great industrial organization as in a government; aside from the question as to whether any limited number of executives could deal with so many diversified problems, in so many places, promptly and effectively. . . .
> I would say that my concept of a management scheme of a great industrial enterprise, simply expressed, is to divide it into as many parts as consistently can be done, place in charge of each part the most capable executive that can be found, develop a system of co-ordination so that each part may strengthen and support each other part; thus . . . welding all parts together in the common interests of a joint enterprise . . . . To formalize this scheme I worked out what we speak of in industry as an organization chart.

The giants were girding for battle wtih strategies that were diametrically opposed. Ford believed in making a single product, standardized to be produced in the greatest volume at the lowest possible price. General Motors believed in a diversity of products to meet every purse, changing with the times to meet public taste. Ford believed in completely centralized control with one man making all decisions—in his case, decisions that were based on hunches. Sloan believed in complete decentralization, with policy determined by groups of specialists after a thorough appraisal of all available facts.

After such an appraisal General Motors adopted a policy for the conflict between Ford and Chevrolet, which Sloan explained as follows: "In 1921 Ford had about 60% of the total car and truck markets in units, and Chevrolet had about 4%. With Ford in almost complete possession of the low-priced field, it would have been suicidal to compete with him head on. No conceivable amount of capital short of the United States Treasury could have sustained the losses required to take volume away from him at his own game. The strategy we devised was to take a bite from the top of his position, conceived as a price class, and in this way build up Chevrolet on a profitable basis. In later years, as the consumer upgraded his preference, the new General Motors policy was to become critically attuned to the course of American history."

While this battle was shaping in the early 1920s, the position of the Model T seemed impregnable. Six million of the 15 million were produced between 1923 and 1925. But paradoxically, while half of all American car buyers were purchasing the Model T, a growing number were becoming dissatisfied with it. By the mid-1920s, faithful old Lizzie no longer represented the common man's concept of personal transportation. It was the lowest-priced car, but it was no longer the only dependable, utilitarian vehicle priced for the masses. The common man wanted something better, and he could have something immeasurably better for a little more money.

The revolution in automobile manufacturing in the twenties was as far-reaching as that which had been sparked by the Model T. Many makers of motor cars had adopted the methods pioneered by Ford and could compete with him—even exceed him—in price cutting. When the Model T touring car sold for $440 in 1920, its nearest competitor, the Overland, sold for $895, a spread of $455. By 1926 the spread between these two, on some models, had been reduced to $50, and there were ten other cars selling for less than $750 and three for less than $500—all offering features that were lacking in the archaic Model T.

The change in the automobile market had been equally revolutionary, for many reasons. Increased buying power during the wave of prosperity that followed the postwar depression, better roads, installment selling, a demand for style beyond the purely functional, engineering advances and refinements were all factors. And there was the new, postwar, woman. In relation to women, Henry Ford still lived in the horse-and-buggy era, when the selection of personal transportation was a purely masculine prerogative. Now the car had become an extension of the home, and the homemaker had much to say about its selection.

By 1925 countless scenes like the following were taking place in automobile showrooms throughout the nation. A husband and wife enter a Ford dealer's showroom. While the husband kicks the tires on the shiny black flivver the salesman extolls its planetary transmission, its low-tension magneto, its two strong springs, its simplicity, its dependability, its low, low price. At this point the woman interrupts to ask what colors it comes in. The salesman smilingly tells her that she can have any color she wants so long as it's black. The man and wife hold a whispered conference and leave the Ford showroom.

They go around the corner to the Chevrolet dealer. While the husband kicks the tires on the shiny blue Chevy the salesman mentions the three-speed gear transmission, the battery ignition that operates the self-starter, the four springs that provide a smoother ride, the demountable rims that make tire changing easier, the gas tank placed safely and conveniently in the rear, the high-pressure lubricating system, the water-pump cooling system, the foot accelerator, and the improved steering mechanism. While he talks, the wife admires the smart lines of the car and leafs through a booklet showing the range of colors available.

There is another whispered consultation. She wants a stylish car. So does he. She wants a green car. He is willing. He wants demountable rims. They both want a self-starter and a transmission that permits driving in low gear without holding a pedal down. They both want a vibrationless, comfortable ride. The price? Well, it's about $200 more than the Ford. "But when you add a self-starter, demountable rims, an ignition lock—all extras on the Ford—the difference is less than $100. And you don't have to pay it now. For $200 down and easy monthly payments the car is yours."

Man and wife leave the showroom, proud and somewhat smug owners of a green Chevrolet—something better than the neighbor's.

This happened so often that Ford sales declined 200,000 in 1925 from the previous year; Chevrolet sales increased by the same amount. Ford was still far and away the leader, but the trend against it had set in. Chevrolet was not the only competitor for whom business was better; Overland, Essex, Star, and others were getting a larger share of the low-priced market. By 1926, while Ford was still the leader, Chevrolet was in firm second place, with 730,000 units, followed by Dodge, Buick, Hudson-Essex, Willys-Overland, Nash, Chrysler, Star, and Studebaker in that order.

Almost everyone at Ford could read the handwriting on the wall except Old Henry. Edsel was now president of the company and pleaded for radical changes in the product, but he had no influence on his stubborn father. The only executive left who was not a yes man was Edsel's brother-in-law, Ernest Kanzler. In January 1926 he laid a six-page memorandum on Henry's desk, outlining why it was necessary to replace the Model T. Henry never commented on the memorandum, but six months later Kanzler was out of the company.

Henry sneered at model changes as "planned obsolescence," which he considered a fraud on the American people. He wrote, "We cannot conceive how to serve the customer unless we make him something that, as far as we know, will last forever." He still considered a car solely in terms of utility. He could not comprehend the changing American taste. He had said that he would not give five cents for all the art in the world, and he could not understand that a car could have an aesthetic appeal. When there was talk of his being the Democratic candidate for the presidency, Will Rogers quipped: "Ford could be elected president all right. He'd only have to make one speech, 'Voters, if I'm elected I'll change the front.' " But Henry didn't listen.

In partial justification of Henry Ford, he did not believe that the Model T would go on forever. But he wanted to replace it with something that was as far ahead of contemporary cars as the Model T had been. Since 1920 he had been experimenting with an eight-cylinder "X" engine that he hoped would be a revolutionary advance in propulsion. After a few were made his engineers realized that this would never be a practical power plant for a light car, but none dared tell Henry. Late in 1926 Ford suddenly ordered experimentation on the "X" engine to cease.

As late as Christmas 1926 Ford still insisted that there would be no new model. "The Ford car will continue to be made in the same way," he proclaimed. No one knows when or why he changed his mind. In the spring of 1927 rumors swept the nation that there would be, at long last, a new Ford. On May 25 the Ford Motor Company made a terse announcement confirming the rumors. On May 26 the 15 millionth Model T rolled off the assembly line. Old Henry made an emotional statement. "The Model T was a pioneer," he said. "It had stamina and power. It was the car that ran before there were good roads to run on. It broke the barriers of distance in rural sections, brought the people of those sections closer together, and placed education within the reach of everyone." He added that the new car would uphold the tradition of the Model T for quantity production, high quality, low prices, and constant service. But, he added, "We are still proud of the Model T Ford car."

An era had ended. In 1927, with the great Ford plant on the River Rouge idle, Chevrolet produced over a million cars to surge into first place. But more than 11 million of the 20 million cars registered in the country that year were Model Ts. It had been a great car—perhaps the greatest that America has ever produced. An entire generation of Americans had grown up during its lifetime. In the history of the automobile industry only one other model has had a longer life. At the extreme other end of the scale from the Model T, the Rolls-Royce Silver Ghost lasted for twenty years—one year longer than the lowly flivver.

Stripped Chassis

Group of mixed-up parts

Near the end of the reassembling

Start for 500-mile run

A TRIUMPH OF AMERICAN STANDARDISATION – THE FAMOUS TEST WITH THR CADILLAC CARS

General Motors Corporation

Interchangeable parts win a trophy for Cadillac. In 1908, three Cadillacs completed this test for Britain's Royal Automobile Club. The chassis were stripped, and the parts mixed up among the three cars. With parts interchanged, the cars were reassembled, and successfully completed a 500-mile run. As a result, the Club's Dewar Trophy for "furthering the interests of the automotive industry" went for the first time to an American car.

FIVE: THE SLIDE RULE COMETH

The representatives of the British Royal Automobile Club stood beside Brooklands race track, polite but skeptical. It was really rather ridiculous for the Americans to try to compete for England's Dewar Trophy, which the club awarded annually for the car that "successfully completed the most meritorious performance or test furthering the interests or advancement of the automotive industry." But in 1908 an American named Henry Leland *was* competing, and he was basing his claim on the workmanship in his Cadillac cars.

Everybody knew that fine craftsmanship was a European tradition. All of the best cars were foreign-made because only old-country artisans could hand-file, grind, and polish parts to perfection. American cars were, in British opinion, "glorified perambulators." Only in foreign cars did every gear mesh neatly with every other gear, every piston slide smoothly and snugly in its cylinder, every part fit perfectly with every other part—*in any given car*. But Leland was claiming that any part in a Cadillac would fit perfectly with the companion parts in *any* Cadillac.

Under the eyes of the auto club observers British mechanics disassembled three Cadillacs and scrambled the pieces. Eighty-nine parts were drawn from the pile at random and replaced with new parts. Then American mechanics stepped forward and reassembled three cars with screwdrivers, pliers, wrenches, and hammers. They put any piston in the pile into any cylinder, connected any rod to any crankshaft. The British ran a 500-mile test on the Brooklands track. All three cars performed perfectly. Sir Thomas Dewar's silver cup was shipped to "Uncle" Henry Leland in Detroit.

The production of standard, interchangeable parts had started in the American firearms industry at the beginning of the nineteenth century, when Eli Whitney invented a machine tool with which unskilled workmen could make identical musket parts. Leland, a machinist and toolmaker, was an alumnus of the Springfield Arsenal and the Colt Arms factory before he moved to Detroit to start a machine shop. He had imported the first set of "Jo Blocks" ever seen in America. These were measuring standards developed by Swedish engineer Carl Johansson that were accurate within four millionths of an inch. That is about the distance that a railroad rail would sag if four houseflies alighted on it to hold a conference.

Leland carried his passion for precision into the automobile industry as the first of the pioneers to replace the rule of thumb with a micrometer. He strove for perfection in parts production—not approximate uniformity. Henry Ford told of seeing two curved-dash Olds runabouts at the first Detroit auto show with engines that were identical except that one was made by Olds and the other by Leland and Faulconer. The former developed three horsepower, the latter almost four.

Henry Leland was worthy of the title of automotive engineer although he had no book learning on the subject and had never seen the inside of a school of engineering. Few in the infant industry had. When the Society of Automotive Engineers was started in 1905, E. T. Birdsall, a consulting engineer who sparked the organization, described prospective members as "all those who could recognize an automobile on Fifth Avenue at sight." This was not entirely facetious. The first president of the Society, A. L. Riker of Locomobile, was a self-taught pioneer in electric vehicles. The first vice-president was Henry Ford, who had little regard for a degree from an engineering college. As to what the S.A.E. might do, Riker suggested that "it would be a great plan to get at some definite names for the various parts of the automobile, because, as we all know, not every manufacturer and dealer calls the same parts by the same names."

Trained engineers of the day were working in the construction industry, shipbuilding, railroading, and for the new telephone and

electrical companies. An M.I.T. diploma had little place in an automobile plant where trial and error was considered a better system
than textbook theory. The idea of engineering laboratories in the
automobile industry was many years in the future. The trickle into
the automobile game of college-trained men was slow at first, until
it was realized that book-taught brains could contribute the essen-
tials for development in three directions: improvement of the materials from which the cars were made—product engineering; the improvement of the car itself—development engineering; and the
improvement of the way in which the car was made—production
engineering.

The first paper read at an S.A.E. meeting was titled "Materials
for Motor Cars." The principal materials, then as now, were iron
and steel. When the automobile was born, America already led the
world in steel production; J. P. Morgan put United States Steel
together in 1901 as the first billion-dollar corporation and the world's
biggest steel producer. The American industry produced vast quantities of steel eminently suited for railroads and bridges, buildings
and ships. This was not the best kind of steel for automobiles, but
few in the United States knew this. America produced the most steel,
but Europe was far ahead in the science of metallurgy.

One of the first big steps in the use of improved steel in automobiles was taken by Ford in the Model T. When he built his first
car, Henry Ford surely knew the difference between iron and steel,
but that was probably the extent of his knowledge of metallurgy.
In his early years of auto building, he observed that many of the
foreign cars were lighter but stronger than their American counter-
parts. As Ford told the story, he was at a race in 1905 in Palm
Beach, where a French car smashed up. From the wreck he picked
up a valve stem that was very light and tough. A French mechanic
told him that it was a European steel made with vanadium as an
alloy.

"I sent to England," wrote Ford, "for a man who understood
how to make this steel commercially. The main thing was to get a
plant to turn it out . . . . Vanadium requires 3,000 degrees Fahren-
heit. The ordinary furnace could not go beyond 2,700 degrees. I
found a small steel company in Canton, Ohio. I offered to guarantee
them against loss if they would run a heat for us . . . . Until then we

had been forced to be satisfied with steel running between 60,000 and 70,000 pounds tensile strength. With vanadium the strength went up to 170,000."

Vanadium steel made possible the combination of lightness and strength in the Model T, and the company extolled it as the last word in a motor car material. Actually, it was later learned that it was used in many places in the car where it did not apply. As trained metallurgists came into the industry, they started to develop many steels for special purposes. Some of this was original research; much of it was borrowed from Europe; but the net result was that the automobile became the end product of highly sophisticated metallurgy.

It was learned that manganese added to steel made an extremely abrasion-resistant material well suited to wearing parts in the car. Nickel-alloyed steel provided great strength and toughness. Alloys containing silicon and chromium produced a heat-resistant steel for exhaust valves. A combination of molybdenum and nickel produced a steel well adapted for transmission and rear-axle gears. Steel could be case-hardened or carburized to give different characteristics to the surface and the interior of the metal. A gear made of tough steel could be carburized to give the surface of the teeth extreme hardness.

In the earliest days of automobile building, iron was iron and steel was steel. Today, the Society of Automotive Engineers lists over a hundred different chemical compositions of steel used in automotive construction, and modern metallurgy and chemistry have introduced other metals and nonmetallic materials in increasing degree. Du Pont points out that their plastics have more than 350 applications in the modern car. It is possible (although not probable in the foreseeable future) that we will someday have cars made largely from plastics, aluminum, and titanium.

Tires and fuel were other materials that required the slide rule of the engineer and the test tube of the chemist before the automobile could become practical. Both the rubber and the oil industries were well established before the birth of the horseless carriage, but their products were not suited to the demands of the new century. Charles Goodyear had made rubber practical in 1839 when, after years of experimentation in trying to "cure" it, he had discovered vulcan-

Goodyear Tire and Rubber Company

The largest single expense in owning a car was outfitting it with tires. A set of four cost up to $500. Above, tire manufacturing in the early days.

ization by bringing a compound of crude rubber and sulphur in contact with a hot stove. An Irish veterinarian named John Dunlop had made the bicycle practical in 1884 by trying to give his small son a smoother-riding tricycle. He wrapped inflated rubber tubes around the edges of the wheels, held them in place by strips of linen tacked to the wheels, and so invented the pneumatic tire.

By the turn of the century Goodyear, Goodrich, Firestone, U. S. Rubber, and others were making pneumatic tires for bicycles. B. F. Goodrich produced the first American-made set for an automobile, rather reluctantly, for Alexander Winton in 1896. Because they felt that there might never be another order for such unusual tires, Goodrich required Winton to pay the development cost of $400 to build a set of outsize, sixteen-ply, bicycle tires for his prototype car.

Until 1905 automobile tires were merely large bicycle tires of the clincher type, which were mounted by stretching them over the rim of the wheel. Even for a three-inch tire, this took superhuman strength or a varied assortment of special tools. The first improvement by tire engineers was the straight-sided tire, with a braid of wire embedded in the bead so that it could not stretch. These were mounted with a flange around the bead and held in place by numerous lugs. With demountable rims, which were developed at about the same time, straight-sided tires made tire changing a much less onerous task and made it possible to carry an inflated spare.

Tires were by far the largest single expense in owning a car. A motorist who got 2,500 miles from a tire considered himself lucky —and a set of tires for a Packard cost about $500. Even a small Model T replacement tire cost $35. Chemists helped to extend tire mileage with tougher rubber compounds. Because it is cotton rather than rubber that gives body and strength to a tire, engineering entered the ancient cotton industry to develop a twisted fiber that would withstand the millions of flexings to which tire fabric is subjected. A big step toward longer life was the cord tire. In early tires the fabric was square-woven. Flexing caused friction between the cross fibers and built up heat that burned the life out of the fabric. In cord tires strong fibers all ran in one direction, held together by flimsy threads. These latter were broken in the course of vulcanization, leaving the cords friction-free.

The first tires had smooth treads, but as speeds increased, some form of tread design was sought. First came a ribbed tread on front wheels to facilitate steering, then many curious nonskid treads, with metal lugs or bits of leather embedded in the surface. About 1908 scientifically designed nonskid treads made their appearance. The most famous of these is the Goodyear diamond pattern—but it was almost not Goodyear's. B. F. Goodrich hit on the diamond pattern as something that was scientifically sound slightly before Goodyear. Goodrich's closest competitor was its next-door neighbor in Akron, the Diamond Rubber Company. Because a tire with a diamond tread might be confused with tires made by Diamond, Goodrich held off. A short time later Goodrich bought Diamond Rubber, so that the pattern and name combination would have been ideal; but by this time Goodyear was using the diamond—and still is.

High-pressure straight-sided tires extended tire life but did little to contribute to a smooth ride or improved appearance. Then in 1922 the low-pressure balloon tire, virtually as we know it today, made its appearance. This was the result of continuous development in materials and design, rather than a specific engineering break-through, but it was a big improvement in safety, comfort, long life, and easier handling; and it contributed to new concepts in car styling.

The only automotive element that did not make revolutionary advances during the first two decades of the century was gasoline. In fact, it deteriorated. The fuel of 1900 was about equal in vola-tility to a modern high-test gasoline. The fuel of 1920 was much lower in octane rating than any modern regular gasoline. The reason lay in the basic process of refining crude oil and the changing eco-nomics of the oil industry.

Petroleum is composed of hydrogen and carbon atoms arranged in molecules of various structures and sizes. It is separated into its many usable products by distillation. In this process the portion of the crude oil containing the smallest molecules boils off at the lowest temperature. As the heat increases, portions made up of progres-sively larger molecules vaporize. Gasoline is composed of the smallest molecules, kerosene is next, then fuel oil, lubricating oil, etc. To get kerosene, it is necessary to first boil off the smaller molecules of which gasoline is formed.

At the turn of the century kerosene for lighting was the industry's big product. Some gasoline was sold as "stove naphtha," but far more was dumped in rivers to get rid of it. It was such a nuisance that one refiner offered a motor maker all the gasoline he wanted if he would pay the transportation costs. Then the spread of electric lighting decreased the market for kerosene at the same time as the growth of the automobile increased the demand for gasoline.

At the refinery the vapors from the still were run through conden-sation pipes, and the resulting liquid was passed through a still house, where the various products were directed to storage tanks by the turn of a valve. The first thing to come through the pipes was gasoline, and in the early days the valve was turned quickly so as to divert the stream to profitable kerosene as soon as possible. As a result, the early gasoline consisted entirely of the very smallest molecules—a highly volatile fuel. Many states had kerosene inspectors to make sure that enough gasoline was taken out of kerosene to make it a safe lamp fuel. As the demand changed, the valve was turned later and later, so that more of the stream went into gasoline and less into kerosene. The resulting addition of the larger molecules to gasoline decreased its volatility and lowered its quality as a combustible fuel.

Until well into the second decade of the century there was little understanding of the characteristics of motor fuel. The demand for gasoline increased so rapidly that the immediate engineering or scientific problem was not how to make a better fuel but how to make enough of it. In 1913 came the first breakthrough, when Dr. William M. Burton of Standard Oil of Indiana perfected a process of thermal cracking. Simply stated, this involved applying high heat to the heavier elements of crude oil under pressure. This caused some of the larger molecules to break down—to "crack" into the smaller hydrocarbons of gasoline. At about the same time a process was developed for precipitating a small amount of highly volatile liquid from natural gas. Called casinghead gasoline, because it was originally found at the head of the oil well casing, this natural gasoline, blended with straight distilled and thermal-cracked products, provided enough usable fuel to turn the constantly increasing number of wheels.

Side by side with product engineering, development engineering in the automobile industry started to progress in two directions. Improved materials made it possible for well-trained brains to develop increasingly better components of the car. The higher powered V-8 engine of the twenties would not have been practical with the materials available at the turn of the century. More spectacular was the contribution by early automotive engineers of new devices that converted the horseless carriage into a practical vehicle.

During the first decade of the century, the speedometer, shock absorbers, the foot accelerator, the electric horn, demountable rims, tire chains, compressed gas, and then electric headlights came into being. The engine moved to the front of the car. Running boards, front bumpers, and folding windshields were added, as was the so-called one-man top—which any two competent men could put up if they knew the proper profanity. The windshield wiper—hand-operated—the rear-view mirror, the rear fuel tank, wire and steel disk wheels, and the rear stop light did not make their appearance until the second decade, which also produced the greatest single invention since the birth of the automobile—the self-starter.

There had been so-called self-starters before Charles Franklin Kettering's invention in 1911. Ransom Olds said he had an electric one on the first production car his company built. There were others operated by springs, compressed air, or gas—and Winton had an incomprehensible device that was supposed to operate by exhaust gas—although there is no explanation of where the exhaust gas came from to start the engine before the engine was running. The great difference between Kettering's starter and all the others is that Kettering's worked.

One could easily theorize that Charles Franklin Kettering did more to emancipate women than all the feminists of the day. Before his invention a woman could drive a car—if the engine was running. But the lusty Amazons who could crank one were few indeed. Then, in one stroke, the dainty female toe became as powerful as the brawny male arm. One might even take a flight of fancy and blame —or praise—Kettering for shorter skirts. It seems more than coincidental that in fifty years before women started to drive, their skirts moved only eight inches upward from the ground. Within twelve years after the invention of the self-starter, they neared the knee. When the clinging skirt impeded female driving skill, modesty bowed to practicality.

Charles Franklin Kettering was far and away the greatest of the automotive inventor-engineers. The boy who was named Franklin for an uncle became the twentieth century's nearest approach to the eighteenth century's great "natural philosopher," Benjamin Franklin. He was also the most highly respected and warmly regarded man in automotive history. Mr. Ford was always Mr. Ford; Mr. Sloan was always Mr. Sloan; but Mr. Kettering was generally and affectionately called Boss Ket. His engineering contributions to railroading and aviation and his side-line interests in the fields of education, medicine, and general philosophy do not concern us here; but to take the least consequential indication of his mental and physical aptitude, he

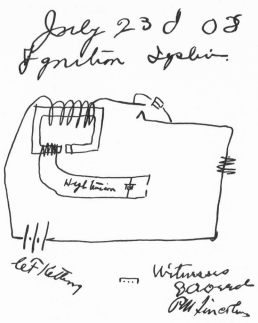

July 23d 08
Ignition System

C.F. Kettering   Witnesses
                        ....

General Motors Corporation

Top: Charles Kettering's original drawing for the patent on the automobile self-starter. Bottom: The first car with a workable self-starter, the 1912 Cadillac.

General Motors Corporation

could write equally well with either hand, could write a different thing with each hand at the same time, and could do it upside down or backwards.

Kettering inspired much of the progress in automotive engineering by his great enthusiasm for the future and his conviction that literally nothing was impossible of attainment in the sciences. He used to tell the motor makers: "I am not pleading with you to make changes. I am telling you that you have got to make them—not because I say so, but because Old Father Time will take care of you if you don't change . . . . Consequently you need a procurement department of new ideas."

After a brief stint of teaching in a one-room school, Kettering had studied engineering at Ohio State, working his way as a summer switchboard installer and trouble shooter for the local telephone company. His first job was in the inventions department of the National Cash Register Company, where, among other things, he invented a small electric motor to open a cash register drawer with an overrunning clutch that would stop the mechanism at exactly the right point. In the midst of inventing this, in 1905, Ket married and set out for Niagara Falls. While changing trains in a small Ohio town, he saw a doctor trying, without success, to crank his car. Ket offered to help and quickly fixed a faulty ignition. As a reward, the automobile owner gave the newlyweds a ride—Kettering's first trip in an automobile.

Kettering's immediate superior at National Cash Register was E. A. Deeds, whose secretary left to work for Henry Leland at Cadillac. Through the secretary, Kettering learned that Leland was dissatisfied with Cadillac's ignition system, but had been told that nothing could be done about it. That was all Ket needed to set him to work on a new type of ignition. At the time, most cars used both a magneto and battery to provide sparks for ignition, with a device for switching from one to the other. The magneto was better at high engine speeds, the battery at low. The dry cells that powered the battery system were good for only about two hundred miles.

Ket devised a new battery ignition that gave one "fat" spark instead of the customary shower of sparks. It prolonged battery life tenfold and made the magneto unnecessary. When Leland bought the idea in 1909, Kettering left National Cash Register to perfect the system. He worked, with a few helpers, in the hayloft of Deed's barn in Dayton. They formed a company called the Dayton Engineering Laboratories Company—DELCO. That was the official name, but the group was generally known as the Barn Gang. It was here that the title Boss Ket originated, although Kettering later said that the only rank in the Barn Gang was that, at times, "one guy was ranker than the others."

One summer day in 1910 Byron T. Carter—the same who had built the Cartercar in the Michigan State Prison—was driving across the Belle Isle Bridge in Detroit. He met a lady in distress—her car had stalled. The gallant old gentleman jumped out to help her. He spun the crank vigorously, and the engine started. Unfortunately, the lady had not retarded the spark. The crank kicked back and broke Carter's jaw—an injury from which he subsequently died. In passing it might be mentioned that this probably happened because Carter was holding the crank properly, with his four fingers around it and his thumb tucked against his index finger. One never put the thumb around the crank, because when it kicked back, as it often did if the spark was not properly adjusted, the result might be a broken thumb or wrist. With the thumb in the proper position the crank usually flew out of the hand without mishap—but not in Carter's case.

Carter was an old friend of Henry Leland. By this time Ket was also friendly with the Cadillac chief. When Kettering remarked, rather idly, that he thought a car could be cranked electrically, Leland gave him an order for four thousand self-starters. But for the Carter incident, Leland might not have been so interested, because every electrical engineer said that a practical electric starter was impossible. It would take, they said, a five-horsepower electric motor to turn over an automobile engine; and the size and weight of such a motor and the batteries to operate it would just about equal the carrying capacity of the vehicle.

The it-can't-be-done defeatists did not know that Ket already had the self-starter half invented. The problem of turning over an engine was basically the same as opening a cash register drawer, and the motor and clutch he had developed for that purpose could be adapted for the automobile. He agreed that it would take a five-horsepower motor to operate an automobile engine continuously but a much

General Motors Corporation

Experts said it defied the laws of electricity, but doing the impossible was routine for Charles F. Kettering. At the Delco plant in Dayton, Ohio, he invented the first workable device that did away with the dangers and inconveniences of the crank—the self-starter. Above, "Boss Ket" adjusts his new mechanism.

smaller motor could be overloaded to turn it over a few times, if it had an opportunity to cool down after occasional use. The device he developed consisted of an adaptation of the cash register motor and clutch with a generator in one unit, operated by a storage battery. The generator, powered by the running engine to keep the battery charged, made possible the more widespread use of electricity in the car for lights and other purposes. The self-starter made its public bow on the 1912 Cadillac—and Henry Leland received another of Sir Thomas Dewar's silver cups from England's Royal Automobile Club.

The self-starter is an example of the unique problem of the automotive engineer. Unlike the chemist, the electrical engineer, the construction engineer, and others, the automotive engineer had no formulas to guide him; he was (and to a large extent still is) working in the future. Kettering told an anecdote to illustrate this.

"When we developed the self-starter," he said, "I was asked by the Detroit branch of the American Institute of Electrical Engineers to give a talk on the electric self-starter, which I did. When I was through one of the members got up and said, 'I don't think we should allow talks like this to be made before our section. This man has profaned every fundamental law of electrical engineering.'

"So I said, 'Well, now, for instance, what have we profaned?'

" 'You are using more current through the wires than our formula allows.' "

Kettering had not made the self-starter as an electrical device per se; he had made it as a piece of an automobile—and there was no formula for this application of electricity.

Progress in product and development engineering was important; but of much greater consequence to the industry and the nation was the advancement of production engineering. In the introduction to his exhaustive work on Ford, Allan Nevins writes, "It was the automobile factory which introduced mass production, in its full scope and meaning, to the world; and mass production has changed the lineaments of our economic and social life more profoundly than any other single element in the history of civilization."

Mass production is widely misunderstood. It is equated in the minds of many with the moving assembly line. This is but one factor —and not the most important one. The moving assembly line bears about the same relation to the entire system of mass production that bookbinding bears to the total work of publishing a book.

Many also believe that standardization of the end product is an essential of mass production—100 million identical black telephones or 15 million black flivvers. Today the odds against two identical

Fords, Plymouths, or Chevrolets following each other down the assembly line are so great that they are almost incalculable without a computer. The same assembly line may handle a dozen or more models in twenty color combinations, with as many upholstery choices; an option of three engines and three transmissions for each model; a big radio, small radio, or no radio; a big heater, a small heater, or no heater; and on and on and on.

Another misconception is that mass production sprang, like Minerva fully armed, from the brain of Henry Ford. The Ford Motor Company certainly deserves the credit for first bringing mass production to its full flower—for blazing a path that others followed to create today's industrial economy and the incredible advance in the standard of living that resulted from the adoption of this system. But all of the elements of mass production were in being and, to some extent, in use before Ford amazed the world with the first perfection of the system.

In describing mass production for the *Encyclopaedia Britannica,* Henry Ford wrote that it is "the focusing upon a manufacturing project of the principles of power, accuracy, economy, system, continuity, speed and repetition." This definition requires some further defining. *Accuracy* means the standardization and interchangeability of parts. *Power* refers to the use of powered handling devices to replace men's muscles—in well-developed mass production nobody ever moves anything by hand. *Repetition* refers to the breakdown of each operation into its simplest components, each of which is performed by a different worker. *Continuity* means the uninterrupted flow of work through the plant. By *system,* Ford probably meant the scientific layout of machinery in such a way that the flow of production never backtracks or diverges. Ford's use of the word *speed* is misleading. *Timing* would be a better expression of the correlation of all the elements of manufacture, material handling, and assembly.

One essential of mass production in the automobile industry that Ford omitted is the use of highly sophisticated special-purpose metalworking machinery. The early automotive engineers contributed more to advanced tool design than all other industries combined, with the result that American machine tools were soon recognized to be the best in the world.

Henry Leland's passion for perfection was the first step toward

The Buick plant in 1912—an early attempt at assembly-line production.

mass production in the automobile industry, although his concern was for quality, not quantity. Others soon realized that if cars were not to remain handmade luxury items, parts must be machine-made with perfect accuracy. Long before there was a moving assembly line, hand-filing and -grinding had become obsolete practices in automobile plants. The Society of Automotive Engineers took another step toward standardization in 1910. They found that the industry was using a most uneconomical diversity of material—for instance, 800 different kinds of lock washers, 1,600 sizes and kinds of tubing. A program of simplification reduced the number of washers from 800 to 16 and the tubing from 1,600 to 17 sizes in 13 thicknesses.

The idea of a system of assembly that moved the work through the plant rather than bringing parts to a point of assembly did not originate with Ford. As early as 1904, Olds was rolling frames past piles of parts, adding a part at each station. Walter Chrysler claimed that he had a rudimentary assembly line going at Buick a year before Ford. He wrote: "Instead of having the whole room filled with tables where frame members were riveted and where other operations proceeded, until, one by one, each table supported a finished chassis, we had the vast room empty of all but four or five tables . . . . Beyond these, extending clear to the far end of the room, was . . . a pair of tracks made by two-by-fours. When a chassis was complete with axles, springs and wheels, a little chain hoist was used to lift it off the table to the floor, astride the track; then it was pushed along from hand to hand; two men put the fenders on, others the gas tank, and finally the chassis got its body. Once we started making cars like that, we had the whole scheme of mass production going, although it was some years before people said 'mass production.' "

People were right not to call this mass production. It was but a little step in the right direction. Scientific mass production was first started by Ford in 1913. The company had moved into its new, well-designed factory in Highland Park—the largest building under one roof in Michigan. Advanced, special-purpose machinery had been laid out under a new, carefully studied system. Each machine had exactly the space required to perform its operations, and not one inch more through which material would have to travel unnecessarily. Each machine was located at the point in a sequential line where the operation it performed was required. Parts and materials were moved largely by conveyors, slides, and rollways. Accuracy in machining parts had been developed to a high degree. Ford made and sold the "Jo Blocks," of which Leland had imported the first set. The remaining element for mass production was the moving assembly line.

According to Henry Ford, the idea for this "came in a general way from the overhead trolley that the Chicago packers use in dress-

The first moving assembly line at Ford's Highland Park Plant in 1913. Parts moved past a row of workers, each of whom performed one operation. The auto industry quickly felt the results of mass production. Car prices spiraled downward, and within one year Ford doubled the wages of the men who worked at his plant.

Ford Motor Company

ing beef." If a product could be more efficiently disassembled on a moving line, it seemed reasonable that the system might be applied to assembly. It was first tried with the flywheel magneto of the Model T.

Under the old system it took an experienced worker an average of twenty minutes to assemble one magneto from a pile of parts. Then the operation was broken down into twenty-nine steps, and as many men were placed shoulder to shoulder in front of a moving belt, each adding a single part as the magneto moved slowly past. On the initial tests, the time for assembly was cut to thirteen minutes ten seconds. After the belt was raised eight inches, the time was further reduced to seven minutes. Experiments were made with the speed of the moving belt—from eighteen inches a minute to sixty. Forty-four inches proved the most efficient timing and made it possible to assemble a magneto in five minutes—in terms of man-hours, magneto production was increased 400 percent.

The moving line system was next applied to engine and transmission assembly and finally, in 1914, to complete chassis assembly. This started with a rope manually operated by a windlass, which was soon replaced with an engine-powered chain on which the chassis moved past the lines of workers at waist height at the rate of six feet a minute. Under the old system, the record for a single chassis assembly was slightly over twelve man-hours of work. Under the new system it was reduced to about one and a half man-hours.

It was no coincidence that Ford doubled wages a year after the mass production system was perfected. Its general acceptance by the rest of the industry led to the great increase in production from slightly over half a million cars in 1914 to more than 3 million in 1924. This increase in production led, in turn, to a sharp decline in car prices. By 1920 relatively unskilled labor could produce about twenty times as much per man-hour as skilled labor had been able to produce twenty-five years earlier.

Although the Ford Company pioneered in production engineering, it stood still in development engineering, resting on the Model T. True, there was an engineering building at Dearborn, but it housed few college-trained men. There was no engineering program and not much equipment. Even dynamometers were in short supply; and a dynamometer is as essential to an automotive engineer as a stethoscope is to a physician. Henry Ford either had not heard or did not

Gravity can be helpful. Wheels are delivered to the assembly line by a gravity conveyor.

Ford Motor Company

heed Charles Kettering's definition of *research in industry:* "Trying to find out what you are going to do when you can't keep on doing what you're doing now."

Other companies were forging ahead in product development, particularly General Motors, which took its great step forward in this area in 1919. Although DELCO was by this time owned by GM through its subsidiary, United Motors, Charles Kettering was still

One way to achieve a "body drop" was this used by Ford. Chassis were assembled on the ground floor—bodies built on the second floor. The twain met outdoors when the chassis rolled off the line.

Ford Motor Company

down in Dayton, running this operation. Durant, Pierre du Pont, Raskob, Sloan, and Chrysler—GM's policy committee—put pressure on the engineering wizard to head up a new General Motors Research Corporation. Ket at first refused, but finally gave in to the blandishments of Alfred P. Sloan, Jr.—with reservations.

"I told Mr. Sloan," he wrote, "that I would take it on three conditions—that I would have no responsibility and no authority, and that I would never be held accountable for the money I spent. I don't think you can run a research laboratory any other way. The minute you take responsibility or authority, you quit researching. You can't keep books on research, because you don't know when you are going to get anything out of it or what it is going to be worth when you get it."

Ironically, the one thing that excited General Motors' interest in Ket at this time turned out to be his only major engineering failure; and it is possible that Pierre du Pont's faith in the failure prolonged the life of the Model T.

At the time there was one successful car with an air-cooled engine, the Franklin. Instead of a radiator, a fan, water jackets, a plumbing system, and a pump, the Franklin engine had only the fan and cast-iron fins on its cylinders to dissipate heat. Kettering was in the process of developing a similar engine with copper fins. The different thermal characteristics of the two metals presented problems, but Ket was sure they could be solved.

Pierre du Pont, who became president of the company when Durant left in 1920, was convinced that the copper-cooled engine would revolutionize the industry. It was proposed to use it initially in Chevrolet. During 1921 and 1922 Chevrolet product development marked time while waiting for the new engine. In 1923 Chevy came out with an air-cooled model that was a sensation at the auto show. There were 759 of them produced. Unfortunately, the car did not work. Sloan, who was by this time president of the corporation, ordered that they be recalled from the field and scrapped. In the boom year of 1923 Chevrolet was left with a water-cooled car that was three years behind in development. Had it not been for this hiatus, it is probable that Chevrolet would have given the Model T stronger competition long before 1926.

The failure of the copper-cooled engine has never been adequately explained. The car division engineers opposed it from the start, and a lack of cooperation between design and production may have been the determining factor. Kettering was still convinced that it would work and tendered his resignation from the corporation to take his engine elsewhere. Here Alfred P. Sloan, Jr., gave evidence of his greatness as an administrator. He told Ket that there was no need for him to resign; the corporation would form a division to make a new car with a copper-cooled engine, and Kettering could head it up—in charge not only of design but of production and marketing. Although Sloan has never claimed credit for the sound psychology he used in this instance, he surely knew that nothing would less appeal to Ket than producing and selling automobiles. Ket did not resign, and this was the last ever heard of the copper-cooled engine. After the Franklin folded in the 1930s, an air-cooled engine did not successfully reappear in an American car until the Corvair, with its aluminum engine, made its bow in 1959.

In the same year that the copper-cooled engine failed, the initial sale of ethyl gasoline was made in Dayton, Ohio—an event that marked the first major breakthrough in improving the quality of motor fuel. This was the result of seven years of research by Kettering and an associate, Tom Midgley.

Internal combustion engines had always knocked under certain conditions. The knock seemed to get worse after Kettering's ignition system came into general use, and disgruntled manufacturers of magnetos insisted that it was caused by pre-ignition from the new battery-generator system. No one connected it with the deterioration in gasoline quality combined with increased engine horsepower. Shortly after, Ket invented a domestic electric power plant with a generator operated by a four-cycle engine. These were first fueled by gasoline, but when insurance companies objected to this highly explosive fuel, kerosene was substituted. The knock immediately became intolerable.

Kettering and Midgley started, in 1916, to find out what made engines knock. They had a one-cylinder test engine with a quartz glass window and an instrument that indicated the pressure changes in the cylinder. They wanted pictures of what happened inside the engine. With a tomato can nailed to two pieces of lath, they made a revolving drum on which they mounted a strip of film with rubber bands. While Ket turned the tomato can, Midgley worked the shutter of the indicator. The pictures proved that the knock was not caused by pre-ignition; it happened immediately after ignition, when an extreme disturbance took place within the cylinder.

The cause, although they did not yet know it, was that the larger molecules in the low-quality gasoline were not sufficiently volatile to be ignited by the spark. When the smaller molecules burned, they exploded the larger molecules—later. This explosion was the knock. The difference in the knocking of kerosene and gasoline led Ket to believe that it had some relation to the volatility of the fuel. From this he reasoned that anything that would cause a fuel of low volatility to absorb heat more readily might improve its combustion characteristics.

As the story is usually told, Kettering remembered that trailing arbutus was one of the earliest plants to bloom in the spring—and trailing arbutus has red leaves. He believed that the red leaves might absorb more heat from the sun and account for the early blooming. This is an interesting anecdote, but Kettering almost certainly knew that, almost two hundred years before, Benjamin Franklin had laid swatches of various colored fabric on the surface of snow in sunlight and found that the darker fabrics sank into the snow and the lighter remained on top. From this he learned that dark colors absorb heat, light colors reflect it. In any event, with or without an assist from arbutus, Ket and Midgley decided to dye gasoline to see whether the darker color would help the larger molecules to absorb heat better.

The most readily available oil-soluble dye was iodine. They poured some into gasoline. The knock disappeared—the problem was solved. But iodine was scarce, costly, and corroded the engine. They tried another dye. The knock came back. They tried colorless iodine. The knock again disappeared. Iodine itself, regardless of color, was an antiknock agent.

Reasoning that if one natural element was a knock suppressant, others might be, they started testing through the table of elements and discovered that an organic nitrogen compound called aniline was a better knock suppressor than iodine. With aniline added to the fuel, they boosted the compression ratio of a test Chevrolet from 4:1 up to 7:1, with great increase in both performance and fuel economy. But aniline had one grave disadvantage—its odor. The test Chevy was nicknamed The Goat. As the search continued all evidence pointed to some compound of lead as being the ideal antiknock agent. They finally found it in tetraethyl lead, a compound that had been in existence merely as a laboratory curiosity since 1853. Today, about 98 percent of all gasoline contains this additive or the more recently discovered tetramethyl lead.

The importance of the antiknock breakthrough was not merely the elimination of knock in existing engines. It made possible engines of higher compression. Gasoline vapor burned under high compression provides more usable energy, which results in more power, or greater fuel economy, or a combination of both, depending on the size and design of the engine. But gasoline of low volatility will not burn smoothly under high compression—it simply explodes and not only causes knock but, if continued, ruins the engine.

Compression ratios before the use of Ethyl were about 4.5:1. They jumped quickly to about 6:1. Continued gasoline improvement combined with engineering advances in engine design raised the ratio to today's top of 11:1. Better all-round performance, greater horsepower, and smoother operation at higher speeds are characteristics of the modern high-compression engine—or the advantage may be taken in fuel economy and lighter weight. In 1947, just before Boss Ket retired, General Motors Research built a test engine with a 12.5:1 compression ratio that was designed to have the same performance characteristics as a then current production engine with a 6.4:1 ratio. The test engine was only three quarters the size of the production engine and went eight miles further on a gallon of gas.

The discovery of the antiknock additive was followed by a number of scientific and engineering advances in refining petroleum that not only further increased gasoline quantity but created a whole new concept of quality in motor fuel. The amount of gasoline that can be extracted from a barrel of crude has been increased 400 percent—from eleven gallons per hundred in the early days to about forty-five gallons today. Modern gasoline is about as far removed from its forebear as an electric range is from a coal stove.

Thermal cracking was superseded, in the early 1930s, by catalytic cracking—the breaking down of larger hydrocarbon molecules in the presence of a catalyst, originally alumina silica. This produced fuel of a basically higher octane rating, even before the addition of tetraethyl lead. Subsequently, polymerization, alkalization, and catalytic reforming were devised as refining processes to reconstruct hydro-carbon molecules to provide gasoline that is hand-tailored to meet varied conditions.

Today every refiner makes a dozen different gasolines at various times of the year, under the same trademark. Though it may bear the same brand name, a gasoline that is sold in Maine is not the same as that sold in Texas; nor is the gasoline that Northerners buy in August the same as what they buy in December. The fuel is changed to meet varying climatic and weather conditions. In summer or in hot climates, gasoline has some of the smallest hydrocarbons screened out because they are so volatile that they might vaporize in the fuel system before reaching the carburetor, causing vapor lock. In winter gasoline is tailored to provide rapid vaporization in a cold engine.

A gallon of today's 100-octane gasoline in a modern high-compression engine can move a ton of weight almost twice as far as the pre-ethyl 50-octane gasoline in the engines of its day. Putting it another way, considering the weight of modern cars, it would cost the American people about $7 billion more each year for fuel to drive today's mileage with the engines and gasoline of 1920.

A breakthrough that eliminated an important bottleneck in mass production of automobiles was made by du Pont chemists in 1924 by a combination of research and chance. The Model T was not colored black because Henry Ford liked this funereal hue. Its sable coat was enamel that could be baked dry in two hours in a 400-degree oven. But enamel was a suitable finish for automobiles only in black or a limited number of equally dismal shades. Cars could be finished in colors only as carriages had been—by the application of several coats of paint and varnish, each laboriously rubbed down and sanded after it dried. The average time for finishing a body by this method was three weeks. On a production of 500 cars a day, this meant 9,000 in process, which would require ten acres of covered drying space. Automobiles were pouring off twentieth-century assembly lines and crawling into the paint shops of antiquity.

Kettering, with his conviction that nothing is impossible in science, believed that there must be something with which a car could be painted in an hour or two and in any color. He asked du Pont to try to solve the problem. Du Pont already had a very quick-drying nitro-cellulose lacquer—essentially a liquid cotton—that was used primarily to spray brass beds to prevent them from tarnishing. Its film was so thin that it would require scores of coats for a car finish. When they increased the viscosity the material would not spray; and when they added new solvents, it dried as it left the nozzle of the spray gun, hitting the car body in the form of tiny colored hailstones.

Next door to the group of chemists who were working on lacquer in the du Pont laboratory was another research unit that was trying to eliminate streaks in motion-picture film. One day in 1920 the technicians on this project filled a drum with a new cellulose-based formulation and stood it outside the laboratory. A power failure shut down their operation, and it was three days before anybody remembered the barrel, which had been standing in the sun. When they opened the drum it contained a thin syrup rather than the jellylike substance they expected. This proved to be the base that the lacquer researchers were seeking.

It took three years of further research and testing to convert the happy accident into *Duco,* a tough, brilliant lacquer in rainbow colors that dried so fast that bodies could be finished on a moving assembly line. In 1924 the "True Blue" Oakland, finished with *Duco,* made its bow at the auto show and started the trend toward colorful cars. Today's peacock-hued parking lots stem from the anonymous individual who rolled that barrel out into the sunlight at Parlin, N.J., and forgot it.

The 1920s marked the changeover from open to closed cars. About 90 percent of the cars made in 1919 were roadsters or touring cars; by 1929, 90 percent were coupes or sedans. The family car, in which all could tour without duster and goggles, had arrived. This was the result of cumulative engineering progress on several fronts—metallurgy, steel processing, machine tools, and spot welding. The closed all-steel body that Dodge introduced in 1924 could not have been made at a reasonable cost ten years earlier.

The early bodies were simply carriage bodies on automobile chassis. Then wood veneer panels gave way to steel sheets screwed to a wooden frame. The body was angular because the sheet steel of the day could be bent but not drawn into molded shapes in a press; nor did large enough presses exist. Cost made the closed car a luxury until 1922, when Hudson and Essex offered a sedan priced only $100 above their touring cars. Typical of other prices of the period was

Cost made the closed car a luxury until the 1920s, when Hudson offered a sedan priced only $100 more than touring cars. This first moderately priced car, the 1922 Essex, started the swing from open to closed cars.

Buick, which priced its touring car at $885 and its cheapest closed car at $1,395, a difference of almost 60 percent.

The Essex coach body was a crude affair, a wooden crate covered with flat metal sheets. But it exposed the great public demand for a popular-priced closed car. Automotive engineers collaborated with steel-production engineers on the development of a continuous rolling mill to produce sheet steel bigger and cheaper. Metallurgists created formulas for steel that could be drawn in presses, and automotive engineers encouraged machine-tool makers to build hydraulic presses big enough and strong enough to stamp out large body sections. Spot welding had been used to a limited extent, but now a jig was devised that held all of the body sections in place while they were instantaneously welded into a complete shell in one blinding flash. By the end of the 1920s, the price differential between open and closed cars had largely disappeared. Later, the public would be asked to pay *more* for a convertible than a sedan.

In 1929 the industry produced 5,337,087 cars—a record that would not be broken until 1949. The American automobile had fully arrived. It did not look like the car of the 1960s, but mechanically the difference was mainly in degree. Today's cars go faster, are safer and quieter, ride smoother, last longer, and are greatly superior in all-round performance, because there has been a constant improvement in detail in every aspect. But, with few exceptions, this is a combination of a great many little things. As an example, Chrysler Corporation lists fifty-nine "automotive firsts" between 1929 and 1960. Typical items on the list are such things as exhaust-valve seat inserts, built-in defroster vents, rotor-type oil pump, powdered-metal filter in fuel tank, power-operated convertible top. There is nothing on the list that is not desirable, but the only one of the fifty-nine engineering advances that stands out, in itself, as being very important, is "full-time power steering."

Power brakes, power steering, and automatic transmissions are thought of as recent engineering developments—but none of them is new. In 1903 the Columbia Electric Truck had power steering. In 1904 the Fisher car had air brakes, with an auxiliary engine to operate the air compressor. The Sturtevant of that year also had air brakes—plus an automatic transmission. There were several automatic transmissions before 1920, all on cars that did not last. When, in 1956, Chrysler loudly extolled their *new* push-button transmission, some old-timers smiled. They remembered the Owens-Magnetic of the middle teen years that was shifted by pressing a row of buttons on the steering column. Most of these early automatic transmissions were electrical—a form of transmission that ended up on diesel locomotives.

These early devices were crude, but they indicated possibilities. Perhaps the long time lapse between possibility and production occurred because the importance of the engineering laboratory was not recognized until the 1920s. An outstanding example of an important improvement that was ignored for more than a decade is four-wheel brakes. In 1908 much of the Glidden Tour was over mountainous terrain in the Alleghanies. Every car had brake trouble except a French Blériot, equipped with four-wheel brakes. Yet it was 1920 before four-wheel hydraulic brakes made their appearance on an American production car: the Duesenberg, new that year. By 1923 they were in general use.

One does not have to be too old to remember the "flat tops"—the closed cars of the 1920s and early 1930s, with their oblong box bodies behind long, straight hoods. Chrysler sounded the death knell of the flat tops in 1934—ironically, with a car that was a failure.

Carl Breer, chief engineer of the Chrysler Corporation, was idly watching a flock of geese as he drove along near Selfridge Field one day in 1927. He noted their effortless, smooth flight and was surprised, as they came nearer, to discover they were not geese but a wedge of planes from the nearby army field. Planes were designed like birds; they were aerodynamically sound. But, reasoned Breer,

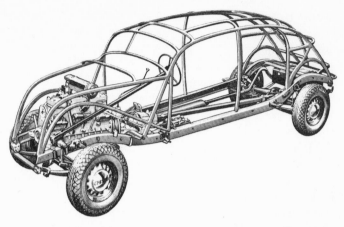

Chrysler Corporation

Watching the grace with which birds and planes moved through the air, Chrysler's Carl Breer reasoned that the same aerodynamic principles should be applied to cars. With advice from Orville Wright and an air tunnel to test his ideas, he found that the best design was a backward sloping curve of equal width throughout the car. His experiments resulted in the revolutionary Chrysler Airflow, the first car to break away from the rectangular flat-top shape.

cars also move through air, although their wheels roll on the ground. And nobody had ever previously considered aerodynamics in relation to car design.

With advice from Orville Wright, Breer had an air tunnel built at the Chrysler laboratory and started to test car shapes. One startling discovery was that the conventional flat top generated less air resistance when it went backward than when it went forward. The ideal shape, aerodynamically, was a parabolic curve from front to back, with a width that was equal throughout the car. To achieve this silhouette it was necessary to move the rear seat forward of the rear axle and to mount the engine over the front axle—two factors that incidentally contributed to a smoother ride. The wider front made possible a three-passenger front seat. When these units were located, a parabolic curve was laid over them from front axle to rear, with the necessary modification for a sloping windshield. So the basic shape of the Chrysler Airflow was established.

When the streamlined car made its bow at the 1934 auto show, the editor of *Motor Yearbook* wrote, "At first glance these cars will look strange to most people, but the writer finds that after you have looked at them for two or three days you become accustomed to them and sooner or later you begin to admire them." Few agreed with him. The fenders were set into the body, so that the car seemed to have none. Everything was curved where people expected it to be straight. The hood was rounded and stubby instead of having the long, sleek shape that, to most people, denoted power. Some people bought, but more people laughed. Only 11,292 were sold the first year. Chrysler persevered for three years with a car that they knew was scientifically sound; but when sales fell to 4,600 in 1937, they gave up the Airflow and retreated to a more conventional design.

They did not have far to retreat. Starting in 1935 most other cars modified their designs in the direction of the Airflow. By 1937 all closed cars were nearer to the basic shape of the Airflow than they were to their own 1934 models. The era of the flat tops was over, and the day of the stylist had dawned.

The Chrysler Airflow, which first appeared in 1935, was a failure—car buyers were not ready to accept its revolutionary appearance. But it marked a turning point in car design, as other manufacturers turned from the boxlike flat-tops to the new curved shape.

Chrysler Corporation

SIX: THE BIG CHANGE

Flappers and flagpole sitters and human flies; bathtub gin and bobbed hair and the big bull market; racketeering and radio and Rotary clubs; mah-jongg and Miami Beach and marathon dancing; petting parties and Prohibition and psychoanalysis; companionate marriage and crossword puzzles and cocktail parties—these are but a few of the phenomena that were spawned or that flowered in that incredible decade, the Roaring Twenties.

It was an era of accomplishment, great and small. A.T.&T. hit 304 on the big board, Babe Ruth hit sixty home runs, and Jack Dempsey hit Gene Tunney for the long count. Communism conquered Russia, Gertrude Ederle conquered the English Channel, and Rudolph Valentino conquered the hearts of America's females. Women got the vote, the drys got the Volstead Act, and knowledgeable wets got a good bootlegger. Speak-easies flourished, youth flamed, and Lindbergh flew the Atlantic.

It was an era of change. Men put on boy's pants—knickers—to play golf, and women took off their corsets to dance. The martini replaced the Bronx cocktail as the favorite tipple of the middle class. Bridge (auction, that is) grew as euchre declined, and the theory of evolution challenged fundamentalism. Strong language and sex talk moved into mixed company and onto the stage and printed page.

Other changes were more meaningful. A revolution occurred in

Automobile Manufacturers Association
Fifth Avenue in the 1920s. The age of the automobile had arrived.

American manners and mores, customs and culture. Victorianism, which had flourished for two generations, died during the last of the teen years. During the twenties, Americans floundered as they sought a new and more modern code of behavior. Many complex reasons have been advanced for the revolution in the American way of life. The war had brought a wider freedom of action to a large number of Americans. It also brought a certain tenseness, the relaxation of which sent the pendulum swinging in a wide arc. Americans tired of making the world safe for democracy with Woodrow Wilson and sought to return to "normalcy" with Warren Harding. Combined with this was a rapid industrial expansion that engendered a seemingly permanent progressive prosperity that provided the people with the wherewithal to procure the niceties of the new normalcy.

The greatest single factor in the big change was a new concept of the role of the automobile. Starting as a rich man's toy or the plaything of sports, it had become, during the teens, a dependable utilitarian means of transportation, accepted by farmers and the middle class. Now it suddenly became a way of life for all Americans. Of this period Mark Sullivan wrote, in *Our Times,* "It is tenable to suggest that the intellectual innovations which came to America . . . were due more to changes in the material world about him than to anything which came to him through the pens of the intelligentsia; that the average man's mind was modified more by the automobile than by any so-called leader of thought." In a sociological study made in a Midwest city one respondent queried: "Why on earth do you need to study what's happening to change this country? I can tell you what's happening in just four letters—A-U-T-O."

Statistics tell part of the story. In 1920 there were 8,132,000 passenger cars registered in the United States. In 1930 there were 23,035,000 for approximately 30,000,000 families. During the decade motor makers produced 31,053,126 cars, to become the nation's leading industry, consuming 20 percent of its steel, 90 percent of its gasoline, 80 percent of its processed rubber, and 25 percent of its plate glass. It took the Ford Motor Company seven years to build its first million cars; it built the tenth million in 132 working days in 1924.

This flood of automobiles owned by all classes of people changed almost every aspect of American life more in ten years than the rail-

Cars of the 1920s. Top, a 1921 Dort touring car. Second, a 1925 Wills Sainte Clair Six. Third, a 1928 Flying Cloud with rumble seat. Bottom, a 1929 Durant.

road had changed it in almost a century. Of the profound influence of the automobile Allen Nevin asserts: "That it helped to change the national psychology and national manners and mores as well as the national economy, cannot be questioned. No other single machine, in all probability, did so much to induce people of provincial mind to begin thinking in national terms; none did so much to knit together different parts of the country; none did more to create a sense of a freer and more spacious life."

The widespread ownership of automobiles ended forever the isolation of the farmer. Although only 12 percent of farm families had running water, 60 percent had a car. When queried by a Department of Agriculture investigator as to why the family had a car and no bathtub, one farm wife replied, with disdain for his density, "Why, you can't go to town in a bathtub!" This preference for a car over a bathtub was not limited to the farm. In a small city survey among factory workers, twenty-six car-owning families lived in such shabby-looking houses that the investigator asked whether they had bathtubs. Twenty-one of them did not.

Farm buying habits were revolutionized. Instead of doing all his shopping in the nearest general store or from a mail-order catalogue, the farmer now went an average of six to eight miles to buy hardware, fourteen for furniture, and twenty for women's fashions. As a result of the farmer's contact with the outside world, the Sears, Roebuck catalogue proclaimed, "The traditional lapse between the acceptance of new fashions in women's ready-to-wear . . . in metropolitan centers and on farms apparently no longer exists." Montgomery Ward and Sears, Roebuck saw the handwriting on the wall; although they did not particularly want to become retailers, they opened their first stores in urban centers in the mid-1920s. The automobile even changed the location of farms—from poor acreage that was three or four miles from a shipping point to fertile soil that was twenty miles or more from the railroad.

A new pattern of urbanization developed rapidly in the 1920s when millions of Americans fled the cities in the great explosion of suburbia. Before the automobile, suburban living had been limited to sites a mile or two from a railroad station. Now, new colonial farm houses, Spanish haciendas, and Tudor cottages—all with garages attached—rose on woodlands, farms, and fields far from the railroad.

During the decade enough lots were laid out between the middle of Long Island and the New York City limits to provide housing for the entire metropolitan population of six million. In 1933 the President's Research Committee on Social Trends reported that the automobile "had erased the boundaries which formerly separated urban from rural territory and has introduced a type of local community without precedent in history." Every sizable city, continued the report, had become a supercommunity—"the center of a constellation of smaller centers."

As the railroads gained crowds of commuters they lost, during this single decade, almost half of their more profitable long-haul passenger traffic. Railroad after railroad gave up its branch lines, and the inter-urban trolley wilted under a network of bus routes. The troubles that are causing today's railroad bankruptcies and frantic mergers were born in the twenties. Social and economic importance started to switch away from the railroad town. Communities that had prospered solely because they were "on the railroad" languished; towns on busy Route 20—or 30, or 40—thrived on the revenue from travelers who used their new filling stations, garages, restaurants, tourist courts, and roadside stands.

Houses themselves changed as they were forced to fight for preference with the family car. They moved closer to the paving line, with the front yard narrowed to make room for a driveway and the back yard constricted to provide space for a garage. Porches, where people used to sit and talk of an evening, were not so necessary to folks who spent their evenings in a car.

A doctor in Michigan described how the automobile changed the practice of medicine. When he started in a small county seat in 1909, with a horse and buggy, there were four other doctors and fifteen practical nurses to serve the town and surrounding countryside. There was no hospital; emergency operations were performed on kitchen tables, and babies were delivered at home. By the end of the twenties there were only two doctors in the community and no practical nurses. He visited several times as many cases by car, and his practice had changed from one of mainly making house calls to one of receiving patients who drove into town to his office. The town still had no hospital, but it had an ambulance, and the doctor was on the staff of three hospitals within a radius of fifty miles. Babies were delivered in delivery rooms; operations were performed in operating rooms.

Ministers did not fare so well. The church had to compete with the car for Sunday time, and the lure of the road was strong. Statistics on church *membership* do not show a decline for the decade, but no statistics are kept on church *attendance*. From pulpits throughout the land clerics denounced "automobilitis" and pleaded with parishioners to use their cars to bring shut-ins to church in the morning and restrict the worship of "God in nature" to the afternoon. Popular ministers preached short sermons and promised to get the congregation out not later than eleven-thirty. Country churches off new roads stood forlorn and deserted.

There was a brighter side to this. Parked cars lined the road adjacent to churches that were on the beaten track—if the service was short—as pleasure-bound motorists paused to worship briefly. Progressive ministers increased their effectiveness by making more motorized pastoral calls, and, particularly in the South, the old practice of circuit riding was revived. A preacher with a Model T could serve four or five congregations each Sunday—and he needed only one sermon.

The 1920s sounded the knell of the nostalgia-laden little red schoolhouse. By the middle of the decade 27,000 buses were carrying rural pupils to modern, multiroomed consolidated schools. In many places the whole labor pattern changed as farmers drove their flivvers into town to take winter jobs, and migratory workers in agriculture and construction moved to wherever there was a market for their services. Families as well as workers migrated as the automobile weakened their roots. Americans had always been restless in relation to their European forebears—witness the covered wagon. The automobile accelerated this quest for opportunity and adventure in new surroundings.

Not only did Americans become nomads, but the automobile started a permanent shift in population. In some places, as in Florida and Southern California, it converted towns into sprawling cities and changed cities into mammoth metropolitan centers. An estimated 1 million people a year went to California to see and spend—and many to stay. The population of Los Angeles increased from 576,000 to 1,238,048 during the decade. In its suburbs Glendale increased its population 400 percent, Huntington Park 500 percent, and Beverly Hills 2,500 percent.

The great Florida boom started in 1925. In 1920 Miami had a population of 30,000, and Miami Beach was a mangrove swamp. During the mid-twenties the annual influx of winter tourists exceeded the entire population of the state, and three out of five of them came by car. A tourist in the perpetual traffic jam on the Dixie Highway counted twenty-eight out-of-state license plates adjacent to his car. Enough of the tourists stayed to give Miami a population of 110,637 by 1930.

The slogan "See America First" was coined in the twenties, and scores of places in the nation became, according to their boosters, "*The* Playground of America." Incidentally, boosting a community or an area became big business at this time. The whole pattern of vacationing changed. Sprawling, shingled resort and waterfront hotels, where the families of the upper class had gone by train for a few summer weeks, were deserted even by their privileged patrons. Nobody wanted to stay in one place that long—there was too much to see, too many things to do. Country boardinghouses where the middle class had spent their summer leisure hung out signs "Tourists Accommodated," and thousands of families along the road who had never previously thought of having the privacy of their homes invaded sought a share of the travelers' gold with neat signs for "Rooms."

Communities established camp sites for "tin-can tourists" who would not or could not spend money for shelter. This was a novelty when Denver, in 1919, set aside a 160-acre camp site for motorists, with running water and sanitary facilities. By 1923, 2,000 communities had municipally owned sites, some, like Los Angeles, with cook stoves, laundry tubs, and hot water—the forerunner of today's trailer camps. Some of the tin-can tourists proclaimed their membership in this loosely knit fraternity by affixing a tin can to their radiator caps. Having little money to spend, they soon became a mixed blessing to wayside communities.

The tourist court was born—rows or semicircles of little cabins. Although some were architecturally "cute," most were glorified chicken coops with light and running water—but from them grew today's lush motels. By 1925 Florida alone registered 178 of these new wayside hostelries that had scarcely existed five years before.

An English writer described her "grand tour" in America: "Turn into a through road anywhere and you will become part of the longest, fastest and most extraordinary procession that ever raised the August dust on the face of the earth . . . . A stream of tourists bowls and bumps along all the open trails from Maine to California. Camp fires and tent villages mark its daily course. It draws Main Street across a continent and changes a sparsely-settled countryside into a vast and populous suburbia."

Through highways became great elongated bazaars, garish with signs and stands and souvenir stalls that catered to the tourists' every whim and vied for his last dollar. Eating habits changed. The old village inn with its leisurely service gave way to roadside eateries with parking space where one could eat on the run. The hot dog, born in Coney Island, became America's favorite national food. In Southern California the drive-in restaurant was born, where one could not only eat without getting out of the car but was served by would-be starlets in smartly cut slacks or short pleated skirts that swished delightfully when viewed from the rear. Short shorts were not yet accepted.

One aspect of the big change that distressed the older generation and the clergy, and which gave sociologists a titillating subject for study, was the new sexual freedom, particularly among young people. Rightly or wrongly, the automobile was denounced as a destroyer of youthful virtue. A bulwark of American morality had always been the difficulty of finding a suitable place for misconduct. Now the automobile took young people far from parental supervision, and a closed car on a dark, deserted road provided the privacy of a bedroom.

There was undoubtedly some fire under all the smoke raised by flaming youth and their improper use of the automobile. One judge castigated the automobile as a "house of prostitution on wheels." That the female still favored the automobile was confirmed by the records of one court in which, during a single month in 1924, nineteen of thirty girls who came before the court for sex offenses reported that the act was committed in an automobile. Petting parties in parked cars were certainly a manifestation of the Roaring Twenties —and it is possible that this custom still prevails. With characteristic restraint the *Harvard Alumni Bulletin* commented that "the motor car induces idleness and is a distracting and unsettling influence."

Youth was not alone in using the new mobility for nefarious purposes. In the opinion of some, tourist courts adjacent to cities were dens of iniquity. Sociologists from Southern Methodist University in Dallas studied the motor courts near their city and found that much of their clientele was composed of local couples who used the facilities for an hour or so. They found one cabin that was rented sixteen times in one night and another that was occupied by 254 couples in ten weeks—109 of them, by their license plates, from Dallas. Somewhat later, J. Edgar Hoover lashed out at tourist courts as "camps of crime." He wrote: "Many of them are little more than camouflaged brothels . . . [where] anyone whom the proprietor even suspects of being a tourist is turned away. . . . There is more money and a faster turnover in the 'couple' trade."

In 1929 sociologists Robert and Helen Lynd published a study in depth of a small Midwest city under the title *Middletown—A Study in American Culture*. It was divided into six sections: getting a living, making a home, raising the young, using leisure, engaging in religious practices, and participating in community activities. In each of these areas they found that the automobile had, during the previous decade, played from a contributing to a dominant role in changing the culture of the community.

They made their analysis of automobile ownership for the year 1923 and found that there were 6,221 cars in Middletown—approximately two for each three families. By the end of the decade it would have been a good deal higher. Fifty-four percent of the total were up-to-date cars, made in 1920 or later. The list of makes is a good cross section of what America was driving in the mid-twenties. Fords accounted for 41 percent, 2,578 vehicles. There were 590 Chevrolets, 459 Oaklands, 343 Dodges, 309 Maxwells, 295 Buicks, 264 Studebakers, 88 Overlands, 74 Willys-Knights, 73 Nashes and Interstates, 65 Durants, 62 Stars, 59 Oldsmobiles, 53 Saxons, and 50 Reos. Chalmers, Franklin, Essex, Hudson, Cadillac, Chandler, Monroe, Paige, Haynes, International, Sheridan, and Hupmobile were each represented by from twenty-five to fifty cars. Sixty-nine other makes had less than twenty-five, including 15 Marmons, 14 Packards, 1 Pierce-Arrow, and 1 Lincoln. A total of ninety-seven makes of cars rolled on Middletown's streets.

The majority of Middletown's population were factory workers, and of the working-class families interviewed, approximately half were car owners. There was a difference of opinion on many things, but on this there was complete solidarity. "We'd rather do without clothes than give up the car," said one mother of nine children. Another said, "We don't have no fancy clothes when we have the car to pay for. The car is the only pleasure we have." A third put it more emphatically: "I'll go without food before I'll see us give up the car"—and many who kept up the payments on their cars when they were out of work may have been doing just this.

A labor leader, when asked what he thought the men in his union were working for, guessed that "twenty-five percent of them are fighting to keep their heads above water, 10 percent want to own their own homes; 65 percent are working to pay off their cars." Factory workers who were making about $35 per week spent an average of one week's income per month to pay for and maintain their car. This had previously been the traditional allowance in middle-class budgets for housing. There were numerous instances of homes being mortgaged to buy an automobile. On the other hand there were several instances where car ownership led to home ownership by making it possible for a worker to move away from the job to an area where owning a home was more feasible.

Many businessmen felt that widespread ownership of automobiles was throwing the whole economy out of kilter. A candy manufacturer reported: "People are not buying candy so much now. How can they? Even laboring men put all their money into cars, and every other branch of business feels it." This was confirmed elsewhere. The *National Retail Clothier* blamed the woes of its industry on the automobile, citing a case of one retailer who "put on a campaign that usually resulted in a business of 150 suits and overcoats on a Saturday afternoon. This season the campaign netted seventeen sales, while an automobile agency across the street sold twenty-five cars."

There was a division of opinion as to whether the car was good or bad for family life. The Lynds reported that, although a high degree of companionship in marriage was not regarded as essential in Middletown, "the automobile appears to be an important agency in bringing husbands and wives together in their leisure, counterbalancing in part the centrifugal tendency in the family observable in other aspects of Middletown's life." Working-class families with cars reported that trips were the chief center of family interest. Several said: "We don't spend anything on recreation except for the car. We save every place

we can and put the money into the car. It keeps the family together."
Others reported that the only times the family was together was at
meals and in the car. The automobile made quite a change in eating
habits of the family. The leisurely Sunday dinner became obsolete in
many homes, and even the evening meal was reduced to a snack so
that the family could get out on the road.

The reverse of this was the criticism that the automobile was a
divisive factor in family life from parents of teen-agers, who complained that the children went motoring, but not with the parents.
The pattern of modern teen-age life is deeply rooted in the twenties
when, as today, a boy was "dead" if he did not have "wheels."
Mothers started to lament, "I don't know where my daughter is," and
daughter would argue: "What on earth do you want me to *do!* Just
sit around home all evening?" Still, 60 percent of Middletown's high
school sophomores to seniors reported that they motored more often
with their parents than without them.

The Middletown study indicates that the automobile was a factor
in spreading the idea of vacations with pay. At that time a paid vacation for a factory worker was unheard of. It was considered enlightened labor practice to permit a worker to take a week or two off at
his own expense and still hold his job when he returned. Several
workers reported that they had done this for the first time after they
got their cars. The manifold uses of leisure that the car made possible
led to the demand for more leisure—vacations with pay.

One material aspect of the big change during the 1920s was the
development of roads. By the end of World War I, with mass production in full swing, America had tremendous potential capacity for
building cars but still had little capacity for their use. During the next
decade the United States undertook the construction of the most
extensive country-wide highway system in modern history. Yet so
great was the automobile explosion that the roads were never adequate to the demands of the new mobility. In 1914 there were seven
cars per mile of improved road. By 1925, although over 450,000
miles of roads were classified as improved and almost $2 billion a
year was being spent on roads and streets, there were thirty-eight cars
per mile.

The lag in getting a coordinated highway system went back to the
early concept of American political philosophy—the respective re-

sponsibilities of the Federal and state governments. Tucked in between the right to coin money and punish counterfeiting and the power to grant copyrights and patents, the United States Constitution grants the Federal government the power to "establish post offices and post roads." In 1806 the government used this authority to start building the National Road between the Potomac and the Mississippi rivers. With the coming of the railroad the government got out of the road-building business in 1837, turning the finished portion of the National Road over to the states. For generations the view was held in Washington that, with railroads to carry the mails, intrastate roads were the sole concern of the states and the Federal government had no right to spend money on them. This state of mind persisted until 1916, when the first Federal Highway Act was passed, under which the government would contribute to road-building costs in states that had established highway departments and would conform to an over-all highway system. By 1919 all states had qualified.

Under exclusive state control road improvement during the first two decades of the century was a hit-or-miss matter. It was not unusual for a motorist to drive along a new hard-surfaced road until he came to a state line marker—where he faced two muddy ruts. The first large-scale effort to correct this was the privately sponsored Lincoln Highway, conceived by Carl G. Fisher as an object lesson in interstate road building.

Carl Fisher had been involved with automobiles from the earliest days. He had compressed carbide gas in tanks to fuel automobile headlights and founded the Prest-O-Lite Company, which flourished mightily until Kettering's electrical system made electric headlights practical. In 1912 Fisher assembled a group of automotive industry leaders and proposed that they sponsor the construction of a hard-surfaced transcontinental road to be called The Coast-to-Coast Rock Highway. The idea met with instant enthusiasm, except for the name. It was felt that the venture should have a patriotic flavor, and despite the opposition of a few Democrats who believed that "The Thomas Jefferson Highway" would be a fine title, "The Lincoln Memorial Highway Association" was formed.

Fisher digested his idea in a letter to Elbert Hubbard. "As you know, Mr. Hubbard," he wrote, "the highways of America are built chiefly of politics, whereas the proper material is crushed rock, or concrete. We believe one magnificent highway of this kind, in actual existence, will stimulate as nothing else could the building of enduring highways everywhere that will not only be a credit to the American people but that will also mean much to American agriculture and American commerce. Will you pitch in and help?"

The specific help that was wanted from Hubbard was a contribution from Henry Ford, with whom the old sage was friendly. The Ford Motor Company never did contribute, although Edsel Ford later made a substantial personal donation. Most of the other leading car and tire producers gave the project extensive support. It is interesting that no oil companies contributed, probably because they were having enough trouble meeting the existing demand for gasoline without trying to create a greater market.

The original plan of the Association called for laying out a transcontinental route, establishing many consuls in each state to promote the highway locally, advising on road-building specifications, and ballyhooing the project with much advertising and propaganda. They settled on concrete as the most desirable road-building material and induced the Portland Cement industry to donate tens of thousands of barrels of their product, which would be given to the states to get the ball rolling. They hoped that the road would be finished by May 1, 1915 so that "a corps of 25,000 automobiles can be taken over this road to the opening of the Exposition in San Francisco."

The idea did not work out quite as planned, mainly because of local and sectional controversies as to the route. The line selected was the most direct path from New York to San Francisco, crossing the Rockies at Great South Pass, Wyoming, and traversing the states of New Jersey, Pennsylvania, Ohio, Indiana, Illinois, Iowa, Nebraska, Wyoming, Utah, Nevada, and California. At the western end Southern California cried loudly that the road should go to Los Angeles. In the east, Maryland, Delaware, and Washington, D.C., protested that anything called the Lincoln Highway *must* go to the nation's capital. President Woodrow Wilson wrote the Association proposing this and was turned down—as was his successor, Warren Harding, when he objected that the route through Ohio did not go through his home town of Marion.

The road, as planned, was never finished, largely because of the selfishness and obstinancy of Utah. The selected route went due west from Salt Lake City, the shortest crossing of the desert into Nevada. By this route the tourist would get quickly out of Utah and spend his money crossing the entire width of Nevada. Utah wanted the road to turn southwest at Salt Lake and traverse most of the length of that state before crossing the southern tip of Nevada and going on to Los Angeles. They would have nothing to do with a direct route west from Salt Lake City. It was 1931 before this controversy was resolved and the Association reluctantly marked an alternate, secondary road in Utah as part of the Lincoln Highway. By this time the road had become U.S. Route 30.

Although the highway was not finished as it was conceived, the project led to a great public interest in good roads and resulted in thousands of miles of construction. The Association used some of its cement, and its own funds, to build "seedling" miles of concrete highway in several states. Local users who rolled smoothly along these short stretches demanded that state and county authorities extend them. Willys-Overland and General Motors paid for constructing several stretches in Nevada and Wyoming. United States Rubber Company paid for an "Ideal Section" of the road in Indiana to demonstrate what a good highway should be. This 1⅓-mile sample was four lanes of concrete on a 110-foot right of way, lighted and landscaped. When it was opened in 1922 it was the best stretch of rural road in the country.

The year 1919 marked the real beginning of a widespread road-building program. Public interest was high. With the war over, Federal funds became available. The army sold 30,000 surplus trucks and other vehicles to state highway departments at a few cents on the dollar. The National Research Council undertook a study to apply some intelligent fact finding to road engineering. And, most important, Oregon passed the first law taxing gasoline. By 1929 every state was collecting taxes on the use of automobiles that in the aggregate came to more than the amount being spent on road building and maintenance. By 1935 motorists were paying one of every eight tax dollars.

It was 1925 before anything was done about marking the growing network of roads to form an integrated highway system, a move that made possible the modern road map. After each state selected

The 1920s marked the real beginning of road building in the automobile era. These paintings indicate two forward steps. With federal help, there were U.S. highways on which the hard-surfaced road did not stop at the state line, as at right. And, below, roads were marked with uniform signs for the first time in 1925.

U.S. Bureau of Public Roads

U.S. Bureau of Public Roads

roads that would be part of a through system the routes were given numbers that did not stop at state lines and were marked with the shield-shaped sign that is still in use. East-West routes were marked with multiples of ten; Route 10 south of the Canadian border to Route 90 through the Southern states. North-South through roads were given numbers ending in 1. Route 1 followed the Atlantic coast from Maine to Florida, Route 11 ran from northern New York to New Orleans, and so on, to Route 101 on the Pacific coast. Warning signs of uniform shapes and colors were adopted at the same time—octagonal "Stop" signs, circular "R.R. Crossing" signs, and diamond "Curve" signs among them.

By the end of the 1920s motorists could travel between most sizable communities on some kind of surfaced road. Most roads were only two lanes; the modern highway was just starting to make

The State of New Jersey was an early leader in modern highway engineering. Above, the first clover-leaf intersection, built at Woodbridge, N.J., in 1928. Below, an early traffic circle at Camden airport.

its appearance. Freeways, thruways, multilane turnpikes, and parkways outside cities were still in the future. A few cities had broad boulevards within their limits. What is now Philadelphia's Roosevelt Boulevard and New York's Bronx Concourse were in being, as was the Bronx River Parkway, the first parkway type of road leading into the suburbs.

Modern highway engineering was in its infancy. The clover-leaf intersection for grade separation at an interchange was patented by Arthur Hale of Maryland in 1916, but the first one was not built until 1928, at Woodbridge, New Jersey. The first piece of truly modern road engineering, the Pulaski Skyway over the Hackensack Meadows in New Jersey, was not started until 1930. The spread of modern roads did not accelerate until the early 1930s, when much of the greatly increased Federal Public Works budget was allocated to road building as a depression repellent.

With all else the automobile industry changed mightily during the 1920s. No longer was it possible for entrepreneurs with little more than enthusiasm to go into the "automobile game." The cost of special tools for mass production and other integrated facilities required a multimillion-dollar investment. It cost more to set up an engineering laboratory than it had cost to establish a factory in the early days. In 1926 General Motors announced a $40 million building program. The little Davids could not fight Goliaths such as this.

There were still many makes of cars on the market—witness the ninety-seven on the streets of Middletown. But many of their makers were already out of business—casualties of the brief postwar depression of the early twenties. They continued to drop by the wayside throughout the prosperous decade. There were 108 automobile manufacturers in 1923; forty-four in 1927. During the twenties only two new companies of any consequence were established: Durant, with his three cars—Flint, Star, and Durant—and World War I Ace Eddie Rickenbacker's, with a car that bore his name from 1922 to 1927. During the peak of the boom Ford, General Motors, and Chrysler had 75 percent of the business, and about three quarters of the balance was in the hands of five independents: Hudson, Nash, Packard, Studebaker, and Willys-Overland.

The big shake-out took place in the great depression of the 1930s, when many great names sadly disappeared, and the stronger inde-

New Jersey Department of Highways

The Pulaski Skyway in New Jersey, on which construction was started in 1930, was the first elevated, limited access, rural highway.

The final company in the Big Three took shape in 1928, when Walter Chrysler bought out Dodge and started to make Plymouths. Just four years earlier he had been unable to get space at the New York automobile show. To display the first cars bearing his name, he rented the lobby of the Commodore Hotel.

Chrysler Corporation

pendents struggled frantically to keep their heads above water. Marmon went, and Cord and Stutz; Franklin and Duesenberg and Pierce-Arrow died. Reo switched from passenger cars to trucks, and Peerless made a more surprising switch—they stopped making cars and started making Carling's Ale. Nash merged with the Kelvinator Corporation and later with Hudson. Graham-Paige hung on, and Willys-Overland squeaked through to later make the famed Jeep. Packard and Studebaker survived the depression to merge in 1954.

The Big Three took shape in 1928, when Chrysler acquired Dodge and started to produce Plymouth. Walter Chrysler was forty-five years old in 1920, when he left General Motors, undertook to save the Willys Company for a fee of $1 million a year, and first had an idea for a car that would bear his name. He was described as "a glittering personality with a rich railroad man's vocabulary, a short temper and a showman's pride." The car that he envisioned was designed by three engineers whom he took from Studebaker: Carl Breer, Owen Shelton, and Fred Zeder. In 1921, while he was still striving to bring Willys out of the hole, he was retained in a similar capacity by the bankers for Maxwell-Chalmers and took with him the plans of the yet unborn car. As part of the reorganization, the Maxwell factory in Elizabeth, N.J., and the plans for the new car were put at auction. Chrysler made a bid but lost to Billy Durant—the first Chrysler car became the Flint.

Chrysler's coadjutors designed another Chrysler, this time for Maxwell. But Maxwell was in financial difficulties, and Walter Chrysler had quietly chartered the Chrysler Motor Corporation in Michigan. The car was ready in 1923, but neither Chrysler nor Maxwell had the money to make it. Walter hoped to attract sufficient attention at the New York Automobile Show to interest money men, but because the car was not in production it was not eligible for space at the show. He hired the lobby of the Commodore Hotel, around the corner from Grand Central Palace, where the show was held, to display his vehicle.

The car, with a high-compression engine in advance of its time, was a mild sensation in the trade. While he stood in the lobby Chrysler was approached by Ed Tinker, president of Chase Securities Company. "We dickered," wrote Chrysler, "seated inside the car with the doors closed and a ring of faces staring at us as if we had been in a fish bowl." Tinker offered to underwrite financing, giving the company ninety-two cents on the dollar. Chrysler wanted ninety-six. Tinker came up to ninety-four cents, if Chase got a bonus. Chrysler held out for ninety-six and no bonus. Tinker walked away.

At this point Chrysler became somewhat panicky. He and B. E. Hutchinson, who would later become treasurer of Chrysler Corporation, took the subway to Wall Street. Chrysler stood on the curb across from the Chase Bank and sent Hutch in. "It was a blustery day in January," he said, "but it was not the cold that made me shiver as I waited. I waited long, too." Hutchinson had to track Tinker down to a barber shop. The deal to establish what would become the Chrysler Corporation was made through a mask of lather.

When Chrysler started in 1924 the car was in thirty-second place in the industry. By 1926 he had climbed to fifth; the next year to fourth. DeSoto was brought out early in 1928, but what Walter Chrysler wanted was a car to compete with Ford and Chevrolet. Although production facilities had been constantly expanded, the company was still buying too many parts to produce a cheap car at a competitive price. Chrysler looked longingly at the Dodge Brothers Manufacturing Company, with its ample forge and foundry installations and its several plants.

John and Horace Dodge had died, within a few months of each other, in 1920. The company continued to operate, successfully but not spectacularly, until 1925, when New York bankers Dillon Read and Company approached the Dodge widows with an offer to buy it for a reputed $150 million to $175 million in cash and stock. Presumably the bankers acquired the company for resale, but for two years they had no offers. When Dodge lost money in 1927, Clarence Dillon approached Walter Chrysler. It was a very interesting bargaining situation. Chrysler wanted to buy, and Dillon knew it. Dillon wanted to sell, and Chrysler knew it. But neither would admit his desire. Chrysler claimed that he did not really need the Dodge facilities but might take them off Dillon's hands if he got a bargain. Dillon claimed that he was not avid to sell but would let this valuable property go if he got a good price, because he did not think that bankers belonged in the automobile business.

They finally agreed that each would put a price on a piece of paper. When Dillon came back ten days later with his paper they took a suite at the Ritz-Carlton Hotel and, without leaving it for five days and nights, haggled out a deal under which Chrysler Corporation acquired Dodge for $170 million in Chrysler stock plus the assumption of liability for $56 million in Dodge bonds. Walter immediately phoned K. T. Keller, Chrysler's production chief in Detroit, who dashed around to Dodge plants with a truckload of previously prepared canvas signs reading "Chrysler Corporation— Dodge Division." The third of the Big Three had arrived. Late in 1928 Plymouth made its bow to challenge Ford and Chevy.

The previous year, 1927, had been rife with news. Lindbergh had flown to Paris; Sacco and Vanzetti had been executed for a killing that most thought they did not do; Mrs. Hall and her brothers had been acquitted for the sensational Hall-Mills double murder that some thought they did commit. All of these received endless columns of newspaper space in this era of sensationalism, but with the exception of Lindbergh's flight, the big story of 1927, in terms of public interest, was the unveiling on December 2 of the new Model A Ford—the second, and more spectacular, Ford to bear the Model A designation. The *Herald Tribune* estimated that a million New Yorkers tried to get into Ford showrooms to see it. In Cleveland mounted police were called out to control the crowds of eager Ford gazers. In Kansas City's Convention Hall the new car had to be mounted like an idol on a high platform so that the tens of thousands of worshipers could view it. *The New York Times* commented that during the decade neither a presidential campaign nor a sports contest ever aroused so much interest as "the fight for the heavyweight national automobile championship between Henry Ford and General Motors."

For months there had been rumors about what Henry was going to do. News of the "X" engine had leaked out and led to the prediction that the new model would be a completely revolutionary car. It was said, with supposed authority, that no matter what kind of a car it was it would be called the Edison, after Ford's good friend in Menlo Park. Nonsense, said others, it was to be a cross between a Ford and a Lincoln called the Linford. Old Henry said not a word. When the company announced to dealers the discontinuance of the Model T nothing was said about when its successor would appear. Everywhere the question was, "Can Henry Ford come back?"

This was a cause for concern among economists and financial experts. When the last Model T rolled off the line in May 1927 and the Ford plants shut down, American automobile production was decreased by one half. If this hiatus in production continued for a lengthy period, it could have a serious effect on the economy, all the way from the steel industry to small-town banks that backed dealers. And it seemed probable that it would continue for more than a year, at least. Ford had no engineers like Kettering or the triumvirate at Chrysler who had been working on what he would do "when he could no longer continue to do what he had been doing." Obviously, a remodeled Model T would not serve the purpose. A completely new car must be designed. Most of its 5,500 parts would have to be engineered. It would have to be tested and revised. And the main factory and the thirty-six assembly plants throughout the country would have to be revamped and largely retooled. Some thought it an impossible job.

But the pessimists ignored a few things. Ford's one-man control had certain advantages for a crash program like this. By his dictatorial methods a new car would be designed almost from scratch and engineered for production in less than six months. General Motors with its decentralized and, in this case, conflicting control had wasted two years on the copper-cooled Chevrolet. Although the Ford Company had no brilliant engineers, it had competent ones who would do as they were told quickly and accurately—and it had the genius of Henry Ford to tell them what to do. It also had a quarter of a billion dollars in *cash* in the banks, and Henry Ford did not care how much of it was spent so long as he got what he wanted.

Actually, some design work had been done in the few months before the Model T was discontinued. Preliminary sketches had been made and general dimensions decided upon for a car that was in no way revolutionary. Henry said: "Edsel and I decided on the wheelbase and size right away . . . . After that it was a matter of working things out on the drawing board until we got them right." The car, at Edsel's insistence, would be much lower than the Model T. The wheelbase would be 103.5 inches, slightly longer than Chevrolet's. Henry still did not really care what the car looked like; he was interested only in performance. This was fortunate, perhaps, because it left Edsel free to design the body without interference—a field in which he had demonstrated considerable aptitude with Lincoln.

Henry insisted on an engine not much heavier than the Model T's and that would produce forty horsepower and a speed of up to sixty miles an hour. He agreed to a water-pump cooling system and battery ignition and, somewhat reluctantly, gave up his planetary transmission for a sliding gearshift. He also insisted on forged steel instead of cast iron wherever it could be used. The Model A had a higher percentage of alloy steel in its make-up than any other car. The engine was outstanding in its acceleration. It could go from five to twenty-five miles an hour in 8½ seconds, a feat then unequaled by any other four-cylinder car and seldom surpassed by sixes and eights.

Engine design was coordinated by an engineer named Eugene Farkas, a favorite of Ford's at the time. Henry, who cared little for books, told him to use the spacious library in the engineering building as his headquarters. When Farkas protested that the room was too large, Henry ordered a partition with built-in blackboards erected across it. Even Clara's loud protests did not deter him from this desecration of the beautiful room. There was a couch under the windows, and here, or in an old easy chair, Ford lounged while the engine took shape on the blackboard. One engineer left a record of how the engine was created:

Mr. Ford had a great preference for seeing things full size, vertically, in front of him. Chalk on a blackboard was the most legible way of seeing them. He could see them at a distance; stand back and get an overall picture . . . . We followed the practice of coloring these drawings, too . . . so you could refer to a red piston or a pink cylinder block, and so on . . . . Mr. Ford could read blueprints, but I do think that in a very intricate drawing that showed a number of sections and views . . . it was a little difficult for him to follow. We kept as many complications out of these drawings as possible.

Mr. Ford would sit and direct us while we drew . . . . You might be drawing a main bearing, for instance, and he would say: "Well now, that's too big. Take a quarter of an inch off that," or "That cylinder wall is too thick, reduce that a sixteenth of an inch," or, "Oh that fly wheel looks too heavy."

In view of the hundreds of thousands of blueprints that are involved in engineering a modern car it seems incredible that a man who refused to look at a blueprint could create a car in this casual manner that would work. But the Model A did work, and very well. A hand-made model was ready for testing in mid-July, less than two months after the demise of the Model T.

Testing at Ford was done as casually as most other phases of product engineering. General Motors already had a large, very scientific proving grounds at Milford, Michigan. Ford testing was done on the public roads of Dearborn. Ray Dahlinger, the chief tester, did not even work directly for the Ford Company; he was the manager of Henry's farm properties. His concept of testing exasperated the engineers. When he brought a car back he either said, "It's God damn good," or "It's no damn good." This was the extent of the test reports. Some engineers made their own tests—one of which led indirectly to a significant forward step. While running at high speed an engineer named Harold Hicks had a crash that propelled him through the windshield. When Ford heard of it he ordered Triplex safety glass for Model A windshields. In 1926 Stutz had come out with a "shockproof" windshield, with wires running horizontally through the glass, and Rickenbacker in the same year had a windshield with a sheet of celluloid between two sheets of glass. But the Model A was the first medium- or low-priced car with safety glass.

Building a car was really the minor part of the problem. Getting it into production in a reasonable time was the greater part of the achievement. While the conversion was in progress the main assembly line had been moved to the River Rouge plant, one of the world's great industrial complexes. Up the River Rouge came ore from the Mesabi Range in Ford ships to Ford docks. At the Rouge plant it became iron in Ford open-hearth furnaces, was converted to steel in Ford blast furnaces, was rolled in Ford rolling mills, was formed in Ford foundries, and finally, after the assembly line was moved from Highland Park, came out the other end of the complex as a finished car—for which even the glass had been made at the Rouge. The plant's ninety-three buildings contained twenty-seven miles of conveyors and were surrounded by ninety-three miles of railroad tracks, all within the complex. Five thousand of its 75,000 workers did nothing but keep the place clean.

The first factory-produced Model A came off the line on October

Ford Motor Company

The gigantic industrial complex at River Rouge replaced Highland Park as Ford's main assembly line. Here, where the Model A was produced, were thirty-seven miles of conveyors, ninety-three miles of railroad tracks, and a hundred buildings. It took five thousand workers just to keep the place clean.

21, 1927, 143 days after the last Model T. But lack of early planning took its toll in getting into full production. By the end of 1927 the Rouge plant was producing only 100 cars a day.

During most of 1928 the man who got delivery on a Model A could choose between pride and profit. His possession made him the envy of his neighborhood, but he could sell it for a gain of up to $200 on an active black market in which some dealers surreptitiously participated. Edsel Ford was kept busy handling V.I.P. orders. When James Couzens, now a United States Senator, ordered a Model A, the Fords insisted on making it a gift, with the same engine number that Couzen's Ford had borne in 1903. Mary Pickford and her husband Douglas Fairbanks had to pay for their Model A, as did Carl Sandburg, Franklin D. Roosevelt, and Princess Ileana of Rumania.

Because of the lag in Ford production, Chevy held its newly gained first place in 1928, with slightly over 1,100,000 cars against a little less than 800,000 for Ford. In the big year of 1929, with the Rouge going full blast, Ford surged to the front with over 1,870,000 cars produced against Chevrolet's 1,250,000. But Ford still had not learned the inevitability of annual model changes, which the sophisticated public was demanding. When Chevrolet brought out a six-cylinder car in 1929 the two-year-old Model A started to look obsolete. When Chevy again surged into first place in 1931 the Model A was discontinued, in much the same way as the Model T, while Ford tooled up to make the first low-priced V-8.

While the makers of the low-priced cars vied with each other to give the masses more for their money in the late 1920s, other more interesting if less meaningful cars were being built for the elite. This was the era when the "classics" came to full flower—*les voitures de grand luxe* that were the ultimate in automobile luxury.

The classic was a combination of elegance and fine engineering in a car of great size and weight. It was durable, dependable, smooth-running, quiet, and comfortable—but not practical. Those who could spend $10,000 to $30,000 for an automobile were not concerned with practicality. The car's most important function was to symbolize its owner's prestige. Perhaps the first classic was the Daimler, one of which was purchased by H.R.H. Edward, Prince of Wales, in 1900. For nearly half a century, through the reigns of four kings, Daimler was the royal car of England, until Rolls-Royce made the first Phantom IV for Princess Elizabeth and the Duke of Edinburgh. When Elizabeth II came to the throne Rolls replaced Daimler as the prestige car of British royalty.

Because fine handwork was the mark of a true classic, most were foreign-made. In addition to Daimler and Rolls in England some of the great names were Hispano-Suiza of Spain, Isotta-Fraschini of Italy, and Maybach-Zeppelin and Mercedes-Benz of Germany. Al Jolson bought three of the last in the 1920s. He gave the cheapest one—an open car costing $21,500—to his wife, Ruby Keeler. The $28,000 town car, with gold-plated hardware and a bird-of-paradise motif woven into the upholstery, was a gift for movie executive Joe Schenck. He kept the third for himself.

The greatest of the classics, at least in size, was the Bugatti-Royale.

Italian genius Ettore Bugatti built cars at a baronial estate-factory in Molsheim, Alsace-Lorraine, surrounded by his kennels, his stable of thoroughbreds, his aviary, his museum, his vineyards, his private distillery, and the village that housed the workers who called him, with reverence, *le Patron*—"the boss." Most of the cars he built were racing sports cars that took more firsts than any other make—perhaps more than all other makes.

In 1927 Bugatti built the first Royale, the biggest car in the world, with a 180-inch wheelbase and a sixty-six-inch track. It had the world's largest straight-eight engine, weighing 238 pounds and measuring four feet seven inches in length. Bugatti kept this car for himself and made ten more that sold for $30,000 each, not including gold hardware and fittings. These were slightly smaller—170-inch wheelbase and sixty-three-inch track. No reason for this change was given, but it is believed that *le Patron* liked the idea of driving a car that was larger than the four Royales that were owned by kings. There is a story that during the German occupation of France in World War II the resistance forces hid a Bugatti-Royale in the Paris sewer, with other works of art, to keep it from the invaders.

A true classic had a body that was individually designed and hand-made for a single car, with much carved woodwork, cut crystal, and, perhaps, precious metals, hand-woven rugs and fabrics and hand-tooled leather. Most of these were made in Europe. America developed the "semiclassic" body for the ordinary millionaire. These were specially designed to fit a certain chassis and built in quantities of fifty to 100. The buyer shipped the chassis of his choice to the body builder and selected his own color scheme and interior appointments.

Most of the American classics were the finest cars of commercial producers, such as Cadillac, Lincoln, Packard, and Pierce-Arrow. Two cars that are no longer with us deserve special mention: the Series E Doble and the Duesenberg. The Dobles—father and four sons—had been building steam cars for nine years before they brought out the Series E in 1924, with a choice of four semiclassic bodies by Murphy of Pasadena. Selling for $11,200, only forty-two were made between 1924 and 1932. At least two Doble owners demanded something better than Murphy's bodies. The Maharaja of Baratpur sent his chassis to London to be fitted with a shooting-brake body to hunt tigers. And there was an actual prototype of the "little old lady in Pasadena" who had her chassis equipped with a hand-made town-car body to make her social calls around Pasadena.

The Doble was the greatest of the steam cars, with performance that outmatched gasoline automobiles in several respects. Whether accelerating or cruising at eighty miles an hour, it moved with uncanny silence, the only sound the hum of its tires. It had tremendous acceleration and could climb any grade on which its wheels could get traction. And it was fast; Howard Hughes' Doble was clocked at 120 miles an hour.

The Duesenberg was the most overwhelming of the American classics, perhaps because of the personalities of the two men who were responsible for it. Fred Duesenberg was a top designer of Indianapolis race cars who started making passenger cars in 1921. The Duesenberg A was the first American car with a straight-eight engine and four-wheel brakes. By 1926 Duesenberg Motors was in financial difficulties and was taken over by Errett Lobban Cord, a young automobile salesman and race driver who had acquired control of Auburn Automobile Company in 1924. After giving the Auburn a new lease on life, Cord wanted to make something better and teamed up with Fred Duesenberg to make the Duesenberg Model J. Cord wanted to make a luxury car. Fred wanted to make a sports car. They ended with a gigantic sports-luxury classic.

When it was introduced in 1929 the Duese was the only American car in a price class with the Doble—$8,500 for a stripped-down chassis. Most owners favored the Murphy roadster body, of which some fifty were made before the Duesenberg went out of existence in 1937, after making 470 Model Js. Although much of the car was made of aluminum, the bare chassis weight was 4,450 pounds. There are a few purists who deny the title *classic* to the Duese because it was not quiet. With four valves to each cylinder and a roaring exhaust six inches in diameter, it could be heard a long way off.

But it was fast. It was a rather frightening experience to have one of these monsters pass by on the road. A stock model was clocked at Indianapolis at 116 miles an hour in 1929 and would have done much better on a long straightaway. With a supercharger, which was later added, a Duese traveled 152.145 miles an hour on the Bonneville Salt Flats.

The Cadillac, Lincoln, and Packard semiclassics of the day were not fast cars; they were built for smoothness, comfort, and style. Seventy to eighty miles was considered a satisfactory top speed. But they had to look powerful and sleek. A mark of all of them was a long, long hood, to give this impression. Although the Packard 8 had a longer engine than the Packard 12, the 12 had a longer hood. Prestige-seeking owners were willing to pay for many cubic inches of empty air around the engine.

Surprisingly, many of the classics weathered the difficulties of the 1930s better than some more modest cars. It was not the depression that killed them—enough people still had wealth to support their small production. As advanced engineering and design produced better-performing, better-looking, and more comfortable smaller cars, the big, heavy monsters simply became obsolete. An example of the conversion to the modern luxury car was Lincoln's Continental.

Edsel built the first of these, in the late 1930s, as a personal plaything. He was in overall charge of styling at Ford—a subject in which his father still had little interest—and designed the Continental solely to please himself, thereby proving his rare good taste and artistry. Although Edsel could have had many engine and other engineering improvements—because there was no thought of mass-producing the car—he accepted a chassis that was mechanically uninspired. He simply did not care. Perhaps this helps to explain why, in Henry's later years, he was unwilling to turn the reins over to his son. He and Edsel looked at an automobile from two entirely different points of view.

The Continental met with such immediate acceptance that it was put into production in 1940 and lasted until 1948. When it returned in 1955 it was made by a new division of the Ford Company specially set up to produce it as a truly fine and exclusive car. It related to Edsel's original car in only two respects. In styling, it had the overall feel of the earlier Continental, which the Museum of Modern Art had featured in an exhibit. And the new division was headed by Edsel's youngest son, William Clay Ford. The automotive historian may label the Continental as a classic of the mid-century.

On October 29, 1929, the big change of the 1920s ended with a resounding crash as the bottom dropped out of the stock market. In the depression that followed, the automobile industry suffered

In 1928 the Model A was a very modern car. The public, who had waited so long, responded with enthusiasm. In New York 50,000 orders were placed the first day; two weeks later the company had 400,000 orders.

along with the rest of the economy, but no more than industries supplying what had been considered basic needs—evidence of the automobile's solid place in American life. In 1931 all manufacturing income stood at 32 percent of the 1929 level; the income of the automobile industry was at 30 percent.

The automobile was now neither a plaything, a luxury or a convenience. It was a necessity as basic as bread. Relief agencies so recognized it; impoverished car-owning jobless were not required to dispose of their vehicles to qualify for public assistance; and not a few traded food coupons for gasoline. Only in America could one see a man park his car and get on the end of the bread line.

A new kind of tourist took the trail in the early 1930s, as the homeless and jobless hopefully moved to pastures that might be greener. The word *jalopy* came into being—no one knows from whence—as old crocks limped along the roads, their windows cracked, fenders flapping, bursting with kids and bedding, furniture piled on the roof, and utensils tied to the bumpers.

The greatest migration was from the dust bowl of the western plains to the lush fields of California, a movement that John Steinbeck immortalized in *The Grapes of Wrath*. His heroes, the Joads, were "Okies" wandering west from Oklahoma. When the motion picture made from the book was shown overseas it confused the rest of the world. It seemed to be reporting a great social tragedy, but it could not be taken seriously. The Joads were presented as homeless, destitute people—fighting valiantly for their very existence. Yet how could this be when they owned an automobile? In Latin America, Asia, Africa, Eastern Europe, and even in parts of sophisticated Western Europe audiences laughed at this incongruity. Everybody knew that only rich people owned automobiles.

"Okies" of the depression days of the early 1930s. With their meager effects piled atop their one prized possession—the car—they sought relief from destitution beyond the horizon.

Automobile Manufacturers Association

The beginning of a famous racing feud. Barney Oldfield and Ralph De-Palma in the 1914 Vanderbilt Cup Race at Santa Monica. Painting by Peter Helck.

SEVEN: POUR LE SPORT

Shortly after World War II a distinctive type of motorist made his appearance on the American highway. He drove a small, angular, open car, usually of English manufacture and most frequently painted red. He wore slacks and a sports coat or a short overcoat, and a mark of his breed was often a cap that sported a tiny peak and seemed to be several sizes smaller than his head. He sat in a seat about three inches off the floorboards, which also seemed too small for him, with his knees jackknifed under the steering wheel. He tooled his small machine in and out among the conventional American-made juggernauts with great assurance and aplomb. When he met another of his kind there were usually horn blasts of greeting and fraternal waves. He appeared to be extremely uncomfortable—and supremely happy. This was the sports car enthusiast—or, in the words of some uninitiated vulgarians, the sports car nut. He was not really a newcomer. He had been in existence as long as the automobile, but this hardy breed had multiplied in America with amazing rapidity—and is still going strong today.

Why the sports car craze started in America at about the end of World War II is a matter of some dispute. Although there was some so-called sports car racing in the middle 1930s, interest was limited to a handful of buffs and the words *sports car* had not yet been heard in the land. To most Americans, a Jaguar was a catlike animal and nothing else, and if one mentioned an M.G. he would be asked, "M.G. who?" Then, suddenly, the M.G. (for Morris Garages) crossed the sea, and the foreign sports car became a way of life for a rapidly increasing cult in America.

It is possible that returning G.I.'s sparked the craze. They met these sporty little machines flitting around in England. They tried them. They were a far cry from the mushy-steering mammoths that the boys were used to back home. They were not so fast as most American cars, but they had far more zip. Their little four-cylinder engines with four forward speeds could accelerate from a standing start to sixty miles per hour in something like sixteen seconds. They were instantly responsive to a touch on a steering wheel with little play, and they cornered around sharp curves with a firm grip on the road and little side sway. Their brakes, which included a hand racing brake beside the driver's seat, were far more powerful in relation to the car's weight than American brakes, so that one could drive at close quarters in traffic with greater assurance. Their chassis were rigid and their springs stiff, making for better control. They did not give a comfortable ride, but they made driving fun, and many Americans who liked to drive for the sake of driving fell in love with them.

Americans wanted British M.G.'s. Britain wanted American dollars. So M.G.'s were exported in quantity as fun cars and later as something of a status symbol for an increasing number of Americans. They were soon followed by small Triumphs, Sunbeams, and Austins from England, and for the more affluent of the hardy breed who wanted and could afford more power and superior status, there came Jaguars from England, Mercedes-Benz from Germany, Bugattis and Talbots from France, and Alfa-Romeos, Lancias, and Ferraris from Italy.

A news release from the Sports Car Club of America gives evidence that the fraternity of sports car *aficionados* who twenty years ago waved to each other so gaily as they passed has grown to a mighty clan. It is captioned "A Million Miles of Racing"—the distance that more than 17,000 sports cars traveled in almost 1,800 races supervised by the S.C.C.A. in a year. This does not include 1,300 timed hill climbs that the club also sponsored, and an indeterminate number of sports car rallies and unsupervised events. Add to this the hotrods of teen-agers that (though the S.C.C.A. may shudder) are a kind of sports car, the souped-up stock-car competitions, and those incredible dragsters that youth finds so fascinating, and it is evident that cars used *pour le sport* are a mighty factor on the American scene.

The first American automobile race held on a track—at Narragansett Park, R.I., on September 7, 1896.

Of course, none of this is new except the nomenclature. The gasoline-powered automobile started as a sports car, and since that snowy Thanksgiving in Chicago in 1895 automobile racing has become the sport that has attracted the country's largest audiences. The all-time record for attendance at an American sporting event is still probably held by the Vanderbilt Cup Race of 1910. Newspaper estimates of the number of spectators who lined the course ranged up to 500,000.

Speed has always had a fatal fascination for man—and the word *fatal* may too often be taken literally. But it was not until the roaring internal combustion engine made its appearance that he could fully indulge his lust for exciting velocity. Speed was considered the most important quality of early cars—in some cases, the only important quality. The automotive pioneers raced their contraptions to attract the attention of backers, as witness Henry Ford. The early manufacturers raced their product—either standard models or special racing adaptations—to attract buyers.

As with all else relating to automobiles, organized racing started in France with a seventy-nine-mile event from Paris to Rouen in 1894. Next year the race was a round trip from Paris to Bordeaux, 732 miles. These pioneer events were followed, in the years around the turn of the century, by increasingly faster and longer races between European capitals—Paris to Amsterdam, Paris to Berlin, Paris to Vienna.

The last of these intercity races was scheduled from Paris to Madrid in 1903. On a Sunday morning 175 starters were lined up at Versailles for over a mile, one behind the other, awaiting the dawn. Ahead of them an estimated 3 million Frenchmen lined the 350 miles of road between Paris and Bordeaux to watch the cars go by. *Lined* is not the proper term. Despite the efforts of police they stood *in the road* to catch the first sight of the approaching speed demons. Then they closed in behind each car as it passed, unmindful of the dust cloud that might obscure another racer. As a result the race never reached Madrid. Casualties among drivers and spectators were so great that the government stopped the competition at Bordeaux and ordered the cars shipped back by freight.

In America, in 1904, William K. Vanderbilt, Jr., posted a cup— reputed to be made of nearly forty pounds of sterling silver— for a road race that would bring some of the glamour and excitement of foreign racing to the Gold Coast area of Long Island, where he and his affluent friends had estates. Public roads of the area were to be closed to normal use during the race.

There was some immediate and rather violent objection to the race from the press and pulpit. One minister thundered, "Oh, the deg-

Barney Oldfield in Ford's 999 on a fair grounds horse-race track.

radation of such a scene! Foolish as a bullfight; as vulgar as reddening the sands in a gladiatorial contest; as revolting as bartering Christ's garments for a few pieces of silver."

The rather lordly wording of the posters that announced the race did not endear the idea to the local yokels, whom the race's sponsors seemed to consider as feudal peasants. The posters proclaimed that "an automobile race of between 250 and 300 miles will be held for the William K. Vanderbilt, Jr., Cup on Saturday October 8th. The start will be at Westbury at daylight. All persons are warned against using the roads between the hours of 5 A.M. and 3 P.M." After outlining the route and graciously granting that the cars would slow down while traversing the main streets of Hempstead and Hicksville, the announcement concluded:

All persons are cautioned against allowing domestic animals or fowls to be at large. Children unattended should be kept off the road.
Chain your dog and lock up your fowl.
To avoid danger, don't crowd into the road.

To this *The New York Times* responded that the "embattled" farmers of Nassau County had announced "that it is their fixed intention to use the highways of the county for their lawful occasions in exactly the same way on the day set for the automobile races as on any other day . . . . They also announce their intention of carrying firearms to protect themselves in case their lives should be menaced by the precipitate scorchers. The speed maniac while he is yet acceptable to reason will probably pay heed to the warning of the farmers of Nassau."

Trouble with the farmers never materialized. The race was to start at 6 A.M. Some of the elite left for the race after midnight champagne breakfasts at the Waldorf the night before; and many of these ended in a colossal traffic jam far from the course when the race ended prematurely. But those with more forethought filled every inn and tavern on western Long Island the night before the race, and farmers found that a cot in the living room or parking space in the yard would command $25, a seat on a roadside porch $5 or $10, and the use of an outhouse whatever the traffic would bear. So long as the Vanderbilt Cup Races were held on Long Island there was never any more talk of "embattled farmers."

The majority of the eighteen starters in 1904 were specially designed foreign-built race cars, including Panhards from France, Mercedes from Germany, and Fiats from Italy, all over sixty horsepower. Most of the American entries were stock touring cars of lower horsepower. The winner was a Panhard, which completed the 284-mile course at an average speed of 52.7 miles an hour. After the second car crossed the line the crowd became so unruly that the race was called, much to the disgust of the American drivers of a Pope-Toledo and a Packard that were running third and fourth.

The next two annual races were repetitions of the first race, but bigger and better and bloodier. The 1905 race was marked by more freak accidents than any of the others. The crowd's favorite was Vincenzo Lancia, who guzzled a quart of champagne just before the start and bellowed snatches of grand opera as he wheeled his 110-horsepower Fiat at an average of seventy-two miles an hour for the first hundred miles. He was leading the race when he made a gasoline stop. As he was about to pull out, Walter Christie came tearing along in a front-wheel-drive car of his own design. Lancia pulled out in front of Christie who, unable to slow down or swerve in time, smashed into the rear of the Fiat and turned end over end, throwing the mechanic in a high arc through the air and sliding Christie along the road. Neither Christie nor the mechanic was badly hurt but the crowd, thinking that Lancia's action had been deliberate, turned ugly, and there was, for a time, imminent danger of a lynching. To those who recall the early days of World War II, Christie's name will be remembered as the designer of a tank.

There were several other accidents, but an American driver named Lytle, piloting a Pope-Toledo, had the craziest of all the mishaps. On a rough piece of road his mechanic bounced out of the car and landed in a field. Lytle never slowed down until he reached the pits, where he picked up a second mechanic and sent an ambulance back for the first one.

The maniacal antics of the crowd were unbelievable. It was rather reminiscent of the scenes in some Spanish towns, where young bulls are driven through the streets and men and boys flirt with their horns as they pass; except that the charging bulls on Long Island could be sudden death. Men and boys crowded the limbs of trees overhanging the road, and it was surely a miracle that none who fell out landed in front of a speeding car. A popular product of vendors was a stick with a feather in the end, which could be used to tickle the drivers as they passed and a woman would cry, "I tickled Lancia" much as modern young females scream, "I touched a Beatle."

By 1906 the Vanderbilt Cup Race was by all odds the most popular sporting event in America, with over a quarter million people lining the course before the 6:15 A.M. starting time. The dirt roads of Long Island had been jammed with cars, headlight to tail light, all night. As they awaited the speeding cars, spectators guzzled beer or champagne, according to their station. One observer commented: "I estimate that ninety percent of them were pie-eyed by eleven o'clock. Why not? None of them had been to bed."

Some twenty thousand people were jammed around one sharp turn, Krug's Corner, hoping for sensational skids—which would have killed or maimed scores of them. Actually, only one spectator was killed here, and on another turn a Locomobile skidded into the crowd, tossed a couple of spectators into the air, and broke a boy's legs. The driver stopped at the grandstand to plead with officials to get the crowd off the road—an obvious impossibility.

In 1907 the American Automobile Association refused to sanction a race because of the uncontrollable crowds. So Vanderbilt and a few wealthy friends built ten miles of private concrete road on Long Island, strongly fenced, which would be part of future Vanderbilt Cup courses and which, between races, the public could use for a $1 toll. A few New Yorkers of a certain age remember driving a mile a minute for the first time on this narrow, twisty, two-lane Long Island Motor Parkway, whose overpasses of public roads rose and fell so sharply that one literally flew off their tops.

In 1908 the Motor Parkway represented almost half of a twenty-three-mile lap of which eleven made up the renewed Vanderbilt Cup Race. This time there were no serious casualties, thanks to the fencing of part of the course. But by 1910 the crowd had learned that the Motor Parkway fencing was not proof against wire cutters and pry bars. The race was so bloody—with four killed and scores trampled by the frantic mob—that this ended road racing on Long Island. The Vanderbilt Cup Race wandered rather forlornly around the country until 1916, once at Savannah, then Milwaukee, next Santa Monica. In 1915 it thrilled the crowds at the Panama-Pacific

Exposition, and then the next year at Santa Monica it expired.

Where strips of hard sand existed, beach racing vied with road racing in the early days. Cape May and Atlantic City in New Jersey were such spots, but the most successful races were on the twenty-mile strip at Ormond–Daytona Beach in Florida. After it was discovered in 1902 that Daytona was the ideal place for high-speed driving, most world records were set there until the scene shifted to the Bonneville Salt Flats in Utah in the mid-thirties. An American, Fred Marriot, was the first man to go two miles a minute, at Daytona in 1906 in a Stanley Steamer. An Englishman, Major H. O. D. Seagrave broke the 200-mph barrier in 1927; Sir Malcolm Campbell first hit 300 mph in 1935; and a third Englishman, John Cobb, topped 400 mph in 1947. A jet-powered car has now unofficially passed the 600-mph mark at Bonneville.

But most early racing was not on sand or roads. It took place on circular dirt tracks that had originally been built for horse racing. From the time Ford raced Winton at Grosse Pointe in 1901, horses had had to share their racing space at resorts with the noisy newcomers. And before the end of the first decade the roar of the death-defying speed demons had replaced the gentle clop of pacers and trotters or the thunder of racing hoofs as the big event of fairs throughout the land.

Idol of this racing circuit was Barney Oldfield, the all-time most colorful figure of American racing. After breaking and rebreaking records in 999, Barney left Ford in 1905 to drive for Winton in the Bullet No. 2. He continued to break records on the road, on sand, and at tracks in a variety of cars. He shattered the long-time Stanley Steamer beach record in a Benz, and his famous Green Hornet was a Peerless. No matter what the car, Barney, for almost fifteen years, could drive it for a record.

Barney was a hero in his time and is still a legend. It is only in recent years that sarcastic motorcycle cops have stopped addressing their victim with the quip "Who do ya think ya are, Barney Oldfield?" And Barney was also racing's bad boy, who, when not on the track, spent much time brawling in bars. Fortunately for him, ex-heavyweight champion Jim Jeffries was a friend, for as Jeffries once said, "I did more fighting in saloons getting old Barney out of scrapes than I ever did in the ring." One of Oldfield's escapades, in

1910, involved another bad-boy champion, Jack Johnson, the first Negro heavyweight world champion fighter.

The morals of Johnson's private life left something to be desired, and for this, as well as his color, he was not a popular champion. There was much talk of a "white hope" who would arise to defeat him. Johnson loved to drive fast cars. This gave Oldfield an idea for becoming the white hope on the track if not in the ring. He challenged Johnson to a match race. The egotistical fighter quickly accepted and bragged that he would become the world's racing as well as boxing champion. The A.A.A. Contest Board said that the match was a money-making hoax and tried to forbid it on the grounds that Johnson was not a licensed driver. Not one to- be hindered by restrictions, Barney went ahead with the race, beating Johnson by more than a mile in each of two five-mile heats on Long Island.

When the triple A sternly suspended Barney from racing, the irrepressible boy from Toledo gathered a stable of paid drivers and started barnstorming fairs in a series of unsanctioned races. If one did not follow the fair circuit and see too many of them, these staged races were more exciting than legitimate events. Barney invariably won the first heat by a narrow margin, after much thrilling hubcap to hubcap driving and dust-throwing skids. The driver whom he had narrowly beaten won the second heat. Then came the tense final clash in which Barney always came up from behind to win by a whisker. Next Saturday the identical performance would be repeated at another fair; and the spectators loved it.

Barney's popularity and unquestioned ability were such that he was soon back in the somewhat reluctant good graces of the A.A.A. In 1914 another great driver, Ralph de Palma—who in twenty-seven years entered 2,800 races and won 2,000—was captain of the Mercer racing team and had readied three cars for that year's Vanderbilt Cup at Santa Monica. Then Mercer decided to double their chances and hired Oldfield to drive the lead car, without consulting de Palma. The Italian-born driver wrathfully quit, and this started an epic feud between the two drivers that raged for years and, incidentally, enriched both participants.

The feud reached its height in 1917, when Oldfield got a sleek, enclosed-cockpit racer, The Golden Sub, built by Harry Miller, whose engines would later dominate Indianapolis. Barney challenged Ralph, who was then driving a 120-hp Packard Twin-Six, to a series of match races at tracks across the country. Oldfield won the first match, on the dirt at Milwaukee, but de Palma struck back with wins at Detroit, Sheepshead Bay, and Atlanta. Barney countered with victories at the Indianapolis Fairgrounds, St. Louis, and Providence. These alternate wins might give rise to the vague suspicion that the contests smacked of the county fair circuses that Oldfield used to stage—a suspicion heightened by de Palma's description of the race at Providence: "Barney had taken the first heat and I had taken the second. In the third heat, which would decide the match, I had built up what I considered to be a safe lead by the last lap. I pulled down on the inside of the banking of the final turn, leaving only a thin space between my car and the rail. Since Barney was behind me on the upper part of the banking, I counted myself a sure winner. Imagine my surprise to see Oldfield cross the track, lightning fast, and shoot by me, hugging the rail to take a five-yard lead. Barney beat me to the flag by the width of a tire." This sounds a little like modern professional wrestling; but tradition claims that the boys were driving not only for a sizable piece of the gate, but for a $10,000 side bet on each race.

Speedway racing, which would become the most prevalent and popular form of American racing until after World War II, may be dated from 1909, when the Indianapolis Speedway was built by four enterprising promoters, led by the same Carl G. Fisher who would later pioneer the Lincoln Highway. The two-and-one-half-mile Indianapolis track was originally dirt, but this was soon replaced by bricks. Hence the Speedway's nickname, Brickyard. Today most of the surface is asphalt, with a token stretch of brick. Although the Indianapolis Speedway has been America's most famous race track for fifty-five years and still draws a bigger crowd to its annual race than any other American sporting event, it must regrettably be said that it is not a very good track. On a banked oval the emphasis should be on speed rather than on the car manipulation of simulated road race courses. Yet the surface and the banking of the curves at Indianapolis are such that cars do not make especially high speeds.

As an example, Chrysler Corporation built a five-mile test track on their proving grounds, which is probably the world's best high-speed oval. Its eight lanes are smooth concrete with curves banked

General Motors Corporation

The first Vanderbilt Cup race, held on public roads on Long Island in 1904, brought loud protests from the townspeople along the way. But the race brought unexpected dividends that quieted their objections. The natives found healthy profits renting cots and parking spaces to spectators.

Automobile Manufacturers Association

The first race at Indianapolis Speedway, August 19, 1909. After this day's racing on dirt, the track was closed and paved with brick.

up to thirty-five degrees in the top lane. The track is so perfectly engineered that the driver of a car going into the banked curve at 140 mph can take his hands off the wheel, and the car will drive itself around the curve in the upper lane if its speed is maintained. On the opening day of the Chrysler track in 1954, the leading cars and drivers from that year's Indianapolis 500 staged a demonstration for the press. Their best laps that year at Indianapolis had been slightly over 130 mph. All of them did about 20 mph better on the Chrysler track, and Billy Vukovich, that year's Indianapolis winner at 130 mph, did a lap at better than 163 mph. A week later Sam Hawks, in an experimental Indianapolis-type car, did a lap at 182 mph.

But regardless of the merit of the oval, the Indianapolis Memorial Day 500 is still considered by most as America's racing classic. It has provided more people with more excitement and thrills than any other event—and in forty-eight runnings has killed thirty-seven drivers and mechanics. It has confirmed the fame of the greatest names in American racing history, including Oldfield, Ralph de Palma and his nephew Pete de Paolo, Tommy Milton, Jimmy Murphy, and the only three-time winners, Wilbur Shaw and Mauri Rose. Eddie Rickenbacker had made a name at Indianapolis before he achieved greater fame as America's number-one ace in World War I, and he was president of the track between the two wars.

The race was first run in 1911 and won by Ray Harroun in a six-cylinder Marmon at 74.51 mph. The next year Joe Dawson won in a National at 78.72 mph. This was the race in which Ralph de Palma, driving a Mercedes, was about ten miles ahead of Dawson on the 198th of the 200 laps when his engine died. De Palma and his mechanic pushed the car past the stands to an ovation from the crowd.

By 1913 the European drivers had caught on to the amount of prize money that could be earned at Indianapolis, and from that year until 1919 the race was won by foreign cars. The Peugeot introduced a new type of car to Indianapolis, with a smaller, faster-turning engine that spelled an end to the mammoth, slowly revolving power plants of the early years. In 1920 American cars came back, when Gaston Chevrolet won in a Monroe at 88 mph. His engine was the prototype of modern high-performance engines with hemispherical

Ray Harroun, winner of the first Memorial Day classic—the 500-mile race at Indianapolis Speedway.

combustion chambers, overhead valves, and twin camshafts. Duesenbergs came to the fore in the early 1920s, and in 1925 the first nine places went to Duesenbergs and cars with engines built by Harry Miller. Miller-powered cars then took over for the next ten years. In 1935 every car that finished had a Miller engine. The idea of calling the cars somebody's "Special," based on who put up the money to finance them, started in 1924, and since then it has been difficult to tell what kind of cars were running. American mass producers came back into the race briefly in the early 1930s, with cars of stock origin. Among the fifteen cars that finished in 1931 were a Studebaker, a Reo, a Chrysler, a Hudson, and a Buick.

By the end of the prewar period the Indianapolis cars had become specially designed vehicles that were not good for anything except racing on tracks of this type. They were very different from road racing cars. Indianapolis cars do not need so much in the way of brakes or a multispeed transmission. They seldom leave top gear except at a pit stop.

Since the war nothing much has changed at Indianapolis. The Offenhauser engine, derived from the Miller, took the latter's place

Modern cars that race at Indianapolis are highly specialized vehicles, specifically designed for this type of racing.

and in turn led to the Meyer-Drake engine. Speeds are continuing to rise and are now in the neighborhood of 150 mph. Crowds and purses have become bigger; the former exceeding 200,000 and the latter $500,000. A. J. Foyt, who won in 1964, received $153,650 for less than three and one half hours' work, plus the Ford Mustang pace car, a TV set, $1,000 worth of clothes, five trophies, a diamond-studded pin, and a "$100 certificate from Dorothy's, Inc." There are many who consider the Memorial Day 500 a rather dull race to watch compared to the newer so-called sports car racing. But, obviously, there are others who do not. In any event, it has become and will probably long remain an American sporting tradition, like the Kentucky Derby. In some respects the two events are somewhat similar. There are those who go to Louisville and see many more mint juleps at the bar of the Brown Hotel than horses at Churchill Downs. Likewise, many who go to Indianapolis picnic in the infield and get but a fleeting glimpse of racing automobiles.

During the 1920s, oval board tracks replaced most of the dirt speedways, dotting the nation from the Rockingham Speedway in New Hampshire to the Pacific Coast Speedway at Tacoma. These were usually a mile or a mile and a quarter, and in shorter races speeds topped those at Indianapolis. By 1927 speeds of 130 mph were commonplace, and a lap speed of 144 mph had been achieved. These board tracks were very expensive to maintain, and when they were neglected, they became so dangerous that the leading drivers stopped competing. Most of the tracks died in the early thirties from lack of public interest.

By 1930 the Miller-powered cars that raced on the boards and at Indianapolis had become so expensive that it was practically impossible for a poor but honest boy to get a start in racing—and there was the depression. In these conditions a few mechanics around the country started to build their own cars and race among themselves; and so the Midgets were born, to become a great craze during the thirties and forties. Literally hundreds of midget tracks came into existence. In Los Angeles a board track was laid in the Rose Bowl and another in the Los Angeles Coliseum. With these, plus smaller Gilmore Stadium and numerous neighborhood and suburban tracks, Los Angeles could accommodate many more racing spectators than Indianapolis, and as one writer put it, "there was racing eight nights a week."

Drag racing, one of the most popular forms of automotive competition, is a contest over a short distance—usually a quarter mile—from a standing start. Some dragsters accelerate from zero to 250 mph in six seconds and have to be slowed down with parachutes. Below, tires smoke at the start beside a driver wearing flameproof face mask.

The cars, with a wheelbase of seventy-two inches, were originally powered by anything the builder could lay his hands on. Harley-Davidson and Indian motorcycle engines were popular, as were outboard motors, until they were disallowed. There were also cut-down Ford, Chevy, Star, and Studebaker engines. One affluent builder had a Bugatti power plant, another an adapted Alfa-Romeo, and a third a Duesenberg. Then Fred Offenhauser, who had been Harry Miller's shop foreman, started to build special Midget engines, and these became more or less standard. The chassis were always the product of individual conception. On the leading circuits the cars were beautifully maintained, with gaudy paint jobs in every color of the rainbow and everything chromed except the driver.

The lure of the Midgets was manifold. The scream of the little engines, the smell of castor oil (which was then the most popular lubricant), the flying dirt, and the crash of rending metal were all factors. But the principal attraction was the proximity of the spectators to the action. Except for a few spots like the Rose Bowl, most midget tracks were quarter-mile ovals of dirt or macadam in arenas that seated from 5,000 to 15,000. The seats were separated from the track by only a six-foot crash wall, so that the cars were running almost in the laps of the front row spectators.

With sixteen cars competing on a quarter-mile track there was always lots of action. This was heightened by regulations designed to give the ticket holder the most for his money. Originally, starting positions were determined as at Indianapolis, with the cars that made the best qualifying speeds up front. When this resulted in too many follow-the-leader races the procedure was reversed, and the slower cars placed in the front rows. This made for a mad melee right after the start, when the drivers of faster cars sought to pass by nudging their slower opponents out of the way. Accidents were plentiful, although seldom fatal, under such conditions. One of the best of the Midget drivers, Bob Swanson, was upside down three times in as many months as a result of his get-out-of-the-way-or-I'll-run-you-over tactics.

Since World War II the complexion and complexity of racing has changed materially. Midgets have largely given way to quarter midgets—the ones that look like toy cars but are not. There is hotrod racing and jalopy racing—and an incredible thing called a Demolition Derby, in which scores of old crocks crash into each other in a field until only one is left mobile. Today's flaming youth are fascinated by dragsters. These roaring beasts run against time from a standing start on a quarter-mile straightaway. A drag competition is a test of acceleration power rather than a race. Some dragsters can accelerate beyond 200 miles an hour in a quarter of a mile and use parachutes to slow down.

Coming up fast in popularity in some sections of the country are go-karts. These are short metal frames with tiny wheels, a seat, and a small steering wheel, powered by a glorified lawn mower engine. There are many half-mile road race type of go-kart tracks, but the sport started on supermarket parking lots on the West Coast—when the store was closed, of course. The go-kart should not be taken too lightly. With twin 12½-horsepower engines one can go in the neighborhood of 100 miles an hour.

So-called sports car road racing is becoming increasingly popular throughout the country. The *so-called* is used because some sports car road racing can be rather confusing to the uninitiated. The cars in the principal events are not sports cars, and the races are not run on roads. Four of the first five U. S. Grand Prix races were won by Coopers and Lotuses—out-and-out race cars. And they race on privately owned race tracks built to simulate road conditions, of which there are now twenty-five around the country.

The same confusion may apply to stock car races, which are very popular in the South, and in which the cars that compete are not stock by any reasonable definition of the word. These sedans may be born on a Detroit assembly line, but by the time they reach the track they bear little resemblance to their sister sedans except in

Daytona International Speedway

The number one road-race course in the United States—Daytona International Speedway. Both sports car and stock car races are held here.

outward appearance. They have been completely disassembled and rebuilt. Brakes, shock absorbers, wheels, and tires have all been replaced with special racing components. The interior of the car has been completely changed, with bracing replacing upholstery. Any possible weak points in the frame have been strengthened. There are regulations as to engine changes, but these do not cover the camshaft, which has been replaced with one that is so "wild" that the racing stock car engine will not idle. The stock sedan that cost its owner some $3,000 when it left the factory may represent an investment of closer to $30,000 when it reaches the track.

The contribution of racing to the development of passenger cars is the subject of a controversy that goes on endlessly among experts. There are those who would attribute to the race track almost every improvement in an automobile since Duryea's little buggy. There are others who would give racing credit for little more than the invention of the rear-view mirror—which was first seen in Ray Harroun's car in the initial Indianapolis 500. The truth seems to lie somewhere in between.

In the early years, before manufacturers had special facilities for testing their product, the race track certainly served as a proving ground. And many things that later became standard were undoubtedly first used on cars designed for racing. Demountable rims appeared first in Grand Prix competition, where the delay in changing a tire was more than an inconvenience; it could mean the loss of the race. The car on which Isotta-Fraschini first used four-wheel brakes in 1910 is said to have been designed for competition. Yet it is hard to believe that rear-view mirrors, demountable rims, and four-wheel brakes would not have come into existence as a matter of course in the development of the automobile, entirely aside from racing.

Yet the controversy as to whether racing helps to improve the breed still goes on at a very high level. General Motors says no. Ford and Chrysler say yes. During the 1950s all of the Big Three started to increase the power of engines in what became known as the "horsepower race." When there was some talk in several states that such high-powered engines were unsafe and that perhaps legislation should be adopted limiting horsepower, the Automobile Manufacturers Association, in 1957, passed a resolution banning factory participation in speed contests or advertising based on speed or horsepower claims. GM still holds to this. In 1962 Ford renounced it and, followed by Chrysler, went back into racing. Now Ford gaily advertises that "Europe's 296 best Rallye cars bow to a new King of the Mountains—the Falcon V-8." And Chrysler, after winning the Firecracker 400 at Daytona with a Dodge, broadcast the comment of its driver, "I've finally found a car I can win with."

Why are Ford and Chrysler back in racing? Cynics say solely for the pubilcity. Lee Iaccoca, vice-president at Ford, confirms this to some extent by stating: "After a Ford wins a race, Ford sales in the area go up. The customer who's seen the race doesn't necessarily pick a high-performance package. What counts is that he buys a Ford." Benson Ford takes a more idealistic view of the company's purpose in racing when he reminisces that his grandfather created the Ford Motor Company based on the accomplishments of old 999 and adds: "We are preparing to enter a new era of automotive transportation. The race track and road rally are the test ground for this new era. Here are being created improved engines, drive trains, suspension systems—all the components that will add up to a vastly improved breed of automobiles."

To this General Motors replies, in effect, "Anything you can do on the race track we can do better on our proving grounds." There would seem to be some merit in this, so far as it applies to racing. All of the Big Three have under their own control much better test roads and tracks and other facilities for proving out engines, drive trains, and suspension systems than are available at race tracks or rallies.

It is probable that the participation of American manufacturers in races and rallies will lead to the improvement of the breed of American sports cars, which, in the minds of sports car enthusiasts, are virtually nonexistent. The Sports Car Club of America, in 1964, classified 104 models of sports cars in eight racing classifications of which only three Corvettes were American-made. In order to be an acceptable member of the sports car clan one must have complete and utter contempt for all "Detroit iron."

This leads to the question, "What *is* a sports car?" One definition might be that it is a car to have fun with rather than a car that is meant merely for transportation. This is, perhaps, too simple; people had a lot of fun with Model Ts, which could never be classified as sports cars. A better definition is that it is a car that is fun to drive if one likes to drive rather than merely to go places. This means it will differ from a conventional American car mainly in promoting greater roadability at the sacrifice of ease, comfort, and carrying capacity.

The driver who likes to drive wants a gear box through which he can manually select the best gear ratio for a particular purpose. This lets out an automatic transmission. He wants quick, close-ratio steering, which gives him action from a one-inch turn of the wheel. This lets out the easier and less-tiring high-ratio steering of passenger cars. He wants stiff suspension that will minimize side sway in cornering. This lets out the soft springs that give family cars a smooth, cushiony ride. He wants better brakes than are supplied on the far heavier Detroit cars. He wants a high-performance engine, regardless of whether it is quiet or vibrationless. He does not care about room for the kids or the pets, the baby's play pen or the appurtenances of the picnic or the camping trip. He would rather be dead than be caught using his car to lug home the results of a day in the supermarket and discount store.

It is true that from the 1920s until the present virtually all cars answering this description were made in Europe. The reasons for this are obvious. Europe never had, until quite recently, a "family horse"—too few families could afford it. Originally, on both sides of the ocean, there were fast, sporty cars for the adventurous to have fun with and more sedate, very expensive transportation for the elite. This changed in America when, by the 1920s, the preferred car was the closed, roomy, comfortable sedan that provided the family with transportation at a price most families could afford. It did not change in Europe, to any great extent, until well after World War II. They kept making their *voitures de grand luxe* for the upper class and improving fast, sporty cars designed to perform well on their narrow, winding, and hilly roads. Whether what came to be known, in the 1930s, as a sports car developed from a race car toned down or from a touring car souped up is a matter on which experts differ.

It was not always thus. Today there are a few Americans who will listen to sports car fans argue the respective merits of Alfas and Jaguars and Porsches and Ferraris and then say, condescendingly,

"But you never knew a Stutz Bearcat." In the teen years and into the twenties there were American cars that would justify in every way the title *sports car*. And of these by far the most famed was the Stutz Bearcat.

Harry C. Stutz built his first car in 1911 in his machine shop, drove it in the first Indianapolis 500 that year, and came in eleventh. This led to the organization, in 1913, of the Stutz Motor Company, which presented a line of cars with the slogan "The Car That Made Good in a Day." The Bearcat of great memory was made only from 1913 to 1916. It was a rough, roaring car capable of an on-the-road speed of about seventy-five miles an hour. It was usually painted white or fire-engine red, sported two bucket seats, and had no doors and no top. Its brass gearshift and brake levers were outside the car. Behind the seats was a large cylindrical gas tank with two knock-off caps, a small leather trunk, and usually at least three spare tires.

This is the Bearcat of the John Held cartoons and Russell Patterson drawings of the Roaring Twenties. It's the car one visualizes when F. Scott Fitzgerald describes the coonskin coat, bathtub gin, flapper era—which indicates what kind of tricks memory can play, because the car had not been made for five years before this era started. The Bearcat of hip flask and flapper days was a very different car—a conventional roadster without bucket seats and with doors and a top.

The Bearcat was not the only pre–World War I American sports car and not necessarily the best. There was the Simplex Speedcar, the Marion Bobcat, the Apperson Jackrabbit, and the Mercer Raceabout. Marmon, Lozier, and Chadwick were other sports car names of the period, and later, there were Auburn and Duesenberg. The Mercer Raceabout was the Bearcat's big competitor at the time and is still better beloved by many old-car addicts. There exists a club called the Mercer Associates that blandly calls itself "an organization dedicated to the preservation of America's most famous sports car." Ken Purdy, noted contemporary writer on automobiles, says: "In my own view, the early Bearcat is a gaunt and ugly piece of machinery when laid alongside a Mercer Raceabout for comparison. It has a high and heavy profile, badly misses the lithe look of the Mercer. Anyone who suggests that I'm prejudiced is dead right. I am." To this a Bearcat fan who remembers the language of the teen years might say, "There never was a worser car than a Mercer," and Mr.

Purdy might retort with a quip of the same period, "You have to be nuts to drive a Stutz."

All these cars were gone by the 1930s, and the nearest thing to a sports car made in America was a runabout with a rumble seat on a conventional Detroit chassis, which developed into today's convertible. America was without a home-made sports car until Briggs Cunningham came along in 1950. A very wealthy man, Briggs devoted some of his fortune to trying to win at Le Mans with a series of cars he produced in West Palm Beach, Florida. Almost as a side line, he would sell a car to a private buyer, detuned for road travel. This was a true sports car, and an excellent one, but being virtually hand-made the cost was fantastic. Cunningham never did win at Le Mans, although he was up front several times, and his cars did well in leading American road races of the early fifties. He gave up in 1955.

In 1953 General Motors recognized the growing interest in sports cars by producing the Corvette, with a unique fiber glass body. A year later Ford followed with the Thunderbird, which the company said was not merely a sports car but "is more truly a personal or boulevard car for the customer who insists on comfort and yet would like to own a prestige vehicle that incorporates the flair and performance characteristics of a sports car." True sports car buffs, with their dedication to foreign makes, accepted neither of them as sports cars. They pointed with scorn to Corvette's automatic transmission and six-cylinder Chevrolet engine and to Thunderbird's optional power brakes, power steering, and electric window lifts. Corvette has since been modified, so that some models are acceptable to the purist; Thunderbird has not yet made the grade with those who seem to equate sports cars solely with road racing.

However, both cars have been accepted as sports cars by hundreds of thousands of less dedicated Americans who believed that a car need not necessarily be a kidney buster in order to make driving fun. Corvette has won some national road races. Thunderbird is definitely not a race car. Either car will do anything that should reasonably be done on the open road—where the true sports car belongs—and do it with a great deal more ease and comfort than most European sports cars.

It is not necessary to race a sports car in order to have fun with it.

A racing car at Daytona. Jim Hall drives a Chevrolet Chaparral.

One who enjoys driving can get his money's worth merely tooling the alert, responsive, handleable little vehicle along a country road on a spring or fall morning. And, although big-time sports car racing has become largely a professional affair, there are some local club races where the good amateur driver can have fun in competition with a car that he can also use to go to the station.

Or the sports car fan can rally, a competition that associates him with others of his kind, provides him and his wife with a fine outing, and may bring them a brace of little silver cups—all without breaking any speed laws or becoming hotrod types. A rally is a contest to determine who can get from point A to point B in the nearest to an exact given time without getting lost or having trouble. Some rallies last a day, some a weekend. The supervising sports car club determines the route, usually over interesting back roads so far as possible, and gives each team a written description of it: "Turn right at Cobb's Mill Inn, left at Connery Brothers store, right at Congregational Church, etc." The course is divided into legs, and an average time is given in miles per hour for each leg. Contestants lose a point per second for being either late or early at the check point that ends each leg. Sneaky club officials hide behind signs and bushes along the route to make sure that contestants maintain an average speed and do not dash up to somewhere near the check point and then dawdle in or drive frantically to make up for time lost by missing the route.

Some dedicated rallyists carry more navigational instruments in their cockpits than a Boeing 707—multiple stopwatches, calculators of various kinds, wheel revolution counters, and numerous other gadgets. Others carry nothing but a stopwatch, a clip board, and a wife. The fun of it is that a husband and wife in a little car with a single stopwatch can beat a pair of mathematical wizards in a power monster if the husband can drive well and carefully and the wife can read the watch and follow the course.

Another form of fun with sports cars is the gymkhana. When British officers in "Injah" adopted this Hindustani word to label competitions in tests of skill on horseback they certainly never envisioned that it would someday be applied to a bunch of noisy little cars making patterns in the parking lot of a closed supermarket, an ideal site for a gymkhana. The event usually involves a slalom course which, like its equivalent in skiing, calls for steering a zigzag path through a series of markers, something that can be accomplished only by a car with sports steering and suspension. Another dizzying event is the clover leaf, named for the pattern that the cars make when circling four markers. A third test involves backing into a space that is very little wider than the car.

All of these are performed, one car at a time, against a stopwatch. The winner is the driver with the lowest average time for all events. Passengers can take part in some gymkhanas by spearing potatoes or balloons from the cars as they gyrate or by balancing golf balls on spoons. Or the passenger can verbally guide a blindfolded driver through the slalom course.

It is obvious that the sports car, or at least the sporty car, is going to become a much more important part of the American scene. Detroit has, as only Detroit can, developed a "family" sports car in such vehicles as Ford's Mustang, Chrysler's Barracuda and G.M.'s Corvair Corsa. The low-priced basic models of these, with bucket seats and stick shifts, are sports cars only in appearance—and appearance does not make a sports car. But there are optional "packages" available for all three that bring their performance in line with their appearance. Corvair Corsa's optional 180-hp turbo-supercharged engine changes a handsome little cat into a responsive little tiger. Barracuda offers an optional heavy-duty suspension and 235-hp engine. For an additional $1,200 to $1,500 the six-cylinder Mustang can be equipped with a high-performance 271-hp V-8 engine, heavy-duty suspension, and disk brakes on the front wheels.

So you may take your pick—a low-priced sporty car that is some fun to drive or a medium-priced sports car that at least matches, dollar for dollar, the importations in performance. As to how the American public feels—aside from those vociferous proponents of European cars—Ford received orders for 65,000 Mustangs during the first *month* that the car was on the market. The sales volume of *all* foreign sports cars in the United States is about 80,000 per *year*.

General Motors Corporation

The General Motors Technical Center, Warren, Michigan, resembles a modern college campus and is staffed by five thousand engineers, scientists, technicians, and designers.

EIGHT: BIG BUSINESS

Bigness is usually relative. Gulliver was a giant to the Lilliputians; a midget to the Brobdingnagians. Billy Sol Estes was a big operator by expansive Texas standards, but a small wheeler-dealer when compared to Ivar Kreuger, the Swedish match king. Many a hero of the high school diamond reveals feet of clay in the big leagues. In most cases the size of the frog is relative to the size of the puddle.

An exception to this is the automobile industry; or, more broadly, the influence of the automobile in the American economic puddle. By any standards, this is big. One out of every six businesses in the United States is dependent for its existence on the manufacture, distribution, servicing, and use of automobiles. One seventh of the country's wage earners—almost 12 million people—earn their living from the automobile. These range from the president of General Motors who gets upward of $740,000 each year for his services, to the ticket seller in a drive-in movie, who may receive $35 a week. Included are close to 1 million people who make automobiles and parts thereof, 2.5 million who sell and service them, over 500,000 who work on roads, and the employees of 11,000 parking lots and garages, 50,000 motels, trailer parks, and tourist courts, 4,000 drive-in theaters, and 578 race tracks; as well as traffic cops, taxi drivers, toll-road ticket takers, waitresses at drive-in restaurants, and workers in metal, glass, rubber, oil, paint, chemical, and scores of other industries. Automobiles use 20 percent of America's steel, 50 percent of its lead, 60 percent of its synthetic rubber, and 70 percent of its plate glass. More than one third of the nation's radios are on the road.

It is almost impossible to find a stopping point for the influence of the automobile industry on the American economy. General Motors alone buys from approximately 55,000 suppliers—ranging from steel mills to walnut vendors—who employ an estimated 12 million people, most of whom do not realize that they are helping to make automobiles. Surely few workers who produce molasses know that part of their product is used to harden sand castings in automotive foundries. Nor do walrus hunters know that there is a market for the hides of their victims in the automobile industry—to make friction drives for coil-winding machines. Crushed walnut shells are used in deburring operations. Ground corn cobs, babies' diapers, pipe cleaners, and sawdust are used in various cleaning, polishing, and drying operations. Guitar picks are used for coil windings, and baby bottle nipples to mask out parts in a painting operation. In all, the largest automobile company contributes some $8 billion a year to the support of these workers in other fields.

Biggest factors in this chain of bigness are the automobile companies themselves. General Motors is the world's largest manufacturing corporation, followed in the United States by Standard Oil of New Jersey and then the Ford Motor Company. The fifteen largest manufacturing companies in the United States in annual sales include the Big Three of the automotive industry and seven oil companies, which owe their places of precedence to the use of their products in automobiles.

Beyond a certain point bigness is difficult to visualize. To say that General Motors' income in 1964 was over $17 billion is rather meaningless. Knock off the last three ciphers, and it would still look big to most people. Perhaps it gives a better concept to point out that General Motors' annual income is greater than that of many of the world's sovereign states. Also, to say that GM is owned by more than 1 million shareholders does not give an impression of its scope. Over 60,000 of these stockholders are institutions—colleges, churches, insurance companies, pension and mutual funds, and others whose income benefits millions of participants. When GM pays a dividend it spreads directly or indirectly to a very sizable share of the nation's population.

What is true of General Motors is more than half as true for the Ford Motor Company, a $10 billion business in 1964. In the same year Chrysler Corporation was seventh on the list of American manufacturing corporations. Even "little" American Motors is in the top 10 percent of the country's five hundred leading manufacturing corporations.

The industry made 7,745,491 passenger cars in the United States in 1964—and an additional 1,561,952 on-the-road commercial vehicles. It produced a large share of the nation's major household appliances; Frigidaire is part of GM, Philco is owned by Ford, and Kelvinator belongs to American Motors. The industry manufactured off-the-road earth-moving and farm equipment, diesel locomotives and marine and aircraft engines, and industrial and domestic air-conditioning and heating equipment. Among the "oddities" of its thousands of diversified products are fabrics and furniture coverings made by Ford and adhesives made by Chrysler. In addition to American cars assembled abroad, GM makes the Opel in Germany, the Vauxhall in England, and the Holden in Australia; Chrysler produces the Simca in France; and Ford manufactures cars called Anglia, Consul, Cortina, Zephyr, and Zodian in England and the Tanus in Germany.

The mammoth size of the automobile companies permits them to carry on research programs that reach into almost every area of the sciences. Some of this work has little or no direct relation to automobiles; General Motors Research Laboratories has perfected a mechanical heart. This division, which Charles Franklin Kettering started with his Barn Gang some forty years ago, is now a part of GM's Technical Center. Located in a complex of buildings far removed from both manufacturing and administration operations, and which resembles the most modern college campus, Tech Center is staffed by over 5,000 scientists, engineers, technicians, and designers. Many of these are working on projects related to future cars—problems of power plants, fuels, processes, and so on. But in the scientific laboratories some projects involve "pure" research into any aspect of the relationship of matter and energy, which involves explorations in chemistry, solid state and nuclear physics, mathematics, metallurgy, thermodynamics, electronics, atomic energy, aerodynamics, magnetism, and much more.

Ford's matching operation is its Research and Engineering Center, which includes its Scientific Laboratory. This, too, is located in a

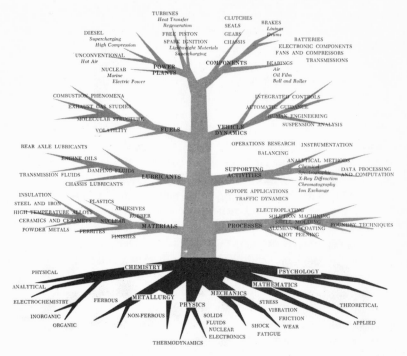

The mammoth size of the automobile companies permits them to carry on research into many areas, some of which have little or no direct relation to automobiles. Above, the areas into which General Motors research explores.

campuslike atmosphere remote from commerce; in fact, it is next door to the delightful Greenfield Village that Old Henry restored as part of his keen interest in Americana and that, symbolically, contains a duplicate of Edison's original laboratory. Ford points with particular pride to a survey by the *Harvard Business Review* that rated its laboratory seventh in a list of the nation's leading research centers in physics and electronics.

The cost of advanced engineering and scientific research is one reason why automobile companies have to be big to exist. Companies that could not afford the multimillion-dollar annual expense to compete with the big fellows in this area were also unable to compete in progressive engineering improvements. But this is not the most important aspect of the merit of bigness. Buying power is a factor, both as to materials and tools. As production tools become more sophisticated, their cost increases by almost geometric progression. It is something of a vicious circle. A company cannot afford to build an automated engine or transmission plant unless it has the volume to keep it busy; and it cannot get the volume to keep it busy unless it can achieve the lower unit cost that the modern plant makes possible. Improved production techniques increase the manufacturer's profit per car, but tooling costs have raised the break-even point at which profit begins. One expert expressed it by saying, "After X number of cars it's almost gravy, but if you don't make X number, you're dead."

Automation in the automobile industry is really an extension of the special-purpose tools that were the basis of mass production. Automatic tools were in existence long before the war; the new factor is control of such tools by electronic systems instead of human hands, plus the combination of several automatic tools into one multimillion-dollar giant of a tool, automatically controlled. Engine-block machining is a case in point. This involves 251 operations that were formerly done on several machines. The block had to be positioned in each machine and, after each operation, manually moved to the next machine. This required thousands of feet of conveyors, lifts, and the expenditure of a great deal of human energy. In a modern plant a rough engine casting goes in one end of a 1,200-foot-long tool, and a finished block comes out the other, completely machined and in-

General Motors Corporation

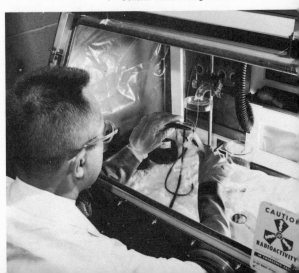

Research activities are carried on in many diversified laboratories, like this Research Isotope Laboratory, where specialized equipment guards scientists from radioactivity.

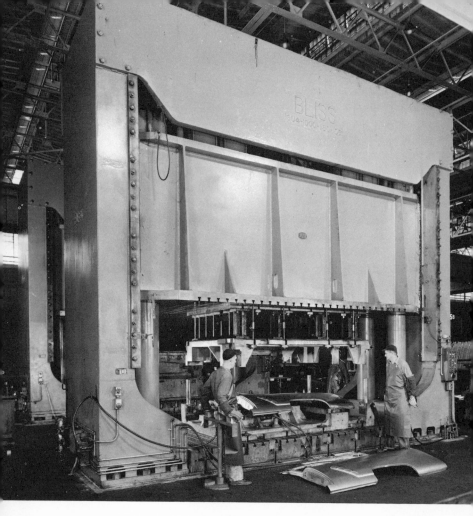

One reason auto makers have to be big to exist is the high cost of equipment. Buying sheet metal presses, with their dies, is a multimillion-dollar investment.

spected and ready for assembly of pistons, rods, and crankshaft.

All the automotive companies have spent hundreds of millions of dollars on such modern equipment, without which they could not compete. This has led to added productivity per worker and to some decrease in the labor force. However, this has not been so great as in such industries as mining, steel, and meat packing—in which, it is said, an automated frankfurter line replaces forty workers with one half of a man. This will not happen in the automobile industry so long as the American public demands such a wide variety of models, changed every year. In the Volkswagen plant in Germany, where there is no model change, 59.5 workers were required per car produced in 1949. Today, in an automated plant, the number is sixteen, a decline of over 70 percent. In American plants frequent changes in the product limit the extent to which it is economical to build extremely expensive tools that might become obsolete.

In presenting his case for a much better deal for the members of the U.A.W., Walter Reuther claims that productivity in the automobile industry has risen an average of 4.9 percent a year for the past fifteen years, a figure that is far higher than the increase for industry as a whole. Automotive management denies Reuther's claim, but offers no figures to combat it.

There is no question that productivity per worker has been increased by automation and other improvements in production techniques. Why, then, has the retail price of cars not decreased? The answer is that real prices *have* decreased—even though today's price tags are almost identical with those of 1958 cars. Today's buyer pays about the same for a car as he did seven years ago, although the cost of virtually all the materials from which the car is made has increased. Unit labor costs have decreased, but labor rates and fringe benefits have materially increased, as has the cost of producing the number of models and personal choices that the public demands. All of this costs car makers money—an increase that is absorbed, without raising prices, by savings due to production techniques and greater volume. And the industry claims that it has built $200 worth of added quality into the modern vehicle. The car makers admit that they could profitably make a car to sell for less than $1,000 if the American public would buy an equal volume of a single basic model, unchanged from year to year à la Volkswagen—a return to the principle of the Model T. But any company that tooled up to make such a car would probably soon be out of business. The most recent example of this is American Motors, whose sales plummeted when they stuck to their more or less standardized Rambler for three or four years.

Automation and other factors that make bigness a necessity for survival in the automobile industry have hurt the smaller manufacturers far more than they have hurt labor. At the end of the war Henry Kaiser formed the Kaiser-Frazer Corporation to build Kaiser and Frazer cars. It bought the Willow Run plant in which Ford had built bombers during the war, and subsequently acquired Graham Paige and Willys-Overland. It gave up production of the Frazer in 1951, briefly made an All-State car for Sears, Roebuck, and now makes only the Jeep. In 1946 Preston Tucker announced a rear-engine car that never got past pilot models; the Playboy, Keller, and Davis cars that were announced in 1948 did not get that far. In 1949 Hupp Corporation quietly retired from the business. In 1952 General Tire bought Crosley Motors and stopped car production. In 1954 Nash and Hudson became American Motors, and Studebaker and Packard merged. Packard gave up the ghost in 1958, and Studebaker stopped United States production in 1964. This narrowed the passenger car business to four companies. *

Coincidental with the death of all the independents except American Motors, the industry entered its modern period of rapid growth. Sales passed 5 million units for the first time in 1949—exceeded 6.5 million in 1950. After dropping back slightly for four years, sales hit a new peak of 7,920,000 in 1955. This was the year of the hard sell, when credit terms were extended to three years. A series of price increases during the next few years, combined with a general public dissatisfaction with the new cars until 1959, reduced sales for the remainder of the fifties.

It has always been a tradition of the automobile business that bonanza years do not follow each other. Except in 1949 and 1950 one outstanding year was always followed by a reaction. This tradition was broken in the 1960s, when there were three banner years in a row: almost 7 million cars in 1962, more than 7.5 million in 1963, and almost 8 million in 1964—some 22.5 million of the 70 million cars now in use in the United States were made during these three years.

Most experts believe that the automobile industry is heading for a new plateau of much higher sales, but they are not sure where this

* This does not include such producers as taxi specialist Checker Motors, which makes a few family sedans; or the new Cord Automobile Company, which assembles a reduced-size version of the old "coffin-front" Cord. Such companies make so few cars that they are a negligible factor in the industry.

Chrysler Corporation

Since World War II, automation has taken over many jobs in the auto industry. Tools that were formerly operated by men are now controlled electronically. In the above photo, a single operator watches over two automated cylinder-head production lines. The panels behind him pinpoint any trouble along the line.

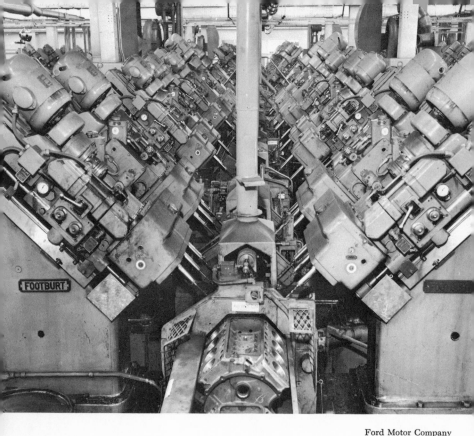

Ford Motor Company

This automated engine-block finishing machine performs 251 operations *were formerly done on several machines—all without help from human ha*

General Motors Corporation

Even inspection can be auto- *mated. This is the control* *panel for a machine that* *gauges cylinder bores and* *stamps the diameter and* *depth on each cylinder. De-* *spite the fact that cylinders* *and pistons are identical to* *within 2/10,000 of an inch,* *particular pistons are still* *fitted to particular cylinders.*

plateau will be. Some believe that an 8-million-car year will soon be considered a bad year. Scrappage is now at about 5.5 million cars a year, and it's going up. This will account for a base that is higher than the total sales of most years in the fifties. New household buying units are expected to increase from 52.6 million in 1960 to 61.2 million in 1970 and account for an additional 1.1 million new cars per year. The number of multi-car households has doubled in the past ten years, and the rate of increase is accelerating due to the wider variety of models available, the increase in disposable income, and the greater influence of youth. This is expected to create a market for at least another 1.1 million cars per year before the end of the 1960s.

Fortune magazine forecast an annual market for 9.4 million new cars by 1980. There are others who whisper of a 10-million-car year by that time, and if all of the trends of the past few years continue, the possibility is not unlikely. Indeed, it is easily possible that this peak will be reached by 1975. Barring a major and lengthy economic recession, the big automobile business may be expected to become as much as 25 percent bigger during the next decade.

It is very likely that this growth will be confined to the present companies, which through their corporate structures and their increasing diversity in products and world markets are well equipped to handle it. General Motors established the pattern for the structure of the modern corporation, both in and out of the automobile business, when back in 1921 management accepted the Organization Study of Alfred P. Sloan, Jr. This study is still the basis of the General Motors organization, which Sloan calls "decentralization with coordinated control." Of this he wrote:

Each of the conflicting elements brought together in this concept has its unique results in the operation of a business. From decentralization we get initiative, responsibility, development of personnel, decision close to the facts, flexibility—in short, all the qualities necessary for an organization to adapt to new conditions. From co-ordination we get efficiencies and economies. It must be apparent that co-ordinated decentralization is not an easy concept to apply. There is no hard and fast rule for sorting out the various responsibilities and the best way to assign them. The balance which is struck between corporate and divisional responsibilities varies according to what is being decided, the circumstances of the time, experience, and the temperaments and skills of the executives involved.

Fortune describes the modern corporation, for which GM was a model, by writing:

> The internal aspect of corporations is evolving as significantly as their relation with the rest of society. In the first half of the twentieth century the typical corporation was a rather simple pyramid with a base of workers who performed repetitive tasks, similar one to another; semi-skilled was the word for them. At the top were a few managers; power was the word for them. Within the managerial group and between it and the workers the flow of authority was all one way—from top to bottom. A very plausible case could be made that this structure tended to crush the initiative and individual spirit of those who worked within it.
>
> This picture is not true of many corporations today, and will be true of fewer tomorrow. The armies of undifferentiated workers have been replaced by better-trained men with more carefully defined responsibilities; specialization is the word for them. The managerial group has expanded hugely, and divides into specialists and generalists. The former have authority based on knowledge. They include not only scientists and technologists, but increasing numbers of experts stemming out of the social arts and sciences—communicators, psychologists, lawyers. The responsibility of the generalists, who appear at many levels, is to integrate and transcend the specialists, in a continuous process of changing operations and evolving purposes. Power there is, but it is a highly "constitutionalized" form of power, appearing in hundreds of focuses and running sideways and up as well as down. The logic of the new structure of corporations requires initiative at every focus of responsibility.

General Motors consists of forty operating divisions, each autonomous so far as the production and sale of its own products is concerned, but assisted, advised, and guided in some operations by ten staff groups. Staffs and divisions are in turn coordinated by three top committees: policy, administration, and finance. It is reasonable to say that no individual in GM ever makes an important decision. Decisions are the result of group discussion among men who have the best knowledge of every aspect of the matter under consideration. If a division manager has a brilliant idea for a new product or a new process, he cannot put that idea into practice until he sells it to the proper groups in the staff and central offices. If the idea stands up under close scrutiny, it will be put into effect, and the division involved will carry it out. Executives of GM are rational and well informed, but, always excepting Charles Franklin Kettering, there is no place for intuitive genius in the Corporation; nothing is ever done on a "hunch."

It is rather surprising that, considering its size, GM is not very fully integrated. Unlike Ford, which makes glass, steel, and fabrics, GM makes none of its raw materials. About 55 to 60 percent of the parts, materials, and services that go into its products are purchased from outside sources. This is so because GM will not go into the business of making an item unless such production can be profitable in its own right. They are not interested in saving a supplier's profit by performing the operation themselves at cost. Their own operation must provide a return on invested capital, pay its own overhead, and return a competitive profit. Under such conditions it is frequently more advantageous to buy from an outside supplier who can operate more economically because of specialization in the item required.

As an example of the always fluid relationship of division, staff, and top management, Alfred P. Sloan, Jr., cites styling and says:

> The combination could not be set once and for all, of course. It varies with changing circumstances, and the responsibility for determining administrative organization is a continuing one. Thus, at one time, the responsibility for the styling of the cars and other products was vested in the divisions. Since then it has been found desirable to place the responsibility for developing the general style characteristics of all our major products in the Styling Staff. This was suggested partly by the physical economies to be gained by co-ordinated styling. In addition, we learned from experience that work of a higher quality could be obtained by utilizing, corporation-wide, the highly developed talents of the specialists. The adoption of any particular style is now a joint responsibility of the division concerned, the Styling Staff, and central management.

Although there are no geniuses at GM, a vice-president of the U.A.W. made the remark—unusual from such a source—that the profits of the automobile companies were due to "what you would have to call management genius—no other word would be strong enough."

The organizations of the other companies are, in general but to a lesser degree, similar to that of GM—"coordinated decentralization." This did not happen easily at Ford. Until the end of World War II the company literally had no corporate organization. In 1944 one news magazine commented, "For months the world straddling empire of Henry Ford has quivered and groaned like a leviathan with acute indigestion." Through the thirties Old Henry kept his usual tight rein on the company, but the hand that held it was becoming feeble, as was the mind that guided it. He had a stroke in 1938 and a second in 1941, at the age of seventy-eight, from which he apparently never fully recovered. In his memoirs, Charles Sorensen wrote: "After his stroke he became a querulous, suspicious old man. He scented conspiracies to grab his business. Often his memory failed him . . . . Previously set opinions about Wall Street and international bankers, the Roosevelt New Deal, scheming motor car compatriots, and his son Edsel's quiet determination to live his own life hardened into an obsession which occasionally flared into hallucination."

Physically, the company did not seem to be tottering in the late 1930s, although it had slipped to third place in sales, behind Chrysler. The River Rouge plant had become the nation's largest industrial complex, employing 100,000 workers when fully staffed. But behind Ford's façade, starting in the early thirties, discord was mounting. Virtually all of Henry's early associates were gone except Charles Sorensen, a big, tough Dane who, as production chief, ruled with an iron hand, seldom argued with the master, and got things done. Edsel Ford was titular president of the company but had limited authority. He was capable but neither autocratic nor ruthless—for which his father considered him a weakling. Old Henry tried to toughen his son, to shape him in his own image as a hard, decisive, quick-thinking industrial leader. Edsel had the strength of character to resist, although his sense of filial loyalty compelled him not to oppose his father openly. Increasingly, during the thirties, Old Henry turned to an incredible little man named Harry Bennett.

Bennett was a tough, fearless bantam. Quick with his fists, he frequently knocked down men twice his size. In the 1920s he had become chief of plant security and had welded a force of ex-prize fighters, wrestlers, former baseball and football players, recently freed jailbirds, and assorted plug-uglies into a small, savage army. Backing up these muscle men he had, throughout the plants, an extensive and efficient spy system. With the rise of Bennett and the aging of Old Henry, the Ford Motor Company was no longer a good place to work. In 1938 a responsible labor leader described it by writing:

There are about eight hundred underworld characters in the Ford Service Organization. They are the Storm Troops. They make no pretense of working, but are merely "keeping order" in the plant community through terror. Around this nucleus of eight hundred yeggs there are, however, between 8,000 and 9,000 authentic workers in the organization, a great many of them spys and stool pigeons and a great many others who have been brow beaten into joining this industrial mafia. There are almost 90,000 workers in River Rouge, and because of this highly organized terror and spy system the fear in the plant is something indescribable. During the lunch hour men shout at the tops of their voices about baseball scores lest they be suspected of talking unionism. Workers seen talking together are taken off the assembly line and fired. Every man suspected of union sympathies is immediately discharged, usually under the framed-up charge of "starting a fight" in which he often gets terribly beaten up.

Harry Bennett's power extends beyond Dearborn to Detroit. In certain localities in Michigan judges and other State officials cannot run for office without a petition with a specified number of signatures. Bennett simply puts such a petition on the conveyor belt, and in one afternoon the prospective candidate has all the signatures he needs.

Bennett also had gangster connections in Detroit and elsewhere to whom he gave concessions in the plants. He justified this, and Ford endorsed it, on the grounds that his gangster friends could prevent the kidnapping of the Ford grandchildren, a constant fear of Old Henry's.

This was the man who, by the end of the thirties, was closest to Henry Ford and, under the old man, had almost dictatorial power in the company. Perhaps Old Henry saw in him some qualities he would have liked in his son. In any event almost everybody in the company, except Sorensen, Edsel, and their few immediate followers, toadied to Bennett through fear. His influence with the old man could cause any of them to be fired, and when key men left or were discharged, Bennett secured their jobs for his own flunkies. To most others Mr. Ford was largely unapproachable, and Bennett issued orders in his name—orders that had to be obeyed because they could not be checked.

Bennett's rise was in large part due to his vicious handling of labor during the turbulent thirties, a matter in which Henry gave him carte blanche under a policy of having nothing to do with unions. None of the automobile companies accepted unionism gracefully. Detroit had always been an open-shop town, and they wanted to keep it that way. They circumvented the provision in the National Industrial Recovery Act that labor could bargain through representatives of their own choosing by establishing "kept" company unions or recognizing weak locals chartered by the American Federation of Labor, which had no real interest in organizing unskilled labor on an industry-wide basis.

It was not until the United Automobile Workers was formed in 1935 and aligned itself with the newly organized, aggressive Congress of Industrial Organizations that labor started to achieve power to make demands. They exercised this, at first, by the illegal but effective sit-down strike, in which employees laid down their tools and camped in the plants, making it impossible for their owners to use them. Chrysler was the first to recognize the U.A.W. as a bargaining agent in 1936, followed shortly by General Motors early in 1937, after a sit-down strike in a key plant that assembled motors for all Chevrolets. This crisis in management-labor relations was not unique to the automobile industry. There were 4,700 strikes in the United States in 1937.

Ford was the nut that the U.A.W. could not crack for four years. Henry proclaimed that the union was dominated by "Wall Street interests" that sought to forge an iron collar around the neck of labor. He proclaimed that, regardless of the law, he would never deal with it, and the shrewd, ruthless Bennett was an able captain to lead the antiunion fight. He virtually controlled the police forces of some cities where the U.A.W. tried to organize Ford assembly plants. Union organizers were unmercifully beaten by Ford goons and ordered out of town by the police. When the union tried to organize one plant, Bennett said tersely that they would close it down and move. Fear of losing the Ford payroll led the municipal government to align itself with the company against the union.

A sit-down strike was impossible at the Rouge because of its size and the well-armed company forces. Also the company employed many Negroes, who, despite the harsh conditions, were better treated at Ford than elsewhere. They were inclined to favor Ford, the devil they knew, rather than the white man's union. When union leaders tried to pass out handbills at a Rouge gate there occurred the famous "Battle of the Overpass," in which Walter Reuther and other U.A.W. leaders were beaten unconscious and kicked down a flight of steel stairs by Ford bullies while police looked on.

By 1941 the general situation had changed materially. The defense program had overcome unemployment. Men fired from Ford could hope to get a job elsewhere. They bravely pinned union buttons on their chests and defied plant security men to take them off. The break came suddenly on April 1, when, over a minor grievance, men walked out at the rolling mill and were followed spontaneously by workers in other buildings. When Reuther and other leaders arrived at the Rouge they found 50,000 workers milling around aimlessly and led them out singing "Solidarity." About 2,500 Negroes and the security force stayed inside and were besieged by the union men.

On the third day of the strike, which had closed the largest plant in America on the eve of the war, Edsel defied his father and opened negotiations with the union. On April 11 he signed an agreement to recognize the U.A.W. as a bargaining agent, and the plant reopened. Contract talks dragged on until June 19, when Bennett presented Henry Ford with a proposed contract. Henry looked at it and tersely ordered: "I don't want any more of this business. Close the plant. Let the union take over."

Two days later Ford representatives signed the contract—and an amazing contract it was. It gave the union not only what other companies had granted but in addition a closed shop, in which new workers were required to join the union, and the checkoff system, under which union dues were deducted from the men's pay by the company. The other companies had to fall in line with this; the automobile industry was completely unionized.

No one knows why Old Henry did an about-face. Undoubtedly his senility had something to do with it. Sorensen says that Henry told him that Clara had issued an ultimatum that if he would not sign a peace agreement she would not stay to see the resulting violence; she would leave him.

During the war years the company maintained its production efficiency despite internal friction. Sorensen still controlled here and was allied with Edsel against Bennett. Henry, who reached his eightieth birthday in 1943, still frequently flared that malign forces—Wall Street, international Jewry, Communists, labor plotters, wild-eyed Washington bureaucrats—were trying to take over his plants. But fortunately, he devoted much time to pet projects like Greenfield Village and village industries. These latter were little water-powered plants that he set up, usually at the site of old grist mills, to make small parts. His idea was that labor with one foot on the farm and one foot in the factory would not be corrupted by unions. He also decided that the soybean was nature's greatest gift to man, both as a food and a material. He established two plants to make parts for Ford cars—horn buttons, switch handles, and so on—from soybeans grown by the Ford Motor Company.

In 1943 Edsel died of cancer, possibly complicated by discouragement and despair. The Secretary of the Navy promptly ordered Edsel's oldest son's release from the Navy. Henry Ford II was twenty-five when he reported to the Rouge to take over his father's burden as a vice-president. The son was mild and modest, but a good deal more aggressive than the father. He respected his grandfather, but he had no intention of letting the octogenarian run the family business into the ground without putting up a fight. He had kept in close touch with company affairs while at Yale and in the Navy. He was appalled at the makeshift administration and the total lack of organization and had little respect for most of the company executives. He disliked Sorensen, detested Bennett. Without being an autocrat, he had, and has, a good deal of his grandfather's drive.

In 1944 Sorensen, almost collapsed from overwork, resigned. He later said that the War Production Board called him in Florida and told him that the President wanted him to manage the Ford Motor Company for the government. He refused and protested against the forcible removal of Old Henry.

For the next year Henry II worked quietly to gather the few capable and reliable key men in the business as his aides and placed them in positions of authority over Bennett men. Bennett first tried to take the young man under his wing, then fumed when he was coldly rebuffed. Henry II held strong cards and intended to play them. With his mother and brothers he held a large block of the company stock, and the War Production Board, still the company's sole customer, had great confidence in him and none in Bennett.

The end of Old Henry's control came suddenly in the fall of 1945. Clara had been pressuring him to relinquish the reins to his grandson. Now Edsel's widow took a hand and announced that if this was not done she would put her stock on the open market. Never, since Henry bought out his original associates, had a share of Ford stock been owned outside the family. The old man gave in. At a board meeting on September 21 he resigned, and Henry II was elected president.

An informed commentator at the time wrote: "Before the directors' meeting had completely broken up Young Henry strode down the mahogany paneled corridor to Bennett's office. He was inside alone with Bennett for several minutes; when he came out Bennett was no longer the boss at Ford."

Old Henry lasted less than two more years; and his death was somewhat ironic. He had been born in an era of oil lamps, wood stoves, and horses and buggies. He had done, perhaps, more than any other man to change the nature of his environment. On the night of April 7, 1947 the River Rouge was in flood. Although the Ford mansion, Fair Lane, stood on a bluff above the rising waters, its power plant was flooded and there was no electricity or heat. At 11:15 Clara heard her husband call. Twenty-five minutes later Henry Ford died, as he had been born eighty-four years earlier, in a room lit by oil lamps and heated by a wood fire.

Allen Nevins wrote that when Henry Ford II "took up the reins of power . . . he drove a chariot which to discerning observers resembled the one-hoss shay at the moment before its collapse." With $700 million in the bank the company might seem to be a rather sturdy shay, but this would not last long at the rate the shay could run downhill now that it was no longer supported by war orders. Young Henry's first thought was "to build a team around here so that we could get the thinking of eight or ten top fellows." He had only three executives of top caliber in the old organization. His first move was to bring in, as executive vice-president, Ernest Breech, president of Bendix Aviation and ex-vice-president of GM. When he took the job Breech commented to his wife that his new boss was only a year older than their oldest son. With him Breech brought three key men to head engineering, production, and finance, all, like himself, General Motors alumni.

Two months after he took control, Henry II received a telegram that would have portentous meaning for Ford's future. It was signed by a Col. Charles Thornton and read, "We have a matter of management importance to discuss with you." Thornton, head of the Office of Statistical Control of the Air Force, was the leader of a group of ten Air Force officers who were seeking peacetime employment as a group. When they met with Ford he promptly hired them. Perhaps he was influenced by a desire to have some associates of his own age; the oldest of the group was thirty-four, the youngest twenty-six. It has turned out to be the most important decision he has yet made. Six of the group have since become vice-presidents of Ford Motor Company, two have become presidents—Robert McNamara and Arjay Miller.

When Breech came to the Ford Motor Company he brought with him several copies of a book entitled *Concept of the Corporation,* written by a business consultant after an eighteen-month study of General Motors. It extolled decentralization, an idea that was already endorsed by all the new key executives and the Air Force Whiz Kids. The new corporate structure under which Ford has regained its mighty stature in the past fifteen years is a close duplicate of General Motors'.

This is not to say that Ford is a junior GM. Because policy is determined in the same manner, it does not follow that policy is the same. Within the automobile business Ford's goal *is* the same—to get as much market penetration as possible at the other fellow's expense. In the overall picture Ford has its own plans and purposes that do not necessarily follow GM's. And there is a slight difference in decision making. One Ford vice-president quipped, "In general we present our plans and Mr. Ford sprinkles holy water on them." When difference of opinion has split a committee meeting, Henry II has been known to make a decision on the basis that, after all, his name is on the building.

Another aspect of bigness in the automotive industry is Big Labor. The U.A.W. is the largest union in the AFL-CIO, exceeded in size only by the independent Teamsters, whose members are also dependent on the products of the car makers. During the last quarter century of growth, labor has fared relatively better than any other segment of the automotive industry. During the depression of the 1930s, wages in Detroit sank to forty-odd cents an hour. Today wages and benefits are nearer $4 an hour.

The labor situation in the industry remained very confused for seven years after the Ford contract completed unionization. In part this was due to the spiraling postwar inflation that led to demands for repeated wage increases. More pertinent was the fight for control within the U.A.W., which was not settled until 1948, when Walter Reuther came to the fore and the communist influence was eradicated from the union. In that year contracts were signed that have formed a basic pattern for labor-management relations ever since.

General Motors claims credit for proposing this pattern, which it calls the "General Motors wage formula." That year, as in previous years, the union presented what the company considered extreme demands. The corporation countered with a proposal that had two unique features. One was the "escalator clause," under which workers received automatic annual cost-of-living increases based on rises in the Consumer Price Index. The other is called the "annual improvement factor" and provides that workers receive an annual percentage increase based on the assumption that industrial productivity is constantly improving. Initially, this was 2 percent, and it has subsequently gone up. In 1949 Ford rounded out the basis for modern compensation plans by signing the first contract with a company-paid pension plan.

There has been no really serious labor trouble in the automotive industry since that time. The last major strike was in 1950, when the union closed Chrysler for 100 days. The rank and file of automotive labor seems to have a very different attitude than they had a generation ago. In 1947, when Ford offered alternatives of a fifteen-cent-an-hour wage increase or a seven-cent raise plus a pension plan worth eight cents, the union membership voted overwhelmingly for the former. In 1964 members of the U.A.W. local at the River Rouge plant voted for early retirement as their prime goal. Higher pay ranked fifteenth in order of preference in this straw vote.

An important factor in the concentration of automotive production in the hands of a few mammoth companies is the annual model change and the public preference for a wide variety of choice in models and variations thereof. Under modern production methods this is such an expensive operation that none but an industrial giant could finance it.

The average American, during his adult life, may have two or three refrigerators and an equal number of changes of furniture or kitchen utensils. But he will own, one after another, upwards of a dozen cars, although four or five would provide him with a lifetime of transportation. Obviously, he does not buy a new car because he needs it. No matter how he may justify the turnover in terms of its being more economical, in the long run, to turn a car in before it starts giving trouble, his action is motivated by emotion rather than reason.

Of course, each new car is a somewhat better car. Each year there are improvements in mechanics and materials, sometimes major ones, but more often so minor that the owner would not recognize them if the salesman and the advertising copywriter did not extol them. But the average American does not buy it because it is a better car or even because it has more goodies and gadgets. He buys it because it is new; because it *looks* new. It has been said that "an automobile is a mobile status symbol, and a mobile status symbol comes as close as you can to defining the American dream."

This practice of an annual model change became an American tradition in the late 1920s, when the long rule of the Model T ended. In the Model A Henry Ford tried to retain his principle of not making changes for the sake of making changes. It lasted only three years. He was forced to fall in line, because his customers switched to his competitors' cars, which did change annually. And from that time forward, the *looks* of a car became increasingly important.

In the beginning of automotive styling was the word of Harley J. Earl; or so says a statement proclaiming that "in 1927 General Motors introduced styling to the automobile industry and set in motion dynamic forces which to-day vitally affect the lives of all Americans." Harley Earl, a designer of custom bodies on the West Coast, was commissioned by General Motors to design the 1927 La-Salle, a smaller car produced by the Cadillac Division. He then joined the corporation to head up a newly created styling section separate from any of the divisions.

Today auto makers, never marked for their modesty, relate the styling of their products to the outstanding artistic accomplishments of the ages. Says Ford in a brochure on styling: "In the contemporary sense, styling is the art of designing beauty into useful things. As a specialized endeavor, it is no older than the present generation; yet styling has been practiced in some form since civilization began. The architects of the past, sculptors, muralists, goldsmiths and tapestry weavers were also stylists, for they used existing materials and technical skills to express the spirit of their time in esthetic terms. The ages of man are identified with great examples of design with style; in Egypt the pyramids; in Greece the Acropolis; in Rome the Colosseum; in Europe the Cathedral at Rheims and the palace at Versailles." And, by inference, in the mid-twentieth century, the American automobile.

Although GM may be correct in saying that the 1927 LaSalle was the first production car to be designed from bumper to tail light by a stylist, the statement that this was the beginning of styling in automobiles requires some interpretation. It was the beginning of styling as a separate operation in the creation of an automobile. Before this there were several cars that had style, but their style was largely functional. The Stutz Bearcat, a very distinctive-looking car, looked the way it did because of what it was; there had been no effort to change its shape to conform to anybody's esthetic concept. Most of the cars of the late twenties—the flat-tops—had hoods over their engines to conceal them and keep them dry and oblong boxes placed behind the engines to hold the passengers. An oblong was the most logical shape for a passenger container. There were differences in appearance and trim, but little effort was made to change the shape for esthetic reasons. The major exceptions to this functionalism were the classic cars with their long, long hoods deliberately designed to give an impression of power.

The general trend of the early efforts at styling was to make short cars look long and long cars look longer. The obvious way to do this was to make the car lower. A shape that is sixteen feet long by five feet high looks longer than a shape that is sixteen feet long by seven feet high. This could be done to a certain extent by decreasing ground clearance and making the wheels smaller. But as the stylists demanded more, they ran head on into the engineers who insisted, with some reason, that there had to be room for an engine and a drive train. "But," said the stylist, "why does the engine need that tall air filter mounted on the carburetor? Why can't you design a flat air filter so that the hood line can be lower? And why does the drive train have to be under the body? Why can't the body be lowered around it?" As the paramount importance of styling became evident, the engineers grudgingly had to give way. They developed a pancake air filter and a hump through the middle of the body floor to house the drive train.

A casualty of the "long, low look" that is still mourned by old-timers was the running board. Today's younger generation has grown up without experiencing one of youth's greatest thrills—riding on the running board. In bygone years this was an exciting adventure for boys who clung to the side of the windshield as the wind created by the speeding car tore through their hair, billowed their shirts, and forced tears from their squinting eyes. This adventure was often a family secret between fathers and sons; mothers had an unreasonable aversion to boys riding on running boards.

In the evolution of styling the automobile went through some rather bizarre periods. There was the chrome age. A simple way to make this year's car look different from last year's was to festoon it with areas of gleaming chromium. Next year the chrome could be moved around so that the vehicle again had a novel appearance—and without building many very expensive new sheet-metal dies. The chrome age reached its peak when most cars looked like mobile Christmas trees. Then there was the tail-fin era. Cadillac came out with tail fins in 1948. The public accepted them as marks of a prestige car. In succeeding years most cars had tail fins. This was a simple and inexpensive change; the fin could be a separate piece welded on a fender made from last year's die. The fins got higher and higher, until Chrysler's "Forward Look" cars of the mid-fifties had fins that seemed to be almost as high as the roof. Nikita Khrushchev, on his visit to the United States, derided American automobiles by placing his hand on a Cadillac tail fin and asking, with seeming innocence, "What does this thing do?"

There is a minor psychological mystery in the attitude of the American people toward the appearance of their cars. The biggest factor in their demand for an annual model change is that they want their cars to look different. But they shy away from any car that looks *too* different. Neighboring owners of Chevrolets, Fords, and Plymouths may argue loudly the respective aesthetic merits of their prize possessions, but they will present a united front in condemning the man in the fourth house as a "screwball" if he buys a car that looks radically different. Too often, when any of the companies bring out a car that departs from a trend, it is an expensive failure. The Chrysler Airflow was an example of this in the 1930s, as was the 1929 Buick. That year, when closed cars were still flat-tops, Buick brought out a new car with curves and bulges in an effort to overcome the boxy appearance. On the first day of the automobile show it was dubbed the "pregnant Buick," and for a

Cadillac started a style trend when it came out with tail fins in 1948. Soon regarded as marks of a prestige car, fins rose higher and higher during the mid-fifties. The Plymouth Fury illustrates the extreme in Chrysler's "Forward Look."

year Buick sales nose-dived. Whether or not the car was aesthetically appealing was beside the point; people did not buy it, apparently because it looked too different.

A more recent example may be found in the Corvair and the Falcon. Both compacts came out at about the same time. The Falcon looked rather like a smaller Ford. The Corvair had a foreign influence that made it quite different in appearance from other cars. Although, at the time, Chevrolet was outselling Ford, Falcon outsold Corvair by two to one because the Corvair looked too "different." Incidentally, this did not bother General Motors, because many of the Falcon buyers were ex-Ford owners, whereas Corvair competed with foreign imports and did not affect Chevrolet sales.

The auto makers' great problem in bringing out new cars is the length of the gestation period. This used to be three years from drawing board to salesroom. Now it is nearer to eighteen months. But in creating new cars, the industry still has to try to determine what kind of a car the public will buy at some future time. Occasionally they misjudge public tastes. The most recent example of this is illustrated by the story of the compacts.

In the mid-fifties, when the so-called horsepower race was on, American cars were getting bigger and bigger. That is what the public seemed to want. It bought almost 8 million of them in 1955. Then a new phenomenon appeared on the highway in steadily increasing numbers—the German Volkswagen, a little vehicle that offered completely utilitarian transportation at a low price—and nothing else. It was followed by Fiats, Volvos, and other foreign cars of their ilk.

Automobile Manufacturers Association

Before the great influx of small foreign cars America had one car that was even smaller, the Crosley, which was made from 1939 to 1952. It was considered a novelty and was never widely popular.

The 1957 Rambler—the first American "compact." By aggressively campaigning against the "gas-guzzling dinosaurs," Rambler cashed in on the popularity of small foreign cars. Its success led the other manufacturers to rush into production with compacts of their own.

American Motors Corporation

At first, the Big Three paid little attention. There had been small American "economy" cars before; the most recent had been the Crosley, which lasted for a few years as a novelty and then faded. As the number of small foreign importations slowly increased, most of the powers that be in Detroit reasoned that they might have a limited sale as second "station" cars in the suburbs, sales that competed with used cars rather than new cars. They were convinced that Americans did not want this type of automobile.

Meanwhile, American Motors had produced a car 176 inches long in 1950—the modern Rambler. It did not make much of a stir until 1957, when American's president, George Romney, labeled it a "compact" and aggressively competed for sales with what he called the "gas-guzzling dinosaurs." Rambler sales started to skyrocket, together with sales of imported small cars. By 1959 the former had 6 percent of the total market and foreign cars 10 percent—up from 0.7 percent in four years. By this time the Big Three had seen the light and put through crash programs to create the Corvair, Valiant, and Falcon. By 1962 cars less than 200 inches long accounted for over 40 percent of the market.

It is obvious that the Big Three had misjudged the public taste; people were not satisfied with simply bigger and bigger automobiles. They announced their determination in no uncertain terms by switching their patronage. But what is even more interesting is that the car makers were right in their conception that Americans did not want merely practical, utilitarian transportation. In large measure American car buyers acted toward the compacts like the woman who saves $10 on a dress and then rewards herself for her frugality by spending $50 on a hat, purse, and shoes. The compacts were quickly loaded with more powerful engines, automatic transmissions, power steering, air conditioning, and other goodies, thereby taking them out of the class for which they were presumably designed. Lee Iacocca, vice-president at Ford, expresses it by saying that the American people demand "economy—no matter what it costs."

What the public was demanding—and what it got—was a much wider range of choice. It really does not seem to want small cars as such. Currently, the smaller cars are starting to get a little bigger; even American Motors, home of the compact, offered a larger car in 1965. But the people have compelled the four principal car makers to provide 323 different models of compacts and standard cars to choose from; plus an almost incalculable number of combinations that can be made with engine and transmission changes, paint and upholstery choices, power brakes, power steering, and numerous other pluses. The assembly line, which was presumably created to produce millions of black Fords, must now handle so many variables that it is possible for a line to run indefinitely without producing two successive identical cars.

To help divine the public taste the sibyls of Detroit display dream cars, or idea cars, of far-out experimental design. Some of these are used as actual test cars for new engineering ideas. Some of them do not even run. When you stand at an auto show, drooling over a dream car, there may be a hidden microphone recording your opinion of it on tape. If that tape discloses that most people who looked at that car commented favorably on its cantilevered steering wheel, you may be sure that work on getting the bugs out of a cantilevered steering wheel will be pushed forward and that you may see this feature in a production car a few years hence.

These display cars range from those that are strictly dreams through those that are likely to be cars of the future, to some that are virtually ready for production. The Corvair Monza was an ex-

In their efforts to gauge the public taste, Detroit stylists rely heavily on dream cars—experimental designs that often do not even run. Above, an experimental car, which later became Firebird IV, begins to take shape in the styling studios of GM.

General Motors Corporation

ample of the last. This deluxe version of a Corvair with bucket seats, a stick shift, and wire wheels was created as a display car and received such immediate acclaim that it went from the show pedestal into production. The Aurora station wagon that Ford displayed at the 1964–65 World's Fair may be an example of the second, which might appear a few years hence with some of its "way-out" unique features modified for production. On the other hand, it seems unlikely that anything like GM's three-wheel Runabout, with built-in shopping carts, will go into production in the foreseeable future.

The idea cars frequently expose elements that are almost certain to represent future innovations in production cars if the public is sufficiently responsive. A simple example of this is the power-operated top in a convertible, which started in a show car. A possible example for the future is a new rear lighting system recently displayed by GM. This involves blue tail lights, amber lights that go on when the car decelerates, and red lights that function only for braking and turn signaling. This would make it clearly evident when a driver slows down or applies his brakes in a line of traffic, because the red and amber lights would stand out sharply in a pattern of blue tail lights.

Despite the great fanfare that takes place each September, when the industry presents the next year's cars in TV spectaculars and gaudy color spreads in national magazines, most of these cars are not new by a dictionary definition of the word. In most years, for most cars, the change is a face lift, which involves alterations of sheet metal and interior and exterior trim, layout, and decorative features. Detroit stylists have a genius for devising various ways for bending sheet metal to make a car look different without costly structural changes. This is not to say that there is not a constant styling and engineering evolution—but it is usually an evolution rather than a revolution. It must be thus. Even with minor mechanical changes a face lift accounts for about $125 of the cost of a car. To build 323 models every year that were new from the tire treads up would increase the cost of cars out of all reason.

The stylist and the engineer are severely limited in what they would like to do by what is economically feasible. General Motors makes a car with a fiber glass body, the Corvette. It might be desirable to make all bodies of fiber glass. But even mammoth General Motors could not tear down, at one fell swoop, the Fisher Body plants in which all other GM bodies are made of metal and replace them with factories equipped to handle fiber glass.

Also, for reasons of production economy, designers must be concerned with interchangeability. Just as interchangeability of parts is an essential of mass production in engines, interchangeability of components is essential to mass production of cars. This is an aspect of the business that Detroit does not like to talk about. The buyer of a Buick would not like to be reminded that, although he paid several hundred dollars more for his car, he is getting the same basic body as the owner of a Chevrolet; nor is the attention of the Mercury buyer called to the fact that the engine in his car is also used in a less expensive Ford.

Ford's 289-cubic-inch V-8 engine starts life in the foundry with the same block as the 260-cubic-inch engine; the difference comes with a shift of bits on the boring line. General Motors bodies, which are offered in 140 styles and 843 trim combinations, start life at Fisher Body with three basic structural types on which are constructed seventy-one basic shells.

Back in 1960 General Motors management decided to make a new body in a somewhat larger size for the 1964 Chevelle. The Body Development Studio and the Advanced Styling Studio—both of which are independent of any production division—were ordered to create a body that would also be usable on the smaller 1964 Pontiacs, Oldsmobiles, and Buicks. When this basic body was approved, the divisional styling studios took over to adapt it to a Chevelle, a Pontiac Tempest, an Oldsmobile 85, and a Buick Special, each distinctive in appearance.

All had to conform on certain elements: common upper structure designs for sedans, coupes, convertibles, and station wagons; a common cowl height; a common windshield aperture. Each could have a separate instrument panel, but the stylists had to use the same basic mechanical components to design four instrument panels that varied in appearance. As an example, Buick and Oldsmobile use exactly the same heater control. One studio installed it horizontally, the other vertically.

Although certain models require separate front ends, rear ends, hood treatments, rear decks, and rear quarter panels, these all must be integrated with the basic body structure and design. The division

The Median, one of three sporty models designed in 1961.

The Allegro was built as an idea car in 1962.

A dozen variations of this car, the Ventura, were designed in 1962.

The first design to be called a Mustang —a two-passenger open sports car.

This approaches the car that finally became the Mustang. It was originally called the Cougar.

An experimental version of the slightly revised Cougar was built in late 1963 and called Mustang II.

This is the final sketch of the production Mustang.

Steps in the styling development of the popular Ford Mustang. The first sketch was produced in 1961. The car was introduced in 1964.

Ford Motor Company

style studios have complete latitude, subject to predetermined cost, on interior trim and decoration, headlights, tail-lighting arrangement, bumper shapes, wheel covers, grill textures, ornamentation, and countless other things. By clever handling of these elements each comes out with a car that looks different but has the same basic body as three other cars.

In a sense, this is rather like the comparison between the European and the American bodybuilders of the old classic cars—but on a large scale. The Europeans built one body for one car. The Americans designed one body, built fifty copies, and varied the cars with paint and trim for less than half the European cost. The Buick owner may not like to feel that he is riding in a Chevelle body, but if the body of his car was specially built for his car only, he would have to pay a good deal more for it.

An example of the birth of a car that is essentially new rather than primarily a revision of an existing car is Ford's Mustang. In 1961 the Corporate Projects Studio at the Ford Styling Center started to play with shapes for some sporty little vehicles. In this Ford, as well as GM and Chrysler, may have been inspired by the knowledge that the bumper crop of post-World War II babies were growing up and would soon be prospective car buyers.

The Projects Studio first sketched three cars that they called the Mina, the Median, and the Open Sports Car. Of these, management liked the Median best; it had the feel of a poor man's Thunderbird. Independently of this, the Studio designed a car called the Allegro and built two of them as idea cars. The Allegros were well received in European automobile shows. The Studio then came up with two more cars: a four-passenger Avventura, of which thirteen variations were developed, and a two-passenger Mustang, an idea car that aroused enthusiasm in shows here and abroad.

But market research, which indicated that the under-twenty-five group ranked a car's appearance as a first consideration, also disclosed that they preferred four seats to two seats by sixteen to one. So, after going through the Mina, the Median, the Open Sports Car, the Allegro, the Avventura, and the Mustang, three styling studios were placed in competition: Corporate Projects Studio, Ford Studio and Lincoln-Mercury Studio. In all, they submitted seven designs, all flowing from the work previously done and the reaction to the idea cars.

The design of the Ford Studio was selected and, at that time, called the Cougar. It was a distinctly different-looking car, with a long hood, short rear deck, and an overall look remotely resembling European sports racing cars. A show car version was made from the initial clay model and presented to the public, labeled Mustang II. This is a case of what was called an idea car actually being ready for production, although, if the public had responded adversely, the project could have been withdrawn.

From that point on it was a question of spending $50 million for tools and fighting the "battle of the inches" to get the car into production. Engineering wanted the hood an inch higher to accommodate the radiator. Styling won this battle, and a new, lower radiator was developed. When Henry Ford II first sat in the rear seat he asked for an inch more leg room. Styling objected that this would impair the overall lines of the car, but Mr. Ford got his inch. After all, his name *is* on the building.

Unlike cars such as the Mustang, which involve fairly radical new concepts in design, most new models are not born in the advance styling studio. They start as a "package" conceived by a divisional product-planning group and presented to management for approval. In putting this package together the group first decides what kind of a car they are aiming at for the future in terms of performance, weight, size, and price. Based on reports from development engineering they take into consideration what mechanical improvements will be ready for the upcoming model and what new materials will be available. These things will determine the car's performance and, perhaps, affect its appearance. From production engineering they learn what new processes may be available that might influence costs and, again, appearance. As an instance, when spot welding replaced riveting, it gave designers much more latitude in shaping metal.

This package contains the broad, overall specifications for the car and goes to styling and product engineering for more specific development. Unlike styling, which is a repetitious operation of producing a new model each year, much of engineering is a continuous operation not initially related to any specific upcoming model. In all four companies, groups of engineers are constantly working on improving each component of the car. Engineering may advise the product-planning group that an entirely new system of brakes, on which they have been working for several years, has reached the point where it

The artist-stylist sketches—the sculpture-stylist interprets his designs in three dimensions in clay.

can be incorporated in the model then under consideration; or that a joint project with an oil company indicates a new fuel that will permit the development of a smaller engine with better performance characteristics.

Meanwhile, other engineers are constantly working with outside industries to improve the raw materials of the car. This work may lead to something big in a specific future model, such as a significant weight saving through the use of lighter metals. Or it may result in many things that are so insignificant that the car owner is not even conscious of them, like substituting plastic for metal in certain bushings where the chemical product will outperform metal or equal it and save fifty cents a car in production costs. Other engineers will work on interpreting the general specifications of the package into detailed specifications, designing hundreds or thousands of parts that will have to be changed because of different requirements in dimensions or performance.

In the divisional styling studios the product-planning package is first interpreted in sketches that indicate the general shape of the new model. Sketches lead to rough clay models, full size, two-dimensional renderings, and finished full-sized clay models. These models are covered with a colored plastic sheet to simulate a paint job, with the bright work finished in foil to represent chrome.

It must be rather frustrating to the artistic temperament of the stylists that the final decision on their work is made by men who have no special qualifications for judging artistic merit. Frederic Donner, Chairman of the Board of GM, was originally an accountant, as was Chrysler's president, Lynn Townsend. Ford's president, Arjay Miller, was a statistician. Most top-management men have backgrounds in sales, finance, production, or administration; nevertheless, theirs is the final word on design.

At times this system has caused problems for the designer. Walter Chrysler's successor in his company was K. T. Keller, a very big and *very* corpulent man. There used to be a story around Chrysler

General Motors Corporation

The most important tool for evaluating a new automobile design is the full-sized clay model. When smoothly finished, it will be covered with colored plastic and gleaming foil to simulate an actual car.

Interior dimensions and arrangements are determined with the aid of a metal dummy that can be adjusted to almost any position of virtually any sized individual.

Glass road on automobile proving ground. As the car moves along, a camera records the contact between the tires and pavement. The photos show what happens during experimentally induced "shimmy," rapid braking, or acceleration.

styling studios, which may or may not be true, that K. T. Keller would not approve any new model in which he was not comfortable in the driver's seat. Because Mr. Keller's requirements for comfort differed widely from those of the average American housewife, there followed a series of Chrysler cars with an inordinate amount of room behind the steering wheel.

While the outside of the car is taking shape, another group of stylists are working on interior design and layout. Seat bucks are built, tested for comfort and for other factors, with real passengers and articulated dummies, and rebuilt again and again. Interior hardware and instrument panels are designed; fabrics, carpets, and plastics are considered for upholstery. Before the car is ready for production, everything that is visible, inside and out, will be the subject of a specific design decision, from the entire front-end appearance, involving grill, bumper, and headlights, to the knob on the crank that raises and lowers the windows.

When the clay model and the interior design are approved, they are reproduced in a fiber glass model, with chromium-plated bright work. This model, which contains actual seats, upholstery, instrument panel, wheels and wheel covers, and so on, is so perfect that it is indistinguishable from an actual car unless one crawls underneath and finds that it is built on a wooden frame. The fiber glass model is principally for show within the locked confines of the styling studio auditorium. Management admires it frequently and shows it on occasion to a few specially honored visiting firemen.

Detroit makes a fetish of this secrecy—surely, to some extent, with tongue in cheek. Although security may be possible in the advance design studios and for certain top-secret engineering projects, all of the companies have a fairly good idea of what competition is doing about a routine model change rather early in the design cycle. Detroit is a closely knit community whose members live, talk, and dream automobiles. There is some personnel changeover among the companies, and two members of the same family sometimes work for different companies. Chrysler once had a stylist whose son was a stylist for a GM division and lived at home. Each man worked in the locked and guarded precincts of his respective company; the companies assumed that they did not talk to each other at home. Outside personnel, such as suppliers serving all the automobile companies,

After running 25,000 miles under all kinds of conditions, test cars are completely disassembled and the parts displayed for inspection by engineers.

are necessarily admitted. Yet the styling studios, engineering laboratories, and proving grounds are rigidly patrolled by company police, and all other outsiders who pass the gates are considered potential spies. There is a good deal of show business in the automobile business.

After final approval, the clay model, rather than the fiber glass one, becomes sacred, because its surface can be worked to finer accuracy. Casts are taken from the clay, from which die models, usually mahogany, are constructed by pattern makers. From them the actual steel production dies will be made. At the same time, a number of hand-made prototype cars are constructed, with each body part hammered by hand over metal blocks and welded into finished cars identical with production models.

All proving grounds have much specialized testing equipment. This wind tunnel can create a 125-mph hurricane.

The next step is pilot-line production, to provide cars for testing. Cars are driven an estimated 40 million miles a year on the test roads and tracks of the industry's proving grounds. If an average driver had started before the pyramids were built, he would not yet have accumulated that mileage. This driving is done under all kinds of conditions, in all kinds of weather, and on all kinds of roads—from concrete so smooth that, when wet, it is more slippery than ice to a Belgian block road that is engineered to give a car ten times the punishment of a normal highway. The test route includes a sand pit, a mud pit, a salt-water trough, and hills up to sixty degrees.

A standard test for a new model is to drive it 25,000 miles and then completely disassemble it. The thousands of parts are laid out on long tables for inspection by engineers. In addition to visual inspection, wear is judged by sophisticated measuring devices and extreme magnification. Internal stress in some parts is determined by X ray.

In addition to roads, the proving grounds have complex laboratory testing devices. A wind tunnel can create a 125-mile-an-hour hurri-

A dramatic illustration of a car in the proving-grounds cold room.

Ford Motor Company

cane. Temperature- and humidity-controlled rooms can create any climatic condition that might be found from Anchorage, Alaska, to the equator. A ride simulator permits engineers to test and measure the reaction of the suspension system to any conditions the car might experience on a road, and an analogue computor analyzes the car's motions. A noise and vibration laboratory analyzes these aspects of the car's performance. Electromagnetic shakers submit the vehicle to conditions more severe than it would ever meet in use, and electronic equipment not only measures noise and vibration but traces it to its source.

Assembly is the final phase. When visiting an assembly plant one is fascinated, standing at the point where the front subassembly—fenders, grill, and so on—meets the rest of the car by speculating what would happen if the front of a white Pontiac were to meet the rest of a red Buick. One can visualize the entire plant shutting down while people frantically search for a white Pontiac on which to put the white front and a red front to put on the red Buick. An accident like that never happens. An intricate system, with schedule and code numbers that start all of the elements of a given car at several different places, makes the elements meet each other at exactly the right time and place, even though in some GM plants Chevys, Pontiacs, Oldsmobiles, and Buicks are all mixed up on the same lines.

Basically the method of assembly, except for the complex control system, is merely a refinement of the system by which Model Ts were assembled. There are four major assembly lines. The engine line starts with engine blocks and delivers complete engines, including electrical systems, transmissions, and accessories. The body line starts with body elements—underbody panels, sides, and quarter and roof panels—which are welded together in precision fixtures, receive their doors and deck lids, and then go through the painting process, accompanied by separate fenders and hood for each specific body. The fenders go on, to become part of a front subassembly with grill and lights, while the body gets its instrument panel, heater and/or radio, if specified.

The chassis assembly line starts with a frame, upside down, to which are affixed suspension components, differential, drive shaft, brakes, and manual or power steering. It is then flipped over, fuel lines and exhaust system are installed, the engine is dropped in, and

HOW AN AUTOMOBILE IS ASSEMBLED.

Left: The frame at the beginning of the assembly line. Right: The rear-axle assembly is added.

Left: After the frame is turned over, the engine is dropped in. Right: All wheel bolts are placed and tightened in one operation.

Left: A finishing operation on the body. Right: The body drop.

Ford Motor Company

Left: The front assembly is added. Right: The car comes off the line.

wheels with inflated tires are added. The final assembly line starts at the body drop, where body and chassis meet. The fenders and grill, as a separate subassembly, are added, then the hood and bumpers, and then air conditioning, if ordered. The car receives its gasoline, oil, and antifreeze, is started up, and rolls off the line under its own power to what is called a roll test stand. Here its operation is checked while it runs on four large drums sunk into the floor, as if on a treadmill.

None of this is as simple as it sounds, although it is done in such an orderly manner that it looks simple. To say that the bodies are painted gives the impression that they go through a spray bath and get a coat of paint. Actually, the steps are these: The body is first washed with a chromic acid solution to etch the metal. After it is rinsed with water and dried, sealer materials are applied to joints and edges. Next comes a black pre-prime coat, which is heavier on door edges and points prone to chipping. Then a red primer coat is added, and the body goes through a drying oven, after which welded seams are coated to make them waterproof. After going through another oven, the body is wet-sanded, washed, and dried again. Finally, the body goes through a brightly lighted spray booth and gets a finish coat of paint. If it is to be a two-tone job, this operation is repeated before it goes into the "reflow" oven, which raises the temperature of the acrylic lacquer almost to the molten state before it dries to impart a "mirror" finish.

As the final step in assembly and testing, the car is picked up after the roll test by an overhead conveyor that takes it down a line on which final processing operations are performed. Next, it is carried through a waterproofing test booth in which a partial vacuum is created in the car, and the car is sprayed with water under high pressure. It then passes through the soft-trim department, where door and ceiling linings, carpets, seat backs, and cushions are added. After a final inspection it gets an O.K. sticker and a coat of spray wax and goes to the loading yard to await a trailer truck or a freight car.

While all this is going on, the plant superintendent sits in an office faced by the glass fronts of several machines, through which pass paper tapes on which a pen is making a straight line. If one of the pens starts to make a squiggle, bells ring, lights flash, and people come charging out of offices. An assembly line has stopped. When this happens all of the policy making, the planning, the "co-ordinated decentralization," the research, the engineering, the styling, and the testing are brought to naught. When a car is born, delivery cannot be interrupted. In the final analysis the health of the giant that gives birth to these 8 million mobile status symbols is dependent on those lines moving, slowly and steadily, but as inexorably as the march of time.

Cities across the country are seeking ways to solve their number-one problem—the traffic jam. In many cases, their efforts result in elaborate superhighways, such as Chicago's Northwest Expressway, above, which shuttles cars back and forth from the suburbs and relieves congestion on downtown streets.

NINE: THE NEW AMERICA

On that night in November 1900 when a handful of New York's Four Hundred turned out to view their first automobile show, there were about 76 million other Americans who did not go to Madison Square Garden. Four out of ten of them lived in cities. The rest lived mostly on farms; the word *suburbs* had not yet been widely heard in the land. Fifty years later, when there were 40 million automobiles in the United States, six out of ten of America's 150 million people lived in urban places. In 1980, when there will be 245 million people, eight out of ten of them will live in urban areas occupying about 2 percent of the nation's land. And these city and suburban folk are expected to own 80 million of the 100 million cars that will then exist.

Therein lies America's most pressing problem and perplexing paradox. By 1980 there will be one car for each 2.4 people in the land, giving Americans far more potential mobility than they now have. But, unless much more is done about roads, the great increase in cars and their concentration in urban areas will leave most Americans sitting in a perpetual traffic jam.

Today, in every large city, in every state capital, and increasingly in Washington, D.C., traffic experts and city and social planners are seeking solutions to this problem. On the West Coast the Rand Corporation—a "think factory"—is spending half a million dollars of Ford Foundation money to study the question of movement in urban America. On the East Coast the Massachusetts Institute of Technology has an equal grant for a similar study. In between there is not a single large city that is not trying desperately and belatedly to plan some way for people to get into it, get out of it, and move around in it. The Automobile Manufacturers Association has given nine separate grants to colleges, universities, and research agencies for urban transportation and traffic studies; and the national government has ruled that no city shall be eligible for certain Federal urban renewal moneys unless its request is accompanied by a workable transportation plan.

Forty-five years ago Henry Ford, who knew little about the subject, said: "One thing you can set down as sure is that cities are doomed. Not immediately, but perhaps much sooner than even the most adventurous are willing to believe." Ten years ago Frank Lloyd Wright, who should have known something about the subject, said, "Further centralizations of any American city are only postponements of the city's end." Some experts of the type who delight in planning people's lives condemn the automobile as the curse of modern urban civilization and maintain that something should be done about the American's attitude toward his "mechanical mistress." In the opinion of one expert: "We have put too much emphasis on the automobile in our daily lives. It is this one-dimensional thinking that has got us into trouble. Looking around the American city one would think that the principal purpose of existence has come to be not a better life, but longer cars to move us greater distances at higher speeds. Too many people apparently think that owning and operating automobiles is why we were born, why we are given an education, why people come together in cities." Another critic claims that America has become a land of Carboys, and adds: "If Gulliver landed on our shores today, he would find not the tiny Lilliputians nor the giant Brobdingnagians, but people who are more like centaurs. They are equipped with four wheels, however, instead of four legs. In the land of the Carboys, Gulliver would have said, the ultimate disgrace is not to be moving."

The embryo of the urban traffic problem started to take shape in the 1920s, with the beginning of the flow of population to the suburbs. At the time the great cry was for better roads in the country. No one recognized that there would be a great urban transportation crisis; people still rode on trolley cars. The road building of the mid-thirties, with Federal aid, was largely to provide rural highways. Also, between the end of the twenties and the mid-forties there was first a depression and then a war, which slowed down automobile expansion. From 1930 to 1946 the number of cars increased only about 5 million, from 23 million to 28 million. The explosion has taken place since the end of the war, when the number of cars has risen about 42 million. Automobile registration more than doubled between 1945 and 1960 and is still rising at an increasing rate.

Meanwhile, the urban population pattern is changing within the metropolitan areas. In 1950, cities contained 49 million people, their suburbs 35 million. By 1970 the suburbs will have 78 million, to 66 million in the cities. And suburbanites insist on using their cars for every move they make away from home; indeed, in the suburbs of many cities they have no choice. In 1946 Americans made about 24 billion local trips by public carrier. By 1960 this was down to 11 billion trips, half of them on buses that use the same roads as passenger cars. By contrast, in 1946 there were 25 billion trips by private cars; in 1960 there were over 50 billion in metropolitan areas. Railroad passenger traffic has declined 80 percent since the end of the war, mostly as the result of losing commuters to buses and cars.

In most metropolitan areas the density of population is steadily decreasing as people spread out from the downtown area of the central city, and the suburbs incorporate previously rural areas. In cities it dropped from an average of 7,800 per square mile to 5,800 between 1950 and 1960; in suburban areas the decline was from 3,200 to 2,600. This makes for a constant increase in the mileage of urban automobile trips. In 1940 urban motor vehicle mileage was 150 billion miles. The mileage in 1960 was 332 billion. By 1980 it is estimated at 800 billion miles. The average urban resident who drove 2,900 miles in 1960 will drive 4,100 miles twenty years later. And suburban car ownership is going up much faster than suburban population. As an example, a study in depth of the Chicago area projects a population rise of 51 percent between 1956 and 1980, an increase of auto registration of 94 percent, and an increase of multi-car families of 170 percent.

The most recent change in the pattern of life in urban America is the flight of jobs to the suburbs. As recently as 1954, 65 percent of jobs were in central cities, 35 percent in the suburbs. By 1975 it is estimated that city jobs will decrease to about 44 percent, and suburban jobs will rise to 56 percent. In some sections of the country this trend is already much greater. On the perimeter freeway circumscribing Boston some 227 companies occupy seventeen industrial parks and employ 28,000 workers (with plenty of parking space). Only thirty-nine companies were in operation in this suburban area prior to the completion of the freeway.

On the edges of many suburban towns near New York, campus-like layouts have been built to house the laboratories and research facilities of such industrial giants as Bell Telephone, Standard Oil Co. (N.J.), International Business Machines, and many more. Other examples of this type of flight from the city to obtain more accessible and congenial working conditions are GM's Technical Center and Ford's Research and Engineering facilities, both of which are well removed from Detroit's central city.

And the automobile industry is adjusting itself to the new decentralized production that is taking manufacturing out of the increasingly inaccessible city. The old plants still exist and hum in Detroit, Flint, Lansing, and other Michigan manufacturing centers, but the modern trend is typified by GM's most recent assembly plant in California. This is called the Fremont plant, because the city of Fremont, a satellite of San Francisco, is the nearest community to it, but one cannot see the city from the plant. Rather, it is located not in relation to a city but on the Nimitz Freeway, twenty-three miles from Oakland. The plant itself occupies 34.4 acres. Its roads and parking lots cover almost twice as much space—77.2 acres—to provide room for 2,143 cars—better than one for each two employees. The 4,100 people who work here are San Francisco suburbanites, but it is probable that most of them seldom see San Francisco unless they are Giant baseball fans; almost everything else they need they will find in the suburban area—and with a parking lot beside it.

In the early days of suburban expansion the downtown area of the central city was still the place to work and to do most shopping. The new groups of houses were merely "bedroom communities," where commuters came to sleep. There were food stores, druggists, plumbers, and doctors in the nearby suburban town, but, except for all but such basic day-to-day necessities, the suburbanite relied on

General Motors assembly plant near Fremont, California, typifies the modern factory—located beside a freeway, removed from the congested city, and with acres of parking space.

the city. The first major change was in food stores. The supermarket had been born in the city, but chain store operators soon realized that the shops on the narrow streets of the suburban town would not be able to compete with a supermarket on the edge of town surrounded by acres of parking space.

Quickly, other stores grouped themselves around the supermarket, to make shopping centers for all the necessities—food, liquor, drugs, laundry and cleaning, and so on. Then the downtown bank opened a branch; a beauty parlor and barber shop made their appearance. Today such shopping centers are providing more and more necessities and leisure-time services. There has been an increase of bowling alleys in such locations, and for the first time in twenty years the number of indoor motion-picture theaters in the country is increasing as movie houses are opened in many local shopping centers.

The next step in decentralized living, was the mammoth single-story discount store surrounded by its acres of parking area either in a shopping complex, or, increasingly, set down in what seems to be the middle of nowhere but beside a good road that leads to adjacent populous areas. One of the first of these was built in northern New Jersey about fifteen years ago. At the time it was built it sat alone beside a through road in the country, near the town of Paramus. Today, it is the center of a line of large retail establishments stretching for several miles along the road, behind vast parking areas that would seem to accommodate all the cars in North Jersey. Most people within a ten- or fifteen-mile radius seldom go into the neighboring cities of New York, Newark, or Paterson to shop—or bowl or skate. They go to Paramus, although few of them have ever seen the actual town. Quality and price of what they buy here are im-

One result of the automobile: the suburban shopping center. This is Detroit's Northland—bounded on three sides by express highways and surrounded by ample parking space.

The J. L. Hudson Company

portant, but of paramount concern is that they can drive to the retail complex on unclogged roads and park conveniently when they get there. Parking space is becoming the deciding factor in the location of many business establishments.

Another modern merchandising trend is the establishment of branches by downtown city stores in suburban towns or in newly created shopping complexes on the perimeter of the city, like Detroit's Northland, the Southdale Shopping Center in Minneapolis, Shopper's World near Boston, and the Roosevelt Field center on Long Island. In New York, Saks Fifth Avenue is still on Fifth Avenue, but it is also in three suburbs. R. H. Macy and Company advertises that it has the world's largest store at 34th Street and Broadway, but it also has seven branches on Long Island and in Westchester County; and when the city of New Haven built an enormous multilevel parking garage in the center of its downtown area, R. H. Macy promptly built a store immediately adjacent to it and matching it level for level.

There is some difference of opinion as to the handling of the parking problem of the city. All planners agree that there is no solution to city traffic unless street parking is eliminated and that no new city construction should be permitted that does not provide off-street parking for the cars it will attract. Some experts are more pessimistic than others. One estimates that if the automobile population continues to increase at the present rate and the proportion of trips into cities remains the same, all of the downtown land area of large cities would be needed for parking by 1980. This is certainly a far-fetched projection. Another engineer figures, more realistically, that a square mile will provide parking space for 90,000 cars, on one level, including aisles to maneuver. If all of the cars in an urban area were to be parked away from home at the same time, they would require between 1 and 2 percent of the land in the area. Because streets take about 20 percent of the land in most cities, it would seem reasonable to provide at least one quarter to one half of 1 percent for those cars that are standing still at any given time so as to leave the streets free for cars that are moving.

The road crisis in urban areas developed from a combination of several factors, principally the fact that most roads are built by states, either with or without Federal aid, and rural areas have had a preponderance of representation in state legislatures, with the

1939 preview of today's highways. In 1939 visitors to the General Motors exhibit at the New York World's Fair were given a glimpse of today's highway system with this miniature scale layout. Few imagined that a quarter century later this type of highway would be almost commonplace.

result that urban areas were consistently shortchanged on the allocation of road-building money. In many places there has been a conflict of interest among various pressure groups—rapid transit interests, Downtown Merchants Associations, and others who are more concerned about what some type of transportation will do for them than they are about what it will do for the area and its population. Every metropolitan area represents several independent city, town, and county governments, each with its own ideas. And the cost of urban highway construction is so great that there is a temptation to build ten to fifty miles of rural road instead of one mile of urban road for the same amount of money, even though the latter may be far more necessary.

First to dramatize a proposed solution to the urban traffic problem was General Motors. In its exhibit at the 1939–40 New York's World Fair was displayed a "City of Tomorrow." Industrial designer Norman Bel Geddes created the model city, based on GM's projections of traffic flow and highway needs in the future. When the plans were completed, there was some discussion among the more conservative elements of GM's top management as to whether the corporation should sponsor anything so fantastic. Bel Geddes had hotels and office buildings with the lower stories devoted to parking, elevated or sunken high-speed highways cutting through the city, pedestrian and vehicular traffic on different levels, perimeter roads encircling the city to carry through-traffic around it and connect the various sections of its suburbs, and, particularly, multilane limited-access highways sweeping through the suburbs into the city with centers of commerce and industry clustered around the interchanges on the highways.

Everything that was shown in GM's "City of Tomorrow" became a reality in less than twenty years. The one aspect of the plan that offers the most promise for preventing the virtual future stoppage of urban traffic is the freeway, but nothing much was done about building them as an immediate result of GM's exhibit.

During the 1940s the Federal government came to the conclusion that the national economy and national defense required a better highway system, and the Public Roads Administration, in cooperation

PLANNED ROUTES OF
THE NATIONAL SYSTEM OF INTERSTATE
AND DEFENSE HIGHWAYS

The greatest public works program in history—a network of highways connecting 42 state capitals and 90 percent of the cities of population over 50,000—was begun under the Federal Highway Act of 1956. Scheduled for completion in 1972, the system is designed for the traffic needs of 1975.

with state authorities, started a study of what became known as the National System of Interstate and Defense Highways. This became a reality in 1956, with the passage of the Federal Aid Highway Act, under which the central government has undertaken the greatest public works program in history by paying 90 percent of the cost of a 41,000-mile network of limited-access highways connecting forty-two state capitals and about 90 percent of cities with more than 50,000 population.

It is planned that this will be finished by 1972 and that it will be adequate for 1975 traffic needs. Actually, most of the mileage will be adequate much farther into the future, but some vital miles will be less than adequate when they are completed. The wide, limited-access highways stretching for hundreds of miles through the country-side are good things to have, for the future. But much of the mileage serves no very necessary purpose today. One reason advanced for not having the system paid for by the user in the form of tolls is that only about 8,500 miles would carry enough traffic to support itself.

The vital mileage of the system now under construction is the 6,700 miles of freeways through urban areas and the perimeter roads around these areas. It is estimated that by 1980 the urban sections of the Interstate system will have a traffic volume per mile of over 50,000 cars a day; the rural sections will have only 10,000. This will considerably overtax the urban routes and leave much excess capacity for the rural sections. By 1980 urbanized areas will have expanded to embrace 9,600 miles of the proposed system.

The Interstate system was conceived as a network to carry traffic *between* cities; any provision for carrying traffic within urban areas is largely incidental. The extent to which urban freeways are being built as a part of this system to serve any given city depends on the city's location in relation to other cities rather than on its particular needs. Hence crossroads cities like Chicago and St. Louis will have complete systems of freeways radiating from them; while Miami, located in the southeast extremity of the country, is served by only one Interstate route. Because of its location, Nashville has one of the most complete Interstate systems of any city of its size; Phoenix, already larger as a metropolitan area and growing more rapidly, is allotted only two roads. Putting it another way, the urbanized area served by each mile of Interstate route ranges from one square mile in Hartford to four in Miami and almost six in Reno.

Obviously the mammoth Interstate Highway program will be but little more than a beginning and a long way from the final answer to the urban traffic problem. If much of urban America—where eight out of ten Americans will soon live—is not to become a permanent traffic jam, a great deal more is needed. Present studies indicate that approximately 16,000 miles of urban freeway will be required to catch up to traffic needs—about 5,600 miles more than the roads that now exist or are covered by present plans.

Urban freeways cost money; a great deal of money. An extreme example is a five-mile stretch of highway crossing the Bronx in New York that cost $22.5 million *per mile*. But no matter how much they cost they will ultimately save money. The limited-access expressway carries about four times the number of vehicles per lane per hour as any other type of road, and moves them at two or three times the speed. It is estimated that the relatively few sections of urban freeways in operation in 1960 saved about 1.69 cents per vehicle-mile in operating costs and 2.66 cents in time saved. By 1980 total operating and accident savings on urban areas of the Interstate system are projected at $4 billion per year; on the rural sections, an additional $1 billion. Annual time savings by 1980 will be about 4 billion hours, 80 percent of it on urban sections. This has been valued at more than $6.5 billion per year. In short, the *annual* savings brought about by the Interstate system by 1980 will equal more than 25 percent of the total cost of the system.

Another aspect of the economics of freeways has to do with land usage. Modern urban planning requires a great deal less land to move a great deal more traffic than the old-style system, in which street layouts were determined by walking rather than riding distances. Under the old system streets took upward of 20 percent of urban land; freeways take from 1.5 to 2 percent to carry the same amount of traffic. Where they are already in use freeway systems take care of about 50 to 60 percent of traffic in the areas they serve; local streets are merely access roads to off-freeway land and do not need to be so plentiful. Commercial centers tend to cluster around freeway access points with local streets in a radial pattern through surrounding residential areas, not in the gridiron pattern of frequent cross streets that were necessary when the housewife had to walk to the corner store.

In many cities a complete and *well-planned* program of building freeways will go a long way toward solving the mounting urban traffic problem and preventing ultimate stagnation. This is particularly true in many western cities that have grown up in the motor age and are automobile adjusted. Los Angeles, which led the parade in building freeways in the early 1950s, is often accused of undesirable urban sprawl. But this characteristic of the city is rapidly being changed. In an article on this change, *Life* magazine recently reported: "Los Angeles, seemingly boundless in size and energy, has taken on the one great attribute it has so far lacked—that of a cohesive city. The tremendous sprawl of Los Angeles across the arid hills and valleys gave it the reputation of being many suburbs in search of a city. The expansion continues. But more and more Los Angeles looks, acts, and sounds like a city . . . . More important than the Dodgers or civic buildings in giving Los Angeles its new personality are the ribbons of freeway which are gradually tying the city's scattered pieces together."

It is possible to get around most of the Los Angeles metropolitan area fairly easily in an automobile, although 95 percent of its travel is by private car. About 6 billion passenger-movements per year are now being made by automobile in the Los Angeles area—almost four times as many as the passengers who use the New York subway and bus systems in a year.

Shortly after it opened, much was heard about traffic congestion on the Hollywood Freeway, a good indication of the necessity for and the popularity of the roadway. This link in the southern California city's extensive highway system was completed in 1954 and was designed to carry an ultimate future volume of 100,000 cars a day. By the end of the first year traffic volume had reached the rate of 168,-000 cars a day. As of 1962 Los Angeles had 242 miles of freeway in use or budgeted against an estimated need, in terms of the 1962 car population, of 515 miles. California is far ahead of any other populous state in its attack on the traffic problem. In 1959 the state passed a bill calling for a 12,000-mile system of freeways by 1980 —almost twice as many miles for this single state as the total mileage of urban freeways provided for the nation under the Interstate Highway system. There are many who feel that even this vast program will be inadequate by the time it is completed.

A factor that may loom large in the way urban America lives is

California Highway Department

Los Angeles is one of few cities in America that has grown up in the age of the automobile. Consequently, it has avoided some of the traffic problems of older cities and has one of the best freeway systems in the country. The Los Angeles Freeway, completed in 1954, was designed to carry an ultimate future volume of 100,000 cars per day. As soon as one year later, its daily traffic was 168,000 cars.

Automobile Manufacturers Association

Model for the "new town" Columbia, which will be built midway between Washington, D.C., and Baltimore. It will provide housing, shopping, schooling, recreation, and community facilities for 125,000 people.

a recent development known by a number of names—satellite cities, planned communities, cluster cities, or, more often, simply as "new towns." The basic concept is a self-sufficient community, in which almost everybody has a car, built outside of the present urban area where rural land is still relatively cheap. At present there are more than twenty such projects in various stages of development, sponsored by private enterprise with much money borrowed from insurance companies.

The typical new town covers about 12,000 acres, nearly twenty square miles, and will have a population of from 60,000 to 75,000.

Generally, it consists of a group of villages, each with its own school facilities, churches, recreational areas, medical facilities, shopping centers, and so on. The villages will be connected with each other, and with a central commercial area, by a limited-access circumferential highway, and the entire community will connect with an arterial freeway running into the big central city. Within the villages, roads will be land-access loops or cul de sacs. The 15,000 to 20,000 dwelling units in the town may range from single-family units to high-rise apartments. In most cases the new town will be bordered by an industrial area, separated from the residential area by topography or landscaping, which will provide jobs for most of the population not engaged in commerce, service industries, and professional work. This is the general pattern of Columbia, a 14,000-acre new town midway between Washington and Baltimore, in which ten villages are grouped around a town center and an artificial lake.

Roads will occupy 4 or 5 percent of the land in a new town, instead of the old 20 percent plus. Most planning stresses the allocation of this space to large park and recreational areas. There will be no traffic congestion, no on-street parking in commercial areas, and no two-way traffic except on cul de sacs. In short, the towns are planned for living in urban areas in the automobile age.

And today planning is necessary for living comfortably in the automobile age. Four out of five households in America have one or more automobiles. The rate is highest in the suburbs—87 percent. It is lowest in cities of over half a million population—61 percent. Virtually all Americans who do not have a car are in the very lowest income bracket or live in big cities that they seldom leave. About 15 percent of all families and 20 percent of all car-owning families have more than one car, and the greatest concentration of these is in the suburbs. The percentage of multi-car households has doubled within the past nine years.

Some statistics on how Americans use their cars are rather surprising. About 60 percent of all trips by car are under five miles, another 20 percent under nine miles. Only 2.1 percent of trips are over fifty miles. The average length of all trips is eight miles, ranging from an average of 4.1 miles for educational, civic, and religious trips, 6.4 miles for trips to work, and 296 miles for vacation trips. About 54 percent of all trips are entirely in urban areas. Another 38 percent are partially within an urban area, leaving only 8 percent as purely rural trips.

Some additional statistics: 69 percent of all people who require transportation to get to work use an automobile, 14 percent of them as passengers. This accounts for 46 percent of all automobile trips. Approximately 85 percent of suburbanites who work in the city drive to work; 94 percent who both live and work in the suburbs use their cars. Family business, other than the work of the wage earner, accounts for 29 percent of all trips and 19 percent of all mileage. Approximately 18 percent of all trips and 34 percent of all mileage are for social and recreational purposes. Educational, civic, and religious activities account for 7.2 percent of all trips and only 3.7 percent of all mileage. Ferrying kids to school, church, scout, and other activities, of which so much is heard, does not loom as large as many believe.

The big driving day of the week in mileage is Sunday, when 28 percent of the longer social and recreational trips are made. The big day in number of trips is Friday, as a result of a combination of work, shopping, and trips for other family business. For some reason, more people drive to work on Monday than on any other day, and far more people visit a doctor or dentist on that day. Over 21 percent of medical and dental trips are made on Monday; no other day accounts for over 16 percent. The items that loom largest in recreational travel are over 15 billion miles driven for hunting and fishing, almost 300 million visits to state parks, and 112 million visits to state forests.

There are about 90 million licensed drivers in the country, 1.2 for each car. This represents about 79 percent of men over fourteen years of age and 41 percent of women. In their thirties, 91 percent of men and 56 percent of women have licenses. The average is pulled down by people over seventy, an age at which only 7.1 percent of women are licensed drivers. There are some 10 million drivers in California, over 11 percent of the nation's total, which may account for some of the congestion on the Los Angeles Freeway. In Nevada and Montana there are fewer licensed drivers than there are registered automobiles. Perhaps the most astonishing statistic is that housewives, of whose chauffeuring activities so much is written in women's magazines, drive only 10 percent of all reported passenger car mileage.

The largest age group of new car buyers are men in their forties, who account for 28.6 percent of all sales. Men in their thirties buy 22.5 percent of new cars, men over fifty-five 20.3 percent, and men under thirty 15.6 percent. The word *men* is used advisedly because almost 90 percent of all new cars are bought by males. About 45 percent of new car buyers have a college or graduate school education, 43 percent are high school graduates. The dropout has only a 10-percent chance of getting a new car. About 85 percent of new car buyers are heads of families, but only 55 percent are the sole wage earner in the family. The most popular car is the four-door sedan, which accounts for one third of all sales. Station wagons account for 19 percent of the business. Two-door sedans and hardtops, divided about equally, represent another third. Less than 7 percent of new cars are convertibles.

It has been said that in America the automobile stands in fourth place in the list of human needs and desires, after calories, sex, and a dry place to sleep. Statistics support housing as a primary desire, and there are no figures on the relative value of a mechanical mistress versus a human one. But it is by no means sure that calories come before automobiles in all household budgets. Given a choice between meeting the payments on the car and a better diet, many Americans unquestionably favor the car.

Many forecasters have been predicting for over a decade that the automobile would become relatively less important as a factor in the economy as the level of disposable personal income continued to rise. With more money to spend on other than necessities people could do and own more things. They could travel, buy boats and swimming pools, and spend more on education and cultural enrichment. It would seem that if more were spent on such things, proportionately less would be spent on automobiles. Strangely, although more money is being spent on other things, proportionately less of the family budget is spent on food and clothing, and the percentage of income spent on automobiles remains amazingly stable year after year. Except during brief periods of recession, the amount spent on buying and operating automobiles since World War II has not varied more than a fraction of a percentage point from 11.5 percent of the disposable national consumer income. And most forecasts now predict that this rate will be maintained as the national income continues to rise.

Despite the critics who condemn the car-centered culture of America—who refer to the automobile as a mechanical mistress to whom American Carboys are enslaved—it must be accepted as a fact that the automobile is not only here to stay but is the biggest single factor in molding the economic and social pattern of America. Most Americans live where they do because of the automobile. Suburban life would be impossible without it, and most Americans live in suburbs. Most Americans buy where they do because of the automobile. And it will not be too long before most Americans work where they do because of the automobile.

This is true of Americans, whose lives are literally run by the internal combustion engine. It is not true of much of America, which is not adjusted to the automobile. Americans patiently carry their great cross of congestion and hazardous driving while their leaders on local, state, and national levels—with few exceptions—are still guided by horse-and-buggy thinking, or conversely, are bemused by missiles and moon shots, atomic energy and satellites. While accepting the atomic age, preparing for the space age, and reaching for the moon, it might be well to give a little more thought to coping with the automobile age. After all, that is the age in which we live.

And it is probably the age in which contemporary Americans will spend the rest of their days—despite many fascinating forecasts of a future in which cars will be replaced by personal helicopters, ground-effect machines, or the more fantastic family rocket ship. Although the tremendous technological advances of the twentieth century belie conservative prophecies for the future, it seems much more than likely that personal transportation will still depend on the wheel for many years to come.

Mass production might bring the price of a small helicopter within the reach of a mass market, but there is as yet no means by which a helicopter could be adopted to the restrictions of crowded parking lots. In the late 1920s, after Lindbergh's flight and as commercial aviation was getting established, almost every prediction for the near future had the small plane competing with the private car and millions of shares of stock were sold in companies that planned to make such planes. This never materialized, because no airborne vehicle has yet been devised that can take its owner directly from his home to the places to which he most frequently wants to go—his job, the shopping center, church, to the doctor, and so on.

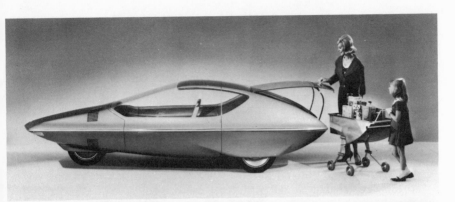

Three ideas for General Motors cars of the future. Top: the three-wheeled Runabout, with a built-in shopping cart. Center: the Firebird IV, designed for fast, cross-country trips on automatic highways. Bottom: the GM–X, a dream sports car.

Much has been written about the future potential of the ground-effects machine for personal transportation. This is the vehicle that travels a few feet over ground or water on a cushion of air. These are already in use as ferries over narrow waters, and the armed services see great promise in them as landing craft or for other special purposes. But before it can replace an automobile, a new means of steering the ground-effects machine must be discovered. It is now steered by a rudder, like a plane or a ship. This does not permit precision steering. Without ground contact no form of control has yet been devised that would permit the use of such a vehicle under the conditions in which automobiles are used. And the ground-effects machine is affected by wind. It is frightening to think of what would happen to a freeway full of such machines on a gusty day.

It seems likely that the American of the year 2000 will still be riding in a four-wheeled vehicle that is a descendant of the one he drives today, although with many significant changes. Its shape will probably be different. With more travel at high speed on improved highways, aerodynamics becomes a much more influential element in automobile design in economy and handling. Two factors seek to resist a car's forward movement: rolling resistance (the friction between the tires and the road) and wind resistance. In cars of contemporary shape these two forces are about equal at a speed of fifty miles an hour, each causing a power loss of about eight horsepower. At the lower speeds at which most driving is now done, rolling resistance, which is not affected by the shape of the car, is more important in lost horsepower than wind resistance.

As speeds increase, rolling resistance goes up very gradually; at 120 mph it involves a loss of less than 20 hp. But wind resistance goes shooting off the top of the graph. At 60 mph, in today's cars, it causes a loss of about 18 hp; at 80 mph, 40 hp; at 120 mph, 120 hp. At high speeds the modern car uses a large portion of its fuel to overcome the resistance of the wind rather than to cover the ground. The average driving speed will undoubtedly double or triple, at least, in future years. With an eye to economy under these conditions, the cars of the year 2000 may well look more like today's airplanes than today's cars.

Another development in future cars that is certain is the continued replacement of steel and iron with metals that are lighter in weight

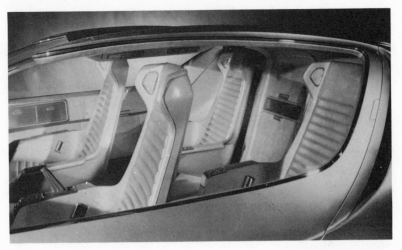

Interior views of two experimental cars. Top: GM's Firebird IV. Bottom: Ford's Aurora station wagon.

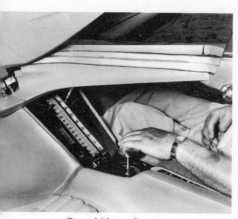

General Motors Corporation

General Motors Corporation

Designs for possible future controls. Top left: Steering, braking, acceleration, and reversing on Firebird III are all on a single knob between the front seats. Top right: Firebird IV is controlled by two grips on the arms of the driver's seat. Bottom left: The Runabout is controlled by two knobs on a panel above the driver's lap. Bottom right: The GM–X has push buttoms and a lever that is reminiscent of the old steering tiller.

General Motors Corporation

General Motors Corporation

and with plastics. Plastics have already replaced metal for many incidental parts of the car's interior, and in the future will almost certainly replace many of the outer surfaces to lighten weight and provide freedom from corrosion.

New ideas for controls are high on the list of innovations that turn up in many dream cars. General Motors, particularly, seems to have an aversion to steering wheels; none of its newest idea cars has one. The Firebird IV is operated by hand grips on each armrest of the driver's seat. The Runabout, the three-wheeled shopping car, has a control console over the driver's lap with two dials that he twists to control the car. The GM–X, a sports car, has a steering bar with an upright handle grip at each end. Except for its more pleasing shape, this futuristic device is very reminiscent of the bar that Barney Oldfield used to steer old 999.

Several idea cars employ a cantilevered steering wheel on a horizontal bar from a center post, which adjusts to a driver's individual requirements and can be swung aside for easier entrance and exit. Perhaps the most sophisticated proposed control system is that of GM's Firebird III, which consists of a single large knob located between the front-seat passengers, so that either may drive. When pushed forward, this accelerates the car; pulled back it applies the brakes; when moved to either side, it controls steering.

The location of the engine in relation to the powered wheels has been the subject of endless discussion and speculation. Should they be at the same end or at opposite ends of the car? Corvair and Volkswagen have been functioning very well with rear engines for years, but have not started a stampede toward rear-engine cars.

In 1929 Auburn brought out a front-wheel-drive car, the Cord, which was, with certain limitations, a technical success. One disadvantage was that it was expensive to maintain, because even a slight bump would disarrange the intricate steering mechanism in the front end. Also, its lack of traction on steep hills gave problems. Because of its advanced design, the "coffin front" Cord was quite popular in Hollywood; and many Cord owners who lived on the sides of the canyons running off from Sunset Boulevard, with very steep driveways, found that they had to park their cars in the road and walk up to the house. Perhaps because of the unfortunate time at

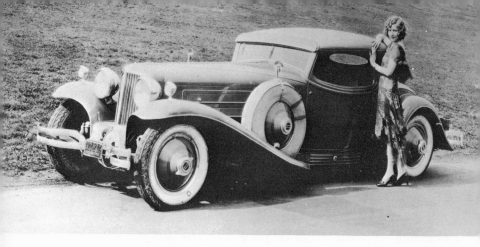

Automobile Manufacturers Association

The 1930 Cord, popular in Hollywood because of its appearance, fascinated engineers because of its front-wheel drive. In this car, all mechanical elements—power plant, transmission, and steering—were contained in the front of the car.

which the car was produced, on the eve of the depression, it died in the 1930s.

The front-wheel drive seems to have some inherent advantages that might, at long last, make it popular with both the public and the car makers. From a production standpoint it would seem desirable to make all the mechanical elements of the car—power plant, transmission, and steering system—as a single unit to which a body and rear wheels could be attached. A front drive eliminates the drive train and the differential and probably the frame. Without the torque created by the rotating drive shaft, which tends to twist the car in the same direction, there would seem to be no need for a rigid frame. A one-piece welded body, with a pair of wheels, would be hitched on behind the driving unit. The front drive would also seem to offer a wider scope to the designer because there would be no engineering restrictions as to what he could do with all the space behind the engine. And the public would not be startled by having the trunk where the engine should be and the engine where the trunk should be.

Engine placement may depend on the type of power plant that will be used in the year 2000. One thing is reasonably certain. It may not happen in this century, but someday the four-stroke internal combustion automobile engine will become as obsolete as the steam railroad engine. On a purely functional basis the automobile power plant is an engineering nightmare. The lateral motion of its pistons must be changed into a circular motion to propel the car, a translation that cannot be made without vibration. Also, the pistons use up a great deal of energy to start and stop four times in each firing. As a result the best commercial automobile engine is able to convert only from 15 to 25 percent of the energy contained in its fuel to useful work. It can produce about one horsepower for each two pounds of weight. This will be improved. The racing engines that Ford adopted for the Lotus are already producing one horsepower per pound. But it is likely that one of several basically more efficient power sources will ultimately overtake the four-stroke engine in terms of weight, economy, and practicality. Prognostications range from the gas turbine to atomic energy.

The closest thing to a new type of reciprocating piston engine is the rotary internal combustion engine that is now in commercial use in a German car, the Spider. American Motors and Renault, France's largest automobile manufacturer, have entered on a joint agreement to research this type of power plant still further. The rotary engine has been around in laboratories for years, but has never been developed as a high-performance engine. The Spider has only ninety-five horsepower. Its basic theoretical advantages are that its power is created by a circular motion, and it runs continuously, thus avoiding both the vibration and the stop-and-go action of lateral cylinders. In this respect it is similar to the turbine engine but runs at a much slower speed.

At the moment there is much fanfare about the *new* turbine engine. This is rather amusing because the first turbine-powered vehicle was built about three hundred years ago in Peking, China, by a Belgian missionary, Father Ferdinand Verbiest. The good Father described his device in a book published in Europe in 1687: "I made a little chariot, two feet long and on four wheels, in the middle of which I placed a vessel full of coals and above that an aeolipile. [An aeolipile is a spherical boiler with a small vent through which a jet of steam escapes. It was devised in Greece in the second century B.C.] On the axle of the front wheels there was a toothed bronze wheel driven by gear wheels by another wheel with four vanes on which the jet of steam was directed."

There was some experimentation with gas turbines in the early years of this century, and a few were used for stationary engines. Henry Ford briefly experimented with one in 1925 but gave it up because of its poor efficiency. The modern gas turbine was triggered by an English invention in 1930, and the first progress was made in the application of this type of propulsion to aircraft in England and Germany. After the war several of the European automobile manufacturers who had gained experience with turbine engines for planes started to apply them to cars. In England the Rover Company has been making experimental turbine-powered cars since 1946 and has produced turbine race cars, front-wheel-drive passenger cars, and rear-engine turbine cars. In France, Renault built, among others, a turbine-powered car that made a record run at Bonneville in 1956 at 192 miles an hour.

In America, Chrysler, General Motors, and Ford have all been experimenting with turbines since the late 1940s. GM has built and displayed a series of four turbine-powered experimental Firebirds. It has also created prototype turbine trucks and buses. Ford, after installing turbines in experimental Thunderbirds and Fairlanes in 1954, concentrated on building a truck engine and has had a demonstration turbine-powered truck on the road for some time. From a publicity standpoint, at least, Chrysler has stolen the leadership by

Chrysler, General Motors, and Ford have all been experimenting with turbine engines since the late 1940s. Chrysler has also built fifty turbine-powered passenger cars and lent them to car owners to get their reactions. Here, the turbine-powered Chrysler.

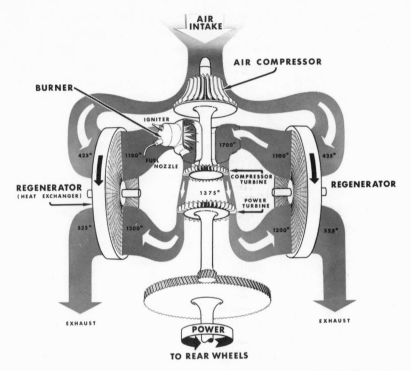

AIR INTAKE

AIR COMPRESSOR

BURNER

IGNITER

425°   1100°   1700°   1300°   425°

FUEL NOZZLE

COMPRESSOR TURBINE

REGENERATOR
(HEAT EXCHANGER)

1375°

POWER TURBINE

REGENERATOR

525°   1200°   1200°   525°

EXHAUST

POWER

EXHAUST

TO REAR WHEELS

Chrysler Corporation

Diagram of the regenerative turbine developed by Chrysler. The intake air first goes through a compressor, where its temperature is raised to 435°. Then, in regenerator, or heat exchanger, heat from the exhaust gases increases its temperature to 1,200°. Next the air enters a firing chamber, where it is mixed with fuel vapor and fired at 1,700°. When the gases of the fuel-air mixture escape from the chamber they expand, causing the blades of the turbine to revolve.

building, after years of experimentation, fifty turbine-powered passenger cars. Starting late in 1963 they have been lending these for three-month periods to average car owners, selected by lot, to get public reactions.

The turbine, like the rotary engine, has the basic advantage of producing power by a circular rather than a lateral motion. It is smaller and lighter than an equivalent reciprocating engine; Chrysler's engine weighs 410 pounds and is said to equal a 600-pound conventional engine in performance. Because of a different method of rating, Chrysler's 130-horsepower turbine engine is supposedly equivalent to a 200-horsepower reciprocating engine. The engine is much simpler than a conventional engine. It has no valves, its electrical system uses only one spark plug, and the number of parts is reduced by 80 percent. It is quiet and completely vibration-free and because it is air-cooled, requires no plumbing system or antifreeze.

Chrysler also claims that tuning up is virtually eliminated, maintenance is reduced considerably, life expectancy is much longer, exhaust gases are cleaner, no warm-up is needed, low temperature starting difficulties are eliminated, and oil consumption is negligible. The engine will operate equally well on a wide variety of fuels. Recommended fuels, in order of preference, are kerosene, No. 1 Diesel or No. 2 Diesel, unleaded gasoline, or a mixture of any or all of these in any proportions. Ironically, the one fuel that should not be used except in an emergency, because of damage to the engine, is the easily available leaded gasoline.

In the Driver's Guide that accompanies its turbine test cars Chrysler states that fuel consumption is about the same as that of a piston engine under the same conditions. In connection with a cross-country test run that they made in two Dodge Darts, identical except for the engines, the company claims that the turbine-powered car used "considerably" less fuel than the conventional car. Looking to the future, Chrysler engineers say that a 400-degree increase in temperature would improve fuel economy over 20 percent. The materials that would permit this higher temperature are still in the laboratory.

How soon there will be turbine-powered passenger cars in common use is a large question. Both Ford and General Motors say that "in the present state of turbine technology" this type of power plant is more applicable to trucks and buses. Ford's truck is a 170,000-pound monster with a 600-horsepower turbine in a tractor that pulls two tandem forty-foot trailers. It has a level road speed of 70 miles an hour and a nonstop cruising radius of 600 miles. Instead of the higher temperature that Chrysler is seeking for greater efficiency, Ford has supercharged its engine. The completion of the Interstate Highway will open a new future for long-range truck and bus service,

The radically designed chassis of the turbine-powered Firebird III has two engines. The turbine engine in the rear powers the car. A two-cylinder, ten-horsepower engine in front provides both twelve-volt and 110-volt electric power for air conditioning, lights, controls, and accessories.

and it is not unlikely that the automotive industry will offer turbine-powered equipment to meet this need.

Chrysler has not committed itself beyond the fifty test cars and intimates that a decision will be guided by the results of these tests. Also, even if the present engine is dependable and generally competitive with modern reciprocating engines, Chrysler will probably not go into production until it has improved the efficiency of the engine either by supercharging or by an increase in nozzle temperature, to permit a claim of further superiority over the reciprocating engine.

The turbine engine may well compete with the reciprocating engine during the next decade and possibly replace it, although on that subject Ford says, quite realistically: "The retirement of the familiar spark ignition piston engine has been predicted regularly ever since the days of its infancy, yet it continues to improve in smoothness, quietness, power and efficiency. The advantages of a continuous process type of cycle such as the gas turbine have long been recognized, and are approaching practical embodiment, but the piston engine is so firmly entrenched in our manufacturing facilities, our service procedures, and our experience that the turbine will have a long battle to dislodge it in the passenger car field."

Regardless of whether or not the turbine engine replaces the reciprocating piston engine in the near future, probably neither is the ultimate power source for the automobile. In theory, electric power is so far superior for this purpose to any internal combustion engine that the technology of applying it will undoubtedly be worked out. At present, there is no electrical system that can compete in terms of practicality with existing gas engines. But during the past few years this has been the subject of concentrated research in several industries—oil, chemical, and electric, among others. Something is almost certain to be developed, whether it be a compact storage device, the production of electricity by a chemical converter, or by solar, atomic, or some other form of energy.

An example of a chemical converter is the fuel cell that is already in use to operate radar and other communications devices. In a fuel cell oxygen and a hydrocarbon—hydrogen, alcohol, or petroleum gas—react, silently and without combustion, to set up a current of electricity. Solar batteries exist that convert sunlight to electrical energy. Atomic batteries are being used in space satellites. But all of these are rather "far out" as potential sources of automotive power. Perhaps not so remote is a lightweight, rechargeable storage battery capable of producing enough power to propel a modern car. In the past few years tremendous advances have been made in developing this type of battery. It is now sparking great changes in the electrical appliance field. Edison Electric Institute has been developing a high-energy battery capable of storing large amounts of power to propel such vehicles as multistop delivery trucks.

Although the auto makers are reluctant to make specific forecasts about future cars, GM, for one, is happy to present its ideas on tomorrow's highways and the control of cars thereon. Their research has developed several things, ranging from a better way of communicating information to tomorrow's driver to a look-ma-no-hands system under which cars drive themselves while the driver looks at television.

Back in the early years of the century it was a great step forward when automobile clubs put up signs to tell motorists where the road went. More than half a century later this is still the only way in which information is communicated to the driver. Road signs are inherently unsafe, because a driver cannot read a sign and watch the road at the same time. Safety signs, such as speed limits, do not impinge themselves on a driver's consciousness. At high speeds and during periods of limited visibility, signs do not offer satisfactory guidance. GM proposes to supplement signs with oral communication to the driver via short-wave radio, either through the car set or a separate speaker.

This could be used in several ways, through permanent installations, using tapes, and through temporary broadcast points, using either tapes or live microphones. A broadcast announcement to motorists entering a town is an example of the former. Many drivers fly past a sign that says "Town of Belleville, Speed 35 MPH," fre-

Experimenting with the "automatic pilot" for cars on the test highway at RCA laboratories, Princeton, New Jersey. In response to electronic signals from the lead car, the car in the foreground starts, accelerates, slows, and stops without any help from the man in the front seat.

RCA Laboratories

quently without even seeing it. With the Hy-Com system there would be a small battery-powered radio transmitter buried under that sign that would broadcast a taped announcement, perhaps in a pleasing feminine voice, saying: "You are entering the Town of Belleville. Welcome. Please note that a speed limit of thirty-five miles per hour starts at this point and continues for three miles. It is then reduced to twenty-five miles for a short distance through the center of town. For your safety and ours, please conform to these limits. Thank you." This would leave the driver in no doubt of where he was and what was required of him, and he would be much more likely to respond to this appeal than to a cold metal sign. When this comes into general use, it is to be hoped that the memory of what billboards did to early highways will still linger and that laws will forbid the broadcast of anything but highway and traffic information on such systems. Otherwise, motorists will almost certainly be subject to many nauseating chamber of commerce radio commercials.

Hy-Com would also prevent confusion and resulting accidents on urban freeways by giving ample notice of upcoming exits. Many visitors complain about the Los Angeles freeways because they do not know where they are going, and, in the fast-flowing traffic, signs do not give them sufficient warning that they are nearing their exit. If a driver is traveling in the left lane of a three-lane highway in a stream of traffic going 60 miles an hour it is small comfort to be advised by a sign that his exit is a quarter mile ahead—off the right lane. Either he chances an accident by abruptly crossing two lanes of traffic, or he passes his exit before he can get over safely. With Hy-Com in use he would have been told five miles back of the upcoming exit and would have had ample time to get in a position to leave the road.

Oral communication can also be used to control traffic at any point by an officer with a microphone using a mobile transmitter. Or it can broadcast information on temporary road conditions. If an accident reduced traffic flow on a busy road, a highway patrolman could drop a portable transmitter beside the road and make a tape recording that said: "This road is temporarily blocked between exits thirteen and fourteen. Please leave the road at exit thirteen and take Oak, Elm, or Ash Avenues to exit fourteen."

Hy-Com is ready for any highway authority that wants to use it. Much farther in the future is an automatic highway on which GM and RCA are jointly working. The latter has, at its laboratory, a quarter-mile loop on which full-sized driverless cars equipped with radio sensors and computers speed up, slow down, or stop automatically. GM has a miniature three-lane highway, with an automatic lane on which sophisticated engineers seriously play with scale models of cars and buses equipped with automatic control mechanisms. The principle of the automatic highway involves wires embedded in the road that broadcast information on the conditions ahead—where the road goes and what is on it. These are picked up by coils on the car and fed to a computor under the dashboard. The computor figures what change is necessary in the control of the car and advises servomechanisms (small electric motors) to operate the brakes, steering, and accelerator as necessary.

All of the things discussed here may happen some time in the future. One might say, based on new technologies still in their infancies, most of them almost certainly *will* happen. But so far as personal transportation is concerned, it will probably be a process of evolution. Americans will move increasingly across their own land in the vehicle that they have grown up with and that, in two generations, has revolutionized their way of life.

History may record the present century as the era of great change. No other similar period has produced so many deviations and so much progress in so many directions—social, cultural, political, economic, scientific, and technological. And of all the changes the most meaningful to the individual American is the automobile. It sparked the technology of mass production, which has created an economy unique in the world—an economy that has virtually eradicated the social gulf between the affluent and the impoverished. By taking Americans beyond the horizon it has conquered provincialism and created the opportunity for wider cultural experience. It has overcome isolation and by so doing has helped to maintain the virility of the roving Americans—their freedom of thought and expression.

Alfred P. Sloan, Jr., ended the account of his years with General Motors with the words, "The work of creating goes on." It will continue to go on to produce a better life for more Americans. And when we speculate about the probable effect of this creativity on our future lives we may remember that there are Americans alive today who stood beside the road and heard their elders pontificate that "it will never replace the horse—never—never."

INDEX

Miller, Arjay, 234, 249
Miller, Harry, 197, 201
Mirrors, rear-view, 135, 201, 206
model changes, annual, *see* styling
Monroe automobile, 165, 200
Motor, quoted, 66
Motor Yearbook, quoted, 155
motoring
    in early days, 21-23
    in the 1920s, 163-164
    modern, 276
Mueller, Oscar, 47, 48, 50
Mustang automobile, 202, 212, 213
Mustang II, 245, 246, 247

Nadig, Harry, 35, 37
Nash, Charles W., 66, 86, 175
Nash automobile, 66, 123, 165, 173, 222
Nevins, Allen, quoted, 105, 116, 140, 160, 233
"999," Ford racer, 59, 60

Oakland automobile, 89, 151, 165
Oakland Motor Car Company, 89
Ohio Automobile Company, 71, 72
Oldfield, Barney, 17, 188, 196-198, 200
    race with Ford "999," 59, 60, 196
Olds, Ransom E., 19, 26, 42, 61-64, 71, 72, 88
Oldsmobile automobile, 13, 15, 19, 23, 24, 31, 32, 62, 63, 64, 128, 135, 165, 244
    1908 model, 88
Olds Motor Works, 62, 71, 81, 87, 88
Otto, Nicholas, 40, 41, 42, 52, 83
Overland automobile, 32, 122, 123, 165

Packard automobile, 2, 71-72, 132, 165, 183, 185
    racer, 194, 198
Packard Motor Car Company, Inc., 72, 81, 173, 175, 222
Paige automobile, 165
paints, body, 150-151

Panhard automobile, 4, 16, 194
Peerless automobile, 23, 81, 175, 196
Peugeot automobile, 4, 42, 200
Pierce, Percy, 26, 28
Pierce-Arrow automobile, 26, 165, 183
Pierce-Arrow Motor Car Company, 81, 175
plastics in automobiles, 130
Plymouth automobile, 87, 175, 177, 239
Pontiac Division, General Motors, 89, 244
Pope, Augustus, 23-24
Pope Manufacturing Company, 80, 81
Pope-Toledo automobile, 2, 23, 24, 25, 194
Pound, Arthur, quoted, 86
Prest-O-Lite Company, 168
production companies, 31, 66, 173
production figures: 1900, 63; 1900-1910, 32; 1908, 87; 1909, 103; 1920-1930, 158; 1925, 123; 1929, 152; 1930-1960, 263; 1950, 222; 1955, 222; 1964, 217, 222
proving grounds, 252-255
Pulaski Skyway, 173, 174
Purdy, Ken, quoted, 209-210

races and racing (*see also* Indianapolis, Vanderbilt Cup)
    Chicago *Times-Herald,* 46-47, 192
    drag, 203, 205
    Ford-Winton, 57, 196
    midget car, 202, 204
    Narragansett, R.I., 191
    Oldfield-Winton, 59, 60
    speedway, 198-202
    stock car, 205-206
    transcontinental, 1909, 107
Rackham, Bennett H., 77, 120
Rambler automobile, 2, 31, 66, 221, 240, 241
Ramsey, Mrs. Alice, 13
Raskob, John J., 92, 94, 146
Reo automobile, 26, 71, 88, 165, 175, 201